Engaged Passions

Searches for Quality in Community Contexts

Research Group Lifelong Learning in Music & the Arts

Hanze University of Applied Sciences, Groningen

Royal Academy of Fine Arts, Design, Music & Dance, The Hague

ISBN: 978-90-5972-387-0

Eburon Academic Publishers
Postbus 2867
2601 CW Delft
tel.: 015-2131484 / fax: 015-2146888
info@eburon.nl / www.eburon.nl

Cover design and lay out: Studio Frank & Lisa, Groningen
DTP content: Peter van Munster

Photo cover: Ninja Kors
Photo Peter Renshaw: Rineke Smilde

Engaged Passions

Searches for Quality in Community Contexts

PETER RENSHAW

Eburon Delft
2010

Contents

Foreword

Quality is key to everything within the arts as well as to the individual artist. When trying to unpack the question "what creates quality?" this often causes raised eyebrows. What constitutes quality within the arts? Why, the highest artistic quality of course! Indeed, there is no debate about that. However, there is more to the definition of quality. When we really consider the arts as a strong means of reaching a broad variety of people trying to make sense of our complex world, it is imperative that quality is considered in a much broader sense than 'just' artistic quality. What is there to say, for instance, about the quality of engagement, of communication and of reaching new audiences in different areas of the community? The contextual variables within collaborative artistic work are as important as the artistic drive underpinning the work. Unfortunately too often, paying attention to the context is marginalized, sadly also by institutions of Higher Arts Education. A broad and deep understanding of the context, beginning with the needs of the people the musicians and artists work with, is imperative.

This is the main message which Peter Renshaw tries to make us aware of. Drawing on his own lifelong passion for both the arts *and* people and his drive to understand the source of people's motivation, the simple question of why people are doing what they are doing has always been central to him. This question underpins 16 interviews, 14 case studies and 14 personal testimonies of reflective arts practitioners ranging from Rotterdam and London to Brazil, and leads to fascinating stories and narratives. The information that can be obtained from these narratives is tremendously rich. Within a wide scope on a local and global scale, it shows what music and the arts can bring to different audiences in the community, be it to children, people in socially disadvantaged circumstances, people in prison or those living with dementia.

The study highlights the different aspects and characteristics of the concept of lifelong learning, where the biographical perspective is as important as the continuing professional development of the artist. It also shows that it is no longer relevant to consider artistic practice as either *l'art pour l'art* or 'artistic social work'. Collaborative creative practice in the community is by definition artistically driven and shows a close interconnection between the creative passion of the artist and what the artist creates in the community. Key is the artist's transformative learning, where she changes her frame of reference when connecting to the context, leaving her individual artistic fingerprints on the creative work.

One of the most impressive aspects of this study is Peter's own passion, where with great integrity he has continuously strived for change. This, together with his huge experience in this field and his great capacity for reflection, makes the study and his interpretation of all the data so unique. This is also why it is important for us to find out why *he* is doing what he is doing, hence our decision to include his own personal perspective in the book.

Rineke Smilde
April 2010

Acknowledgements

This book would never have happened without the drive, commitment and inspiration of Rineke Smilde. Over 15 years we have spent many hours discussing the challenges confronting musicians and conservatoires as they face up to a changing world. Throughout this time Rineke has been honest in her criticism, constantly nudging me to deepen and extend my vision as part of my own lifelong learning. For this, and for her friendship, I will always remain deeply grateful.

The main narrative running through the book hangs on the testimonies, case studies and interview responses of the 20 musicians, artists, theatre practitioners, arts managers and educationalists, who have so openly shared their experience, time and trust with me. In busy, pressurised lives this generosity is not taken lightly. It is hoped that their integrity and engagement will serve as an example to others working in the field. Certainly for me, their stories reaffirmed my view about the rich possibilities that can accrue from collaborative engagement with other sectors and communities.

Special gratitude goes to those critical friends who have been there for me in different circumstances over many years. Their honesty and insightful questioning have always been stimulating and have often pointed me in a new direction. Notably, there is John Stephens, a sage of music education whose enthusiasm and ideas continue to be catching and absorbing. I also much value the lively, informed views of Sean Gregory and Helena Gaunt of the Guildhall School of Music & Drama, both of whom continue to ignite my reflective spirit.

In addition, I have benefited enormously from many conversations with two of the contributors whose voices resonate throughout this enquiry. Linda Rose brings her wealth of experience in the development of teachers and musicians into the ground-breaking work of Music for Life. Judith Webster has been challenging me with her critical perspective from the moment she was appointed to run the Community and Education Department for the Royal Philharmonic Orchestra. The work of both Linda and Judith demonstrates a deep understanding of the synergy between the personal, the professional and the artistic in the reflective development of musicians and artists – a main thread running through the book.

Finally, I am indebted to Peter van Munster and Linda Hendriks for their care and attention in guiding the text to publication. Such professionalism is never taken for granted.

Last but not least, there is Milena, my wife, who vowed she would run a mile if I ever embarked on writing a book. But she is still here as a constant support and at times, a very critical friend – which I need and much respect!

1

Change and challenge

1.1   Introduction

The main thrust of this book has underpinned most of my work over the last 25 years or more. During this time there have been a large number of initiatives encouraging arts practitioners to interact and collaborate with organisations in the community who felt that their practice would be enriched and enhanced by engaging in the arts in some way. As these projects took root, musicians and artists, for example, often found themselves confronted by competing agendas that took them outside their customary boundaries. Increasingly they were expected to respond to social, cultural, educational and political pressures arising from the demands of diversity, social inclusion, regeneration and globalisation. For many practitioners this was daunting because their training had not prepared them to adapt to the challenges of these rapidly changing circumstances.

The shift in conditions and expectations, the growing awareness of responding to different contexts, raised the knotty problem of 'quality'. How were they expected to define and evaluate the quality of their practice when they were launched into situations for which they had not been trained? How were training organisations expected to reappraise their attitudes and priorities regarding a professional preparation rooted way back in the past? Basically, how can one propel conservatoires and Higher Arts Education institutions into the 21st century?

The search for what might count as 'quality', especially in the many diverse contexts within which arts practitioners work, lies behind this enquiry into quality and community engagement. It has been commissioned by Professor Rineke Smilde, Director of the Research Group in Lifelong Learning in Music and the Arts (LLMA), which is positioned in Prince Claus Conservatoire, Groningen and the Royal Conservatoire, The Hague, The Netherlands. The enquiry reflects the philosophy underlying the work of the Research Group but it also has a global reach, drawing on policy discussions in UK and on individual voices from The Netherlands, England, Germany, Brazil and Sweden.

The backbone of the enquiry comprises 16 in-depth interviews, 14 personal testimonies and 14 case studies from arts practitioners, managers, project co-ordinators, teachers and evaluators. The interviewees were invited because they embody a wide range of experience and perspectives: musicians, visual artists, theatre practitioners and educationalists working in community neighbourhoods, schools, arts centres, conservatoires, orchestras, youth opera, a samba school, prisons and homes for people with dementia. The central question addressed by the enquiry is:

How do arts practitioners determine what constitutes 'quality' in their engagement with cross-arts and cross-sector projects within different community contexts?

The interviews, testimonies and case studies provide a rich source of data, ideas, comment and controversy, illuminated by examples of effective practice. They are also inspirational because in each case the motivation of the artists, their passion, demonstrates a dual commitment – to 'people' and to 'art'. Their engagement with the community is driven by both a moral and an artistic imperative. This is very honest and refreshing in a world so frequently dominated by self-seeking instrumental goals.

The dialogue with the interviewees runs like a thread through the enquiry, constantly raising questions that have become signposts for the narrative of the book. For example:

What is the motivation of the arts practitioners in this enquiry?

How far are effective partnerships dependent on practitioners making meaningful connections with the context in which they are working?

To what extent does community engagement entail establishing reflective dialogue, 'conversation', with partner organisations?

What factors need to be taken into account when determining 'quality' in a community context? (e.g., quality of project; quality of practitioners; quality of process; quality of end-product)

What is the impact of community engagement for the learning and development of practitioners? (e.g., approaches to learning and development; the place of mentoring and co-mentoring; reflective learning, evaluation and assessment; shifting the culture of organisations)

These key questions need to be examined in relation to the current challenges confronting arts practitioners, arts organisations, conservatoires and Higher Arts Education institutions. This is the main aim of the book.

1.2 'Community engagement' in the context of this enquiry

The problem of building a common vocabulary within the area of 'community arts' is widely acknowledged, especially as so many sectors are now collaborating in different aspects of community development. It is no longer rare for arts practitioners to be working within the domains of education, health care, social services, criminal justice, business, environment and ecology. Within all these contexts the quality of engagement is of paramount importance, but definitions of quality will vary depending on the purpose and context of the particular project and on the nature of the activity.

In 2002 a very useful mapping exercise was carried out by William Cleveland as part of his work as Director of the Centre for the Study of Art and Community in Minneapolis (see Cleveland, 2002). For the purposes of this enquiry the following definitions are helpful.

Community-based activities are those that are created and produced by and with community members, combining significant elements of community access, ownership, authorship, participation and accountability.

Arts-based community development comprises arts-centred activity that contributes to the sustained advancement of human dignity, health and productivity within a community (e.g. educating, inspiring, mobilising, nurturing, healing, building community capacity and sustainable development).

Cross-sector community development that is necessarily collaborative because community issues are multidisciplinary, multi-agency, multi-stakeholder and multi-sector by nature.

Arts-centred programme work which is especially relevant to this enquiry into 'quality':

> Our study of arts programmes in community and institutional settings has led us to conclude that the most two critical contributors to success have been a clear artistic focus and the high quality of the artists involved. The most successful programmes have been developed by artists making art, not artists doing something else. These artists have created art programmes, not therapeutic or remedial programmes that use art as a vehicle. This does not mean that they were not concerned with solving problems or unaware of the therapeutic or self-esteem-building effects of their efforts. Quite the opposite, in fact. They often contend that these benefits are the unavoidable consequence of making art. It is their belief that they do the most good by concentrating on the empowering qualities of the creative processes and not on the diagnosis or treatment of what is 'wrong' (Cleveland, 2002).

From his considerable experience in the USA William Cleveland criticises the notion of *outreach* which has become a much over-used term:

> Numerous well-meaning 'outreach' efforts have failed because the initiating partner has underestimated the complexities of the environment in which they were attempting to work. The term 'outreach' itself assumes a centre, a source, and a destination or target. Many 'undeserved' communities have been subjected to a cycle of outreach and abandonment that has undermined local efforts and produced a legacy of bitterness. Many are now demanding that community-arts investments and partnerships focus on developing a capacity for self-determination and self-service (Cleveland, 2002).

Cleveland stresses the point that those outside partners, agencies and practitioners initiating projects have the responsibility of learning as much as possible about the social ecology of the environment they are working in. This is well illustrated in this enquiry by Eugene van Erven's Case Study of The Story Kitchen in Haarlem and that of Clare Chacksfield's account of her multi-faceted project Eastfeast in East Anglia. Both these projects are organically linked with their respective communities (see Appendices, 6.3 A and 6.2 A).

Many of the points raised in this mapping exercise of community arts and community cultural development are explored in a recent two-year study of community music in Australia conducted by Sound Links (2009). This comprised a research project of Queensland Conservatorium Research Centre, Griffith University, Brisbane, in partnership with the Music Council of Australia, the Australian Music Association and the Australian Society for Music Education. A number of prominent characteristics of community music-making were identified, many of which are relevant to this enquiry into quality engagement. For example:

Relationship to space

> Connections to location
> Connection to cultural identity and cultural heritage
> Pride of place
> Balance between physical and virtual spaces

Social engagement

> Commitment to inclusiveness
> Engaging the marginalised 'at risk' or 'lost to music'
> Providing opportunities
> Empowerment
> Links to well-being
> Relationship to audience

Support/networking

> Links to the local community
> Links to other community groups
> Links to local council
> Links to business
> Links to local service providers
> Connections to national peak bodies

Dynamic music-making

> Active involvement open to all
> Responsiveness to ambitions and potential of participants

Short- versus long-term orientation
Flexible relationship between audience and performers
Balance between process and product
Broad orientation facilitators

Engaging pedagogy and facilitation

Sensitivity to differences in learning styles, abilities, age and culture
Nurturing a sense of group and individual identity
Commitment to inclusive pedagogies (ranging from formal to informal)
Embracing multiple references to quality
Recognising the need to balance process and product
Attention to 'training the trainers'

Links to school

Locating activities in schools
Identifying mutual interests
Sharing of equipment and facilities
Marrying formal and informal learning
Exchange pedagogical approaches
Realising activities as part of the curriculum
Support and commitment from school leadership
(Sound Links, 2009)

The findings of this Sound Links research echo much of the developmental work in community music that has been growing steadily in the UK for over 25 years. Leaders in the field include Community Music London, Community Music East, More Music in Morecambe, The Sage Gateshead, Sound Sense and Youth Music. All these organisations run professional development programmes to support their work, whilst some universities and colleges are beginning to provide specific training opportunities in community arts: for example, the MA, Postgraduate Diploma and Postgraduate Certificate in Cross-Sectoral and Community Arts at Goldsmiths, University of London.

The quality issues at the centre of this enquiry are equally relevant to the fields of community music and community arts as to those of the arts organisations and practitioners represented in this study. But further important questions will be explored that have a special resonance with the work of training organisations like conservatoires and Higher Arts Education institutions that have yet to fully address the challenges of community engagement and the changing cultural world.

1.3 Challenge of changing cultural landscape

The question of 'quality' in a cultural world increasingly challenged by diversity of practice, diversity of forms, diversity of contexts and diversity of opportunity, has become a major issue for debate by government, funding bodies, arts organisations and Higher Arts Education institutions. The nature of this global 'conversation' has both a complexity and urgency that impinges on practice at local levels and in different sectors and communities. It cannot be ignored but neither should it be allowed to stifle the creative energy of individuals and organisations. In the current era of accountability and measurement the more subtle, reflective processes used to 'ensure' quality must not be allowed to be hijacked by the mechanisms of Quality Assurance.

In many ways we are now living through an exciting cultural revolution that is challenging well-worn assumptions about arts practice and is inviting us to redefine how artists of all kinds can engage more meaningfully with society as a whole from birth until death. The debate in UK has been particularly lively and far-reaching. For example, in an influential Consultation Paper, *Culture and Learning: Towards a New Agenda*, for the British think-tank DEMOS, John Holden (2008) points out that "the growth of the creative economy, issues of identity, diversity, the influence of culture in international relations, digitisation and new technology have fundamentally changed both the position of culture in society and the lifelong educational needs of present and future generations" (p. 8).

It is often argued that in the process of shaping this 'new agenda' traditional standards of excellence will be jeopardised, but this view does not hold up as individual practitioners, cultural organisations and funding bodies increasingly interrogate what constitutes quality and excellence in their broadening remit of work. Cultural leaders, who want to see the arts taking into account such key factors as diversity, social inclusion, regeneration and globalisation, insist that arts organisations and Higher Arts Education institutions should become cultural catalysts that understand there are different forms of excellence rooted in different social, cultural and educational contexts. Making these connections and responding to them creatively are an essential part of what it is to be an engaged and responsive artist or cultural organisation.

Central to this re-engagement is a search for forms of excellence that embody the vibrancy of innovation and risk-taking. In the review commissioned by the British Government's Department for Culture, Media and Sport, *Supporting Excellence in the Arts*, Brian McMaster (2008) makes a strong case for ensuring that innovation and risk-taking become the motor for extending artistic boundaries, for deepening creative processes, and for exploring the possible interconnections between different arts, cultures and sectors. Such alliances and partnerships can generate new art forms and new collaborative processes of learning that inevitably raise questions about reappraising traditional ways of looking at quality. McMaster (2008) maintains that innovation and risk-taking are both linked to the concept of excellence. "For something to be excellent it has to be relevant, and for it to be relevant it has to be continually reinterpreted and refined for and by its audience. Risks have to be taken, innovation must be central to the process" (p.10).

This dynamic perspective will resonate especially with those cultural institutions working collaboratively with schools, colleges and other organisations within the wider community. Many of them are breaking new ground as they listen to and engage with the voice of young people and wider audiences. Learning, engagement, participation and collaboration have become the new 'buzz' words. Such nuances are reflected in the shift from 'education' to more flexible terms like 'discovery', 'creative learning', 'learning and engagement', learning and participation', 'creative projects', and 'creative development' in cultural organisations (see Robinson and Greenstreet, 2006 and Holden, 2008).

These views were fleshed out further through the consultation process initiated by John Holden's (2008) paper. The responses and results of the investigation were published as a report on culture and learning that includes formal and informal learning, the arts and heritage (see Culture and Learning Consortium, 2009, *Get It: The Power of Cultural Learning*). The report suggests that we take a broad, inclusive approach to cultural learning that "must embrace all forms of learning, all types of learner, and all aspects of culture. It must acknowledge cultural learning as a lifelong pursuit, from a child's early years through to the third age" (p.18). The responsibility lies with cultural organisations and their educational and community partners to develop collaborative programmes that aim to foster creativity within many diverse contexts.

The importance of this commitment to creativity and cultural learning was also emphasised in the report of the House of Commons Education and Skills Committee (2007) on the place of *Creative Partnerships* in the school curriculum in England. It came out with a strong recommendation that "the DCSF (Department of Children, Schools and Families) reviews policies such as Every Child Matters and personalised learning to ensure that creativity is established as a core principle in learning and development" (p.4). Reflecting on the benefits of the Government scheme *Creative Partnerships* (commenced in 2002), the Committee states that "at its best, when *Creative Partnerships* starts with a school development plan and builds a strong relationship between teachers and creative practitioners, it can significantly expand the capacity and ambition of a school to teach creatively" (p. 4).

(Also see the 2006 Roberts report *Nurturing Creativity in Young People* and the 1999 NACCCE report *All Our Futures: Creativity, Culture and Education*).

There is no doubt that at policy level in the UK the emphasis on creative learning, cultural learning, personalising learning, collaborative learning, informal learning and lifelong learning places considerable demands and responsibility on the professional arts sector as it strives to find ways of enabling young people and adults to shape a cultural landscape that makes artistic and social sense to them. Achieving this entails forging new partnerships and engaging in new participatory programmes that focus on enhancing creative and cultural learning.

This challenge to re-engage people in their creative and cultural lives raises fundamental questions as to what might count as quality and excellence in the wide range of contexts in which artists work. It also has major implications for the learning and continuing professional development of all kinds of arts practitioners – performers, improvisers, composers, choreographers, artists, DJs, curators and creative producers. Many of these practitioners are increasingly extending their roles and working closely with teachers and other community leaders. In the near future this is likely to become the norm as flexible patterns of work are embedded in their portfolio careers – a point clearly flagged up in Youth Music's (2002) report *Creating a Land with Music* (p. 4).

The need for conservatoires to realign their priorities was made explicit by Rineke Smilde (2009a) in her PhD dissertation *Musicians as Lifelong Learners*.

> The conservatoire needs to constantly fine tune and adjust itself to the needs of the profession, and vice versa. This requires a reorientation by the conservatoire, where a shift in culture has to be accompanied by a reappraisal of what actually counts in today's world. Portfolio careers are the result of the big changes in the music profession and should not remain on the periphery of the conservatoire, but instead become part of core business (p.252).

This point of view was also reinforced by Einar Solbu (2007) in his presentation to an international Seminar addressing *Trends in the Music Profession in Europe: Lifelong Learning and Employability*. Solbu, Senior Advisor to the Norwegian Ministry of Foreign Affairs and Vice President of the International Music Council, argued strongly for conservatoire training to reflect the 'real life' of the workplace when he stated that:

> The various situations in which musicians work today – and I mean work seriously as musical artists – (...) require a range of different combinations of qualifications: in performance, in creation of music, in arranging music, in improvisation, in establishing the interest for music among various audiences, in transmitting knowledge of music, in understanding people's response to music,

in involving people in music (and people may be little children, or youngsters or elderly people etc.) in speaking about music, in instructing people in music-making, in recording, in creating or manipulating music electronically, in running a music business, in working as a freelance artist, in relating to the commercial music industry, in initiating projects, in working with artists from other fields of art, etc. (p.2).
(See Lectorate & Polifonia DVD: *Dialogue in Music*, 2007)

As arts organisations and Higher Arts Education institutions begin reappraising their priorities and redefining their core purpose, they are likely to start charting a new direction that is more in line with contemporary trends and developments. Perhaps some could well become flagships for change and renewal.

1.4 Further trends and developments

Engagement and participation

One of the most significant trends in the UK at the moment is the collective move towards the Cultural Olympiad in 2012 – a 'movement' that embodies the values of aspiration, inspiration and achievement. With its special focus on harnessing the talents, energy and creativity of young people, particular attention is being given to developing forms of participation that connect people, getting them to work together and to celebrate their engagement with their local communities. Every effort is being made to engage young people and give them the opportunity to shape their own pathway, to develop a sense of progression through their personalised journey.

Enabling young people to choreograph their individual pathway is a challenge for any arts organisation because it can only be achieved through genuine dialogue, through meaningful conversation between young people and arts practitioners. As young people are given a voice in determining their own pathway – a journey that may well include the creative use of digital technology or the creation of multi-media installations – there can be a redistribution of knowledge, reflecting a changing relationship between young people and professionals, and between the nature of art forms and practice.

Such significant cultural changes are part of the DNA of many contemporary-minded arts organisations, but there are others (like some orchestras and conservatoires) who may well feel threatened by trends that fail to resonate with their well-established priorities. It is difficult to build up meaningful connections between young people, community partners and those organisations that are resistant to change. And yet the future is going to demand new learning and performing environments that extend existing boundaries and deepen creative processes that engage community participants of all ages without compromising quality. Quality remains the sine qua non of community engagement under all these changing circumstances.

An orchestral response to change: *LSO Discovery*

In UK the seeds for orchestras and opera companies beginning to develop a community and education brief go back to the early 1980s when the Arts Council of Great Britain announced that Education should be seen as an integral part of the work of its revenue-funded clients. The need to diversify and create new audiences was picked up by the pioneers of this development: notably, the London Philharmonic, the London Sinfonietta, the Scottish Chamber Orchestra, the City of London Sinfonia, the City of Birmingham Symphony Orchestra, the Royal Opera House and English National Opera (Baylis Programme). By the mid-'80s all Arts Council clients receiving public subsidy were expected to develop education and community programmes as part of their remit. This raised some major challenges for orchestras as they had to consider ways of extending their profile without diluting the quality and integrity of their artistic work.

Crucial questions had to be asked. For example, in what ways might orchestras be expected to connect meaningfully to their particular communities? Was this new-found interest largely funding driven or did it reflect a serious concern for their deeper engagement with 'education'? How far could 'education' be seen as relevant to the core artistic business of promoting concerts? To what extent should 'education' be linked to audience development? How far could education work be artistically driven – what does this mean in the context of a school? Could 'education' be seen as one way of connecting the work of composers, performers, workshop leaders and audiences? What were the implications for the learning and development of orchestral musicians and composers? How would such major developments impact on the culture of an orchestra? Would there be any spin off on the work of conservatoires? All fundamental questions that are still in the process of being explored – sometimes more reluctantly than enthusiastically!

One significant example of this development can be found in the London Symphony Orchestra, who launched its education and community programme in 1989. LSO Discovery, as it is now called, has one of the most diverse and wide-ranging profiles of any orchestra. It both generates and responds to change from its community base in LSO St Luke's – the UBS and LSO Music Education Centre. From an interview in Zone Magazine, Philip Flood (2009) Head of Discovery, outlines its four main programmes:

Community work in and around St Luke's with the Gamelan, choirs, early years programme, adults with learning difficulties, family concerts, developing 'urban music' using music technology.

Education work with schools in the local Borough of Islington and across East London, together with adult education and lifelong learning activities, and teacher education development programme using LSO models of practice.

Developing young talent, which is at the heart of the Future Partnerships Programme, with which the LSO engages with young instrumentalists of every ability. This is funded by the DCSF (Department of Children, Schools and Families) and comprises four strands:

Celebrate and Inspire Concerts: 3 at St Luke's and 3 at the Barbican in which young players sit alongside players from the LSO with prior workshops in schools.

Projects in the Boroughs: including informal LSO concerts, a fusion orchestra to develop improvisation and creative work to improve ensemble playing.

Developing and Nurturing Young Talent: in which LSO On Track works with 50 gifted players, 5 from each Borough, over the next 4 years. They will attend concerts and rehearsals; have mentors from the orchestra; develop ensemble playing; and learn the progress routes through to music college and possibly to joining orchestras in the future.

CPD programme: initially developed in the Borough of Hackney through a modular programme of work to enable non-specialist teachers at Key Stage 2 to be able to deliver music successfully to their children. It is intended that the programme will also be developed in 10 Music Services across East London eventually involving over 100 teachers.

At *postgraduate level* conducting master classes are run by Valery Gergiev. In addition there is the Panufnik Composers Scheme where six emerging composers are chosen to create short new works for the Orchestra. Its new commissioning scheme, UBS Soundscapes: Pioneers, will commission three works every season for the next three years.

Underpinning this comprehensive set of initiatives is the *digital programme.* This comprises an interactive digital network including video conferencing to transform what happens locally for the benefit of the wider national and international community. The *digital programme* includes master classes, artists' interviews, teaching children in primary schools, and career days where potential players of the future can talk to orchestral members thereby gaining invaluable access to the LSO.

The Head of LSO Discovery points out that the Orchestra is now completely engaged with the programme. Members of the Orchestra take part in school and family events. At least three-quarters of the Orchestra participate in other activities and some prioritise the work as their main interest, so much so that the Orchestra has invested substantially in player training to work successfully in these areas.

In conclusion it is interesting to note the long-term vision underlying the DCSF-funded Future Partnerships Programme. In the words of Philip Flood:

> We are strategically focusing on East London where we very much see LSO St Luke's as a musical hub, a real centre of excellence for music-making with road shows in the Boroughs and at the Barbican linked to the LSO repertoire. The London University Institute of Education will be evaluating the work of our projects and exploring the relationship between the Orchestra and the Music Services and the communities of the boroughs. These projects are not one-offs but their impact will be measured in 10-15 years and should give us a significant insight into what makes best practice in music education (Zone Magazine, 2009).

The diversity and scope of LSO Discovery is impressive, especially as the culture of the Orchestra has adapted and responded with skill, ingenuity and commitment. It is now interesting to see the way in which these developments impact on the training of teachers and professional musicians. This is especially relevant to the combined work of the Barbican-Guildhall campus and to the groundbreaking orchestral initiative – the Centre for Orchestra – instigated in 2009 by the LSO, Barbican Centre and the Guildhall School of Music & Drama.

A response to change in music education: Musical Futures

One influential development in music education in UK over the past few years has been the project Musical Futures. Initially directed by David Price and later co-ordinated nationally by Abigail D'Amore, Musical Futures commenced in 2003 with generous funding from The Paul Hamlyn Foundation. The aim was to find:

> new and imaginative ways of engaging all young people, age 11-18, in meaningful music activities. The starting point for Musical Futures was to understand the factors affecting the apparent disengagement of young people with sustained music-making activities, at a time in their lives when music is not only a passion for young people, but plays a big part in shaping their social identity (D'Amore, 2009, p.10).

As is outlined in the Introduction to the Resource Pack *Musical Futures: An approach to teaching and learning* (D'Amore, 2009, p. 9):

> Musical Futures is an approach to teaching and learning. It is a new way of thinking about music-making in schools that brings non-formal teaching and

informal learning approaches into the more formal context of schools... It is based on the belief that music learning is most effective when young people are engaged in making music, and when their existing passion for music is acknowledged, reflected on and built-upon in the classroom.

At its heart is a commitment to:

Find ways of engaging all young people in the 11-18 age range in meaningful, sustainable musical activities

Make music learning relevant to young people, and connecting their in-school and out-of-school interests and experiences

Enable young people to experience practical music-making, to understand the processes of music-making, and for music-making to contribute to their overall social, educational and personal development

This tends to happen in Musical Futures by:

Students (age 11-18) working through a variety of non-formal and informal teaching and learning styles, ensuring that their individual learning needs are met

Valuing students' personal musical interests

Motivating students first, before moving them into other musical and learning styles

Making use of aural learning, that fully integrates listening with practical music-making, improvising and composing

Teachers and practitioners flexing their teaching and learning styles to act as facilitators and through showing rather than telling, guiding and modelling rather than instructing

Students acting as peer leaders

Technique, notation and other forms of written instruction being part of the process, but rarely the starting point

Very few teachers can be expected to deliver such a challenging approach without the support of other practitioners from the wider profession. Informed partnerships are critical to the success of Musical Futures as it sets out "to break down some of the traditional barriers between classroom, instrumental teaching, the extended curriculum and students' own interests, and encourages partnerships between schools and external providers wherever possible" (ibid, p.25).

The expectations arising from Musical Futures resonate with the cultural and musical interests of many young people but they also raise critical questions about the learning and development of teachers and music practitioners, many of whom need to be re-skilled in order to be able to respond creatively and flexibly to the many changing contexts that they are likely to encounter.

In *Creating a Land of Music* (Youth Music, 2002) it was argued that the four central roles of composer, performer, leader and teacher could be seen as a 'genetic code' for the contemporary musician (p.5). In an early report for Musical Futures, *Simply Connect* (Renshaw, 2005b), the multi-faceted nature of being a musician was recognised as crucial to delivering high quality work in collaboration with schools and other community environments. Effective musical leadership was seen to embrace many diverse roles, including those of composer, arranger, facilitator, improviser, performer, conductor, teacher and catalyst. (Also see Einar Solbu, 2007, at the end of Section 1.3).

Musical Futures is beginning to influence approaches to music education in a significant number of schools in UK, but for change to take root and be sustained, there will have to be a major transformation in the learning and development of teachers and music practitioners. Both MusicLeader (www.musicleader.net) and Soundsense (www.soundsense.org) have begun to address this pressing issue, along with other organisations like The Sage Gateshead, the Connect team at the Guildhall School of Music & Drama, the Centre for Excellence in Teaching and Learning at the Royal Northern College of Music, the Education and Community Programme at Trinity College of Music and the Postgraduate Diploma in Creative Leadership at the Royal College of Music. But there is still a long way to go before anyone would claim that there is consistently high quality music education provision throughout the UK. So much depends on the quality, scope and relevance of the training.

A response to change in conservatoires and the music profession
Lifelong Learning in Music & the Arts, Prince Claus Conservatoire, Groningen and Royal Conservatoire, The Hague

In The Netherlands one major initiative stands out in its search for identifying new priorities and mapping new paradigms in the learning and development of professional musicians. In 2004 Rineke Smilde set up an applied research project to study the comprehensive area of Lifelong Learning in Music (www.lifelonglearninginmusic.org). The many different facets of this work have a strong European perspective but they also reach out globally to include North and South America.

In September 2008 the research was extended for a further four years with a wider brief that has become the central focus of the Research Group in Lifelong Learning in Music and the Arts (LLMA). This is a joint research group of the Hanze University of Applied Sciences in Groningen (Prince Claus Conservatoire) and the Royal Academy of Fine Arts, Design, Music and Dance (Royal Conservatoire) in The Hague. It forms part of the Centre of Applied Research and Innovation 'Arts and Society' of the Hanze University.

Much of the conceptual framework underpinning the research can be found in Rineke Smilde's PhD dissertation, *Musicians as Lifelong Learners: Discovery through Biography* (Smilde, 2009a). Many of the key arguments also resonate with the main thrust of this mapping exercise into what counts as 'quality' in the context of community engagement. For example:

> Changes in the social-cultural landscape are helping to shape a very different workplace for musicians

> Flexible portfolio careers require finely tuned transferable skills and a more entrepreneurial attitude towards work

> Musicians now have to perform different roles as they are expected to respond creatively to cultural and educational contexts that go beyond the concert hall

> Increasingly musicians have to work collaboratively with professionals in other fields – in cross-arts, cross-cultural and cross-sector contexts (ibid, pp.1-2)

In order to illustrate the impact of these changes on the personal and professional lives of musicians, Rineke Smilde (2009b) used biographical research that focused especially on examining the relationship between the life, educational and career span, and learning styles of the 32 musicians interviewed. The analysis of the learning biographies is helpful in providing a framework that can inform our understanding of those significant events and 'educational interventions' that help to shape our learning at different stages of our lives (Smilde, 2009a, p.3).

The research questions that underpinned Rineke Smilde's study are equally pertinent to the thinking underlying this enquiry into 'quality'.

> What knowledge, skills and values are considered necessary to function effectively and creatively as a (contemporary) musician?

> How do musicians learn and in what domains?

> What does the necessary conceptual framework of lifelong learning for musicians entail and what are the implications for education and learning environments?

Further important subsidiary questions were also raised in the research:

> What are the main changes for the European music profession?

What are the likely implications for the professional training of musicians?

In what ways do conservatoires respond to these developments? (Smilde, 2009a, p.3)

The findings of this research could well be used when devising relevant learning and development programmes for musicians in conservatoires and other related training organisations. (As an example, see the discussion of the Joint Music Master for New Audiences and Innovative Practice in Section 5.1). They also embody the principles underlying the European Universities' Charter on Lifelong Learning (2008):

1. Embedding concepts of widening access and lifelong learning in their institutional strategies.

2. Providing education and learning to a diversified student population.

3. Adapting study programmes to ensure that they are designed to widen participation and attract returning adult learners.

4. Providing appropriate guidance and counselling services.

5. Recognising prior learning.

6. Embracing lifelong learning in quality culture.

7. Strengthening the relationship between research, teaching and innovation in a perspective of lifelong learning.

8. Consolidating reforms to promote a flexible and creative learning environment for all students.

9. Developing partnerships at local, national and international level to provide attractive and relevant programmes.

10. Acting as role models of lifelong learning institutions.
    (EUA, 2008, pp.5-7)

In the process of preparing this Charter on Lifelong Learning it is clear that universities recognise the social and economic challenges that lie ahead due to the increasing speed of globalisation, the demographic transformation of Europe into ageing societies and the rapid pace of technological change (ibid. p.3). The drive to create more inclusive and responsive universities is also challenging Higher Education institutions, including art colleges and conservatoires, to become more "aware of the need to engage in and reinforce dialogue with society more broadly – with employers and employee organisations, as well as with parents and students. This can best be achieved by strengthening partnerships at different levels, with particular attention to the local level where needs are most acutely perceived and expressed" (ibid. p.4).

The principles underlying the Charter on Lifelong Learning are also embedded in the four research strands within the Research Group in Lifelong Learning in Music & the Arts (2009): (www.lifelonglearninginmusic.org/researchprojects)

1. Transformative learning in music and the arts

How musicians and artists learn and how they can fulfil a meaningful role in society by adopting a reflective and entrepreneurial attitude.

2. Cross-arts and cross-sector practice

What might constitute a mutually effective collaboration between art forms and between art forms and organisations or companies? In what way can collaborative projects present an artistic challenge for the musicians and artists involved?

3. The conservatoire as partner in professional practice

In what ways can conservatoires and other Higher Arts Education institutions develop fruitful collaborations with external partners? What are the criteria for a fluent dialogue for collaboration in various contexts? How can they reach mutual agreement about definitions of quality and values?

4. Healthy ageing through music and the arts

What influence does music-making have on the wellbeing and cognitive skills of elderly people? How can creative workshops for the elderly best be developed? What is the meaning of working with music with elderly people suffering from dementia? Research into these questions is about finding new audiences and broadening work perspectives for professional musicians.

Each of these research strands is closely connected to the findings of this enquiry into 'quality' and community engagement. But it is also hoped that the work of the Research Group will help to deepen and extend the practice of conservatoires and Higher Arts Education institutions. At the heart of its thinking is the importance of dialogue and of making connections through creating mutually beneficial partnerships both within global and local contexts. Its mantra could well be – connections, context, conversation, community, creativity and collaboration.

1.5 Challenge of quality and community engagement

This enquiry into 'quality' is firmly rooted in the thinking underlying the Research Group in LLMA but it also reflects the shift in priorities at cultural policy level in UK and further afield. It aims to address the challenges confronting the professional arts world as it comes to terms with the many cultural, social, educational and technological changes raised earlier in this chapter. There is now abundant evidence to demonstrate that the cultural landscape is in a process of ongoing change, with the result that priorities and frames of reference have to be continually reappraised and redefined. Individual musicians and arts practitioners, along with their cultural organisations, have little alternative but to learn to accept this change and adapt to a creative future that is uncertain and unpredictable. In many ways they have to become active agents in their own destiny – they have to know how to make sense of this new landscape, how to see and seize new possibilities, how to make new connections, how to engage with the many challenges that may take them well beyond their own art form. Basically they have to escape from the limitations of a 'silo' mentality and engage in the intrinsic messiness or complexity of the 'real' world.

The danger of being trapped within a limited, disconnected frame is of course, relevant to most walks of life – finance and the banking world being no exception. In her riveting book *Fool's Gold*, Gillian Tett (2009), a social anthropologist and an Assistant Editor of the Financial Times, makes the following observations that could apply equally to the narrow mindset of those musicians, for example, who remain intractable about extending their social and cultural horizons:

> These days I realize that the finance world's lack of interest in wider social matters cuts to the very heart of what has gone wrong. What social anthropology teaches us is that nothing in society ever exists in a vacuum or in isolation …A 'silo' mentality has come to rule inside banks, leaving different departments competing for resources, with shockingly little wider vision or oversight. The regulators who were supposed to oversee the banks have mirrored that silo pattern too, in their own fragmented practices. Most pernicious of all, financiers have come to regard banking as a silo in its own right, detached from the rest of society. They have become like the inhabitants of Plato's cave, who could see shadows of outside reality flickering on the walls, but rarely encountered that reality themselves (pp.298-299).

This acute observation holds a certain resonance for those cultural organisations, conservatoires and Higher Arts Education institutions where some individuals, like some bankers, remain stubbornly resistant to engaging with the world as it really is. Despite some enlightened developments in recent years, many conservatoires especially view any activity that is not seen as 'core business' as being of marginal value and therefore of not reaching the standards of excellence expected from conventional performance in the concert hall. Of course, this position is increasingly being challenged by those professional musicians, teachers and students who see the world through a different prism. Nevertheless, entrenched attitudes remain deeply embedded in an outmoded culture and it takes courage and imagination, not to mention creative and leadership skills, to engage with the challenges of working in the wider community.

But this engagement brings with it a responsibility to address the question of 'quality' and this enquiry sees itself as one voice in a much wider conversation about definitions and assessment of quality. For example, in *Creating a Land of Music*, the Report for Youth Music (2002), a clear statement was made about the need to develop a coherent framework for evaluating quality.

> It is increasingly recognised in the professional arts community that no single immutable standard of excellence can exist. Any valid view of excellence has to be defined in relation to context and fitness for purpose. All musical activities must strive for excellence, but the criteria used to judge this will vary depending on the aim and context... An urgent task, therefore, is to produce a common framework for evaluating and assessing quality that accords with diversity of need and purpose across all music genres (p.11).

These two principles of 'fitness for purpose' and 'relevance to context' are implicit in the strong Case Study of Eugene van Erven. In his search for determining quality in community art, especially in the context of community-based theatre, he makes the following perceptive observation:

> The quality of these projects cannot be judged by assessing a single performance alone with criteria borrowed from a mainstream arts discourse. Of course one can judge the quality of the song arrangements and the technical ability of the professional musicians involved in the concert (...), but one should also look at their sensitivity towards the neighbourhood singers, and how the songs communicated with this particular audience. Furthermore, one should consider how the concert fitted into the sub-projects that preceded it and how it will feed into others that are still to follow... The outsider's artistic assessment of these kinds of projects, in short, should be balanced by an assessment of the social and ethical quality of the work viewed in its totality. Such an overall view is not complete unless it is informed by the perspectives of participants, intended local audiences and other stakeholders. Community arts require a new kind of critic – and new kinds of artists (Appendices 6.3 A).

The force of these comments runs like a thread throughout this enquiry and their significance is recognised by the Research Group in Lifelong Learning in Music & the Arts. It is hoped that the main thrust of the enquiry will help to clarify and strengthen the quality of arts engagement within the wider community.

2

Passions and perspectives

2.1   What drives people to do what they do?

The previous chapter places the question of quality and community engagement in the wider political, cultural and educational arena. It describes some of the policy drivers that help to determine funding imperatives and shape the agendas of many cultural organisations. It would be naïve to deny the significance of these external factors. Without arts councils, foundations, funding bodies, local authorities and numerous government initiatives, the whole cultural infrastructure would be sorely impoverished. Although most individual artists and practitioners understand the wider parameters that help to shape their workplace, many also have deeply felt personal reasons for their engagement with work beyond the concert hall, theatre or teaching studio.

From the interviews, testimonies and case studies that are the backbone of this enquiry (see Appendices 6.2 and 6.3), it is clear that each person has been enriched by their own distinctive journey and that the experiences embedded in their narrative provide the source of their motivation for doing what they are doing now. This is hardly surprising. But what is especially striking is the common ground shared by the people interviewed. Certain shared principles, values and attitudes underpin their personal, social and artistic commitment. In all cases their artistic identity lies at the core of how they see themselves. But although an artistic impetus might be the primary motor that drives them, their values and principles also play a significant role in shaping their decisions and determining their priorities. In a nutshell, their engagement is driven by both an artistic and moral imperative.

The title of this enquiry, *Engaged Passions: Searches for Quality in Community Contexts,* is deliberately placing an emphasis on 'engaged passions' – on the depth of intrinsic motivation and commitment that feeds the artists' engagement with the community. 'Passion' lies at the heart of what they do but this is not the untamed passion of the 'noble savage'. It combines a vibrant creative energy, a vigorous spirit with a finely nuanced sensibility towards their participating audiences.

For Ken Robinson (2009) personal passion and natural aptitude are the two main features of people being 'in their element'. He considers that:

> When people are in their Element, they connect with something fundamental to their sense of identity, purpose, and well-being. Being there provides a sense of self-revelation, of defining who they really are and what they're really meant to be doing with their lives (p.21).

For the people involved in this enquiry, there is little doubt that they feel 'in their element' through their engagement with the wider community. Without exception they all have passion and aptitude, but the full force of what they do is given direction by their moral compass, their sense of justice and social responsibility. A commitment to 'people' is considered just as important, if not more important than their commitment to 'art'. That is why they feel 'in their element'. An artist who is primarily obsessed by their talent, aptitude and passion for their art can easily become excessively self-absorbed and trapped in a bubble – rather like Gillian Tett's bankers at the end of Chapter 1. This self-referential mentality plays no part in community engagement, which necessarily entails the artist connecting to a wider context in their search for shared social, cultural and artistic meaning.

The main thrust of this position is argued strongly by Howard Gardner (2008) in his book *Five Minds for the Future.* Alongside 'The Disciplined Mind', 'The Synthesizing Mind' and 'The Creating Mind', Gardner emphasises the central place of 'The Respectful Mind' and 'The Ethical Mind' when people from different disciplines, backgrounds and cultures collaborate and work together. 'Respect for persons as ends in themselves' (rather than using people as a 'means' to an end) is the over-riding moral principle that guides and regulates our actions in relation to others (see Downie and Telfer, 1969, pp.15, 37). It entails accepting and tolerating differences, understanding other people's points of view, valuing who they are as individual persons, recognising that they have a unique voice that needs to be heard. This lies at the core of the moral imperative that underpins any form of community engagement.

To illustrate the way in which music can transcend differences and bring seemingly different people together, Gardner (2008, pp.121-122) takes the West-Eastern Divan Orchestra as an example. Started by Daniel Barenboim and the late Edward Said in 1999, the orchestra is premised on the moral principle that each individual musician – young Israeli and young Arab from Palestine, Jordan, Syria, Lebanon, Egypt and Iran – has the right to be respected as a person despite the conflict and alienation they experience in their daily lives at home. The music (largely European classical) transcends boundaries, whilst the act of making music together builds bridges and fosters a shared understanding in an otherwise hostile world.

Barenboim sees a symphony orchestra as a 'template for democracy'. He has said that "when you play in an orchestra you have to express yourself, and simultaneously listen to what others are playing and saying" (Church, 2009, p.4). The metaphor of 'conversation' has a strong resonance with this moving example of 'engaged passion' in a very disparate, fractured community. The musical conversation at the heart of the West-Eastern Divan Orchestra is succeeding in bringing about better understanding and heightened mutual respect, qualities that are central to having a 'respectful mind'. Drawing on the words of Barenboim and Said (2002, pp.6, 10 & 11), Gardner (2008) points out that:

The joint activities of making music together by day and talking through difficult issues in the evening have the effect of bringing members of the two groups closer together. As explained by Barenboim and Said, "They were trying to do something together, something about which they both cared, about which they were both passionate (…) The transformation of these kids from one thing to another was basically unstoppable (…) In cultural matters, if we foster this kind of contact, it can only help people feel nearer to each other and this is all" (p.122).

Daniel Barenboim would be the first to insist that passion by itself will not produce quality, but it is a sine qua non for igniting the spark in others, for creating the conditions for other people's creativity to flourish, for providing the inspiration that will draw others into a creative process that matters to them. Both the artist and participant become fully engaged and neither wishes to be fobbed off with work of questionable quality.

2.2 Examples of what drives the arts practitioners in this enquiry

As was indicated earlier in this chapter, the interviews, testimonies and case studies in this enquiry demonstrate that each person subscribes to the qualities, values and attitudes that are implicit in the fundamental moral principle of 'respect for persons'. Their engagement with the community manages to marry their passion for their art and for people with their passion for creating quality artistic experience that respects and listens to the voices of all participants. Time and again the human qualities raised include:

respect; empathy; tolerance; compassion; honesty; generosity; patience; integrity; authenticity; openness; curiosity; ego-less

A clear example of a project leader being driven by her commitment to the values underpinned by the principle of 'respect for persons' is found in the testimony of Linda Rose, who founded Music for Life in 1993. In her description of her sensitive and at times, uncertain journey exploring the place of music in dementia care, Linda states that:

Music for Life is not a methodology but rather a journey to embark upon with the possibility of emerging from the confusion to find something of oneself along the way. Its values and beliefs are transmitted from one to another, just as some sense of what is important was transmitted to me. This has been and still is subject to constant testing and integral to my own personal and professional development... The project has taken with it so many people from so many different walks of life and encouraged them to support and participate – and fund. This is a constant source of amazement and delight for me for they are recognising and sharing this set of values, a belief in what is essentially human and important in life – a need to relate and respect (6.2 J).

In their different ways all the managers and practitioners interviewed describe how they aim to connect to the people they are working with, unlocking their creative potential, developing their skills and understanding within a supportive environment, free of competing agendas and the possible constraints of 'political correctness'. One interviewee made the perceptive observation that "political correctness can become a tyranny – it can lead to dysfunction and can stifle creativity".

The personal testimonies provide a rare window into seeing what drives people to be so committed to what they do in such a wide variety of contexts. For example, Sara Lee, Artistic Director of Music in Prisons, experienced a transformative moment during her first gig in HMP Wormwood Scrubs, where she spontaneously performed a work composed by one of the inmates. The response from his peers was so respectful and deeply moving that Sara has been working in prisons ever since. These are the kind of feelings that still drive Sara:

> 25 years on and although quite different, my passion is still there. Increased knowledge has only brought more of a desire to make what the man and the audience felt available to more people, as I believe music and the process of creating it makes a massive difference to people's lives. The content of my work may have changed but the same things about it still make me happy, make me angry and drive my motivation to continue.
>
> Over the years it has been amazing to be in a position to offer people who need and deserve it, a voice, the chance to be heard and a new opportunity. For me, the work throws up more than just the challenge of guiding disparate groups of people through a music project. I love music and am fascinated by people and what makes them tick, so it is a privilege to be able to use these two things in combination in my working life. It is remarkable that you can go into such a dark and austere place yet be able to create something beautiful within it. The combination of containment and musical freedom is a paradox but there is something really exciting if a little bizarre about giving people in prison this metaphorical freedom (6.2 H).

Similar strength of feeling and insight can be found in two testimonies from totally different parts of the world – Sweden and Brazil. Anna-Karin Gullberg is the Co-leader and Founder of a radical project, BoomTown Music Education, in the regeneration area of Borlänge, Sweden. Reflecting on her motivation, Anna-Karin says that:

> (...) my driving force is at least two-headed: my conviction that as persons we are much more interesting and happy, and our relations more giving and fruitful if we are honest, real, authentic, alive, engaged, enthusiastic, bold and beautiful! To achieve this you have to be guided to look into yourself – into the content of who you are – and not only to the outside, to the form (...) My other driving force is the fact that from birth I have had a feeling that I am here on earth to make a difference. I have always had a spiritual (not a religious) perspective on life, on meaningfulness and a kind of seriousness when it comes to fighting for equality,

growing in consciousness and reforming institutions to support spiritual evolvement (6.2 D).

Moving to Brazil we find Heloisa Feichas whose mission is to transform the way music is perceived and learnt in the School of Music in the Federal University of Minas Gerais. She is aiming to strengthen links between the university and its wider community which suffers from major social problems, social inequality, poverty and poor quality education. Heloisa points out that:

> Finding a way of inspiring students (from the Music School) to be active in the world has been my target: working with a pedagogy that allows the students to discover about themselves; helping them to unlock different doors according to their needs and their consciousness; also provoking them to look at the world outside the Music School and to understand its needs and what we as artists can do to transform it...

> All this work is important for me because I want to make a difference to the world in which I live. The motivation for me to be involved in all my educational projects is to influence people (students) to be critical and conscious in the world. I believe we can change things through passion, through commitment and developing our knowledge and skills. This means engaging in a constant process of learning and searching, always using our sense of curiosity and creativity. It is fascinating to think about expanding a community of musicians that are also learners, thinkers and creative artists (...)

> The artistic and social criteria for judging the effectiveness of my musical work has to do with the level of happiness, motivation, joy and pleasure in doing it, which will consequently affect other peoples' feelings – also in the pleasure of attaining new knowledge and expanding it (6.2 B).

Sara, Anna-Karin and Heloisa might or might not see themselves as 'subversive' but each one of them cares passionately about connecting and responding to people so that their individual voices can be heard and respected. To achieve this they have had to ask searching questions that have inevitably challenged the status quo. But they have succeeded – they have been listened to and the 'system' has been nudged forwards in order to respond to the changes that have been generated from within.

Linda Rose is also very perceptive as she traces her own inner journey about how Music for Life gradually unfolded.

> In trying to build a picture of why and how Music for Life came about, I have had all sorts of conversations, both with myself and with others. I am told that yes I am curious, that I like to be connected and that I am secretly subversive. I like creating unexpected and what initially seem to be impossible relationships between individuals and groups of people. I love watching people find themselves and know, from my own experience, this happens slowly. I like the challenge of changing systems but know this happens slowly too, and am patient.

Once the sporty, active participant I have changed into the observer, looking on and processing. I like to watch people, anywhere and everywhere, at railway stations, in traffic jams, in restaurants, or engaged on our projects. I am interested in the places, the contexts in which people live their lives and how they respond to them, or are shaped by them. I believe that all people are creative until the very end of their lives and that empowering people to find themselves is the most meaningful thing I can do in my life. All of this I suppose underpins the growth of Music for Life (6.2 J).

Linda's belief that "all people are creative until the very end of their lives" would be shared by Clare Chacksfield who directs Eastfeast in East Anglia – a very successful multidisciplinary project that draws on the arts, horticulture and education. For Clare the 'metaphor of growing' lies at the heart of the Eastfeast process. This forms the basis of a collaborative 'learning journey' that acts as a 'catalyst for change'.

There is something that continues to captivate me about this work as it embraces all the things that feed me – metaphorically, spiritually and literally. The importance of sustainability as part of our way of life goes beyond the parameters of the day job and is a part of our mission, to enable young people to have authentic contact with the real and tangible outside world so they can protect it for future generations to enjoy (...)

I am captivated by the transformational potential that a nexus of relationships between the arts, horticulture and education seems to have (...) My daily work reminds me of the meaningful and therefore potentially therapeutic effect on people's wellbeing that this alchemy of art forms can create. As a team we take a subversive interest in being an organisation that is a catalyst for change, and part of the changes we see come about as a result of the combination of disciplines (6.2 A).

The 'metaphorical', 'spiritual' and 'literal' aspects of Eastfeast – that is, its essentially holistic nature – is a constant source of inspiration for Clare and her team, who see the project mirroring the ebb and flow of life. Similarly, Ninja Kors' commitment to a holistic philosophy is partly rooted in her experience of playing the gamelan whilst a student in ethnomusicology at the University of Amsterdam. The feeling of 'one-ness' within the 'gong phrase' is described quite poetically by Ninja in her testimony.

To fall into place in this massive but subtle wall of sound. To hear the notes coming to you through the throng of brass keys. To hear ornamentations do their somersaults and skipping jumps, only to land on their feet again at the end of the gong phrase. The gong phrase! Not landing on the count of one, like in most western music which leaves the rest of the bar to its own devices. No, the gong phrase ends on the count of eight, the final beat. The whole phrase works towards that beat, and every note comes together on that final note. The gong phrase carries within itself a sense of one-ness. It is strongly connected with the culture that developed it: the religious notions, how the universe fits together, how a community is formed. And most of all, it is a musical principle that gives identity to the music itself (6.2 G).

Ninja carries this holistic perspective into her work at the World Music & Dance Centre in Rotterdam. It is absolutely central to how she sees the connections between projects, community engagement and sense of personal and musical identity.

In many of the testimonies the roots of people's motivation can be found in a significant moment in childhood – a person, event or thread of experiences that once evoked powerful feelings but which continue to burn away inside them and prompt them to act in ways that do full justice to their deeply felt principles. There is a sense of necessity and urgency that drives each person to strike out and strive to make a qualitative difference to other people's lives.

In England, if there is one person who has made a significant mark on music education over the last 50 years or more, it is John Stephens – former teacher, County Music Adviser, HM Inspector, Staff Inspector for Music with the Inner London Education Authority, founder of the Music Education Department at Trinity College of Music and adviser to numerous major organisations such as Youth Music, the Britten-Pears School in Aldeburgh, The Sage Gateshead, the Royal Opera House and all of the London Orchestras. It is a formidable track record and one from which I personally have benefited over the last 30 years. John has always been there for me as a key sounding board. This was especially the case when I gave birth to the Music Performance and Communication Skills Project at the Guildhall School of Music & Drama in 1984. Even now he continues to be a shrewd listening ear and critical friend.

John's commitment has always been focused on young people, teachers and musicians and he has never wavered in bringing the professions of music and education closer together. At the end of his testimony John asks himself those fundamental questions that continue to drive him and which could well act as an example for others who wish to make a difference in music education.

> What forces have sustained and nurtured this belief in the value of music and the importance of the educational process? Why am I still excited by the performances of students and young people? What depths of curiosity compel me to continually ask 'why?' in almost every musical encounter? How does the political imperative drive me to the 'What would happen if ....?' question. Like pebbles on a beach, picking up one to examine only reveals another. I'm a beachcomber and, fortunately the landscape is rich with opportunities for reflections (6.2 K).

Perhaps John started out his life in Portsmouth as a musical 'beachcomber'. During his Wartime childhood no one particular event stands out as of over-riding influence, but there is no doubt that he was hungry to experience any music that came his way – from the Royal Marine band to the 'wireless' and the church. Opportunities for music in school only came to John when he was 16, but by then he had built up an eclectic musical palette which helped him be receptive to the many experiences that came his way. But more than that, he also began to develop a feeling for the power of music in people's lives. For example:

> By the year of my eighth birthday, the marines from Eastney barracks had all gone off to be cockleshell heroes in the Second World War whilst I, an evacuee, began to learn, first the piano and then the violin. Nightly visits to the air raid shelter in the garden were set alongside an increasing interest in music. I later realised that the 'Home Front', as the civilian population was called, found great comfort and support from musical activity and I too absorbed the cultural environment of the time: listening, between news bulletins, to music programmes.

> I keenly mastered Bach's *Jesu, joy of Man's Desiring* because Dame Myra Hess, a notable pianist of the day, had made her mark with a piano arrangement for her regular war-time recitals at London's National Gallery. As I now realise, this was an age in which music was valued for the emotional and spiritual support it provided in a stressful time: Vera Lynne's *There'll be Blue Birds over the White Cliffs of Dover* and other popular songs had significance to all the families whose fathers were away fighting for King and country whilst their wives valiantly coped with trying to maintain as normal life as possible (6.2 K).

When it came to leaving school at aged 18 John was in no doubts about the direction he wanted to take. No one could have been clearer!

> By this time an enthusiasm for music – making and listening – had focussed and I strongly wished to share with others the feelings and excitement I had in this involvement: it was akin to a missionary zeal. I found in music a deeply rewarding emotional involvement, satisfaction and fulfilment that I realised I had the capacity to pass to others. Thus when my dad asked what I wanted to do with my life the answer, as I clearly recall, came directly – 'to teach music' (6.2 K).

For Renee Jonker, Director of société Gavigniès, a foundation for sponsoring music, childhood memories are also very strong and he is always keen to find out what drives people towards music. In his testimony he says how fascinated he is to ask musicians 'when were they born in music?' Answering this question himself, Renee, who has a very broad view about the nature and place of the arts in society, makes the following response:

> My personal moment of 'birth' must have been on a Thursday evening and not 'in' music but 'through' music. On Thursdays my parents would leave for Rotterdam to sing in an opera choir (...) In those days Thursday evening was the time of the VPRO broadcasting, devoted to avant-garde cinema and theatre. This was my window on a world that was strange, confusing, seductive, mysterious and magical at the same time, but in any case a lot larger than the world I had been living in. The movies of Fellini, Pasolini, Fassbinder, Herzog, Wenders, Truffaut, Visconti, Godard, the absurd theatre of Wim T. Schippers, the unique documentaries of Cherry Duyns and Hans Verhagen – they all had a great impact

on developing my taste for art. After seeing these kinds of films on television, it was only natural that I should enjoy the music of Cage and Ligeti, which of course made me a complete outsider with the other kids in school (6.2 F).

To understand Eugene van Erven's passionate commitment to community art one also has to go back to his childhood. At the moment Eugene lectures in the Theatre Department of Utrecht University, directs a triennial International Festival of Community Arts in Rotterdam and is a researcher in the Community Art Lab, Utrecht. As a child Eugene experienced the stark contrast of rural village life on the Belgian border and that of an urban working-class neighbourhood in Utrecht. Another significant influence was his marriage to a Caribbean nurse with whom he has travelled worldwide. This social and cultural background has helped to:

> (...) lay the foundation for a life of intercultural communication and, together with the village theatre that my uncles and aunts were involved in back in the rural south, for my lifelong interest in community art. I believe in the power of art made in close collaboration with the people who live in these places and for whom active involvement in the arts is not self-evident (6.3 A).

For Robert Wells, Programme Leader, Professional Pathways, at the Guildhall School of Music & Drama, the expectations of his parents and teachers had a profound effect on the opportunities offered during his childhood. Unfortunately, Robert was placed in a failing secondary school in which teachers had low expectations of the students. When he was 15 the school was 're-launched', with a new building and an almost complete change of staff. This change led directly to Robert becoming a musician.

> When the school was re-opened we got a new music teacher. Unlike my previous teachers he was inspirational. Realising that we were all likely to fail the music course we were doing, he started after-school clubs and even opened the school on several Sundays for us to have additional lessons. Interestingly, given the lack of interest most of us had for school, the majority of the class turned up to these additional sessions. After about a term he pulled me to one side and asked if I would be interested in studying A Level music at the school, a course he was looking to introduce the following year. His belief that we could meet his high expectations, that we could be successful, was exceptionally powerful and transformed my life.

> The belief that others can achieve great things if placed in a supportive environment has informed and affected my own teaching. This was probably most evident whilst I worked at NewVIc, a sixth form college in East London (...) NewVIc was a revelation – an oasis. The college, only a few years old, was in the heart of London's East End, which is deprived and diverse in equal measure. The attitude of the tutors was that the students could achieve any goal they set themselves. As staff we were encouraged to try new ideas, challenging ourselves, the students and a number of orthodoxies surrounding how best to teach the performing arts. This environment proved to be hugely beneficial both to the students and the staff (6.2 M).

The source of many people's motivation is inevitably connected in some significant way to childhood, school or family. For others, they are shaped by how they respond to a traumatic event like an accident. Life-choices and future direction often have to be completely reappraised when a person is suddenly confronted by the unexpected. This happened to Judith Webster, when an accident in her final year at university prevented her from entering the music profession as a violinist. At the beginning of her Case Study outlining her journey into music therapy, Judith describes how she re-oriented her motivation and re-directed her energies and commitment.

Everything changed for me at the beginning of my final year studying music at Birmingham University. Like many musicians, I had mapped out my intended career. Following university, I was to go to music college as a postgraduate followed by a short career as a professional musician in an orchestra (maybe 10 years), followed by something more down to earth after I had fulfilled my lifelong dream and got it out of my system. Then I had an accident, crushed my left hand, and began to get to grips with the most important lesson of my life. You can't plan your own destiny, and if you try to, fate might get in your way, and you may well be blind to the most creative opportunities which lie right in front of you.

So, from the outset my personal journey towards being a music therapist was littered with judgements around quality and hierarchies associated with different musical skills in the music world. The pinnacle was to be a player; if you couldn't do that then you would teach. I went abroad to have a think.

Music therapy was always a natural bringing together of two important aspects of my life in a truly creative context; my music, and my tendency to be drawn to challenging social contexts that forced me to think and grow – at that time evidenced through voluntary work. However, I had already considered and rejected music therapy as a career path, prior to university, as to me it felt like second best. Now that fate had closed the door on a potential playing career (as a violinist), I had to take another look at who I was and what I might do. There was never any question about it being in music, but I have always been driven by personal conviction and was incapable of simply drifting into an alternative career if it did not feel right.

There followed a two-year journey towards music therapy, and subsequently, through the work itself, a discovery of my true musical and personal strengths and how they could be expressed in the context of music therapy practice (6.3 M).

Returning to The Netherlands, for Marga Wobma-Helmich, the new Director of Education, Participation and Programming at the National Ballet and Nederlandse Opera, music has always been an integral part of who she is. Marga grew up in a home "filled with music". The seeds of her passion for music were sown in her childhood. As she points out:

The question whether I wanted to play an instrument was never asked; the only question was which instrument I wanted to play. Asking the first question would have felt the same as asking if I wanted to grow up. It's a useless question because growing up is a given fact of life. Just like making music. The only question is how you want to grow up or how you want to become musically active (6.2 N).

Marga was formerly responsible for developing the education programme of Het Concertgebouw in Amsterdam. In this capacity she felt her motivation, energy and commitment to quality all came together. In her testimony she writes:

> What keeps me motivated to do my work is that my energy comes from a natural resource. I love what I do and I have the opportunity to keep on developing in many different ways – as a creator, as a facilitator and as a leader. Quality is always an issue in all areas – for the performances and projects, for the preparation, in how you communicate your ideals, in how you try to motivate people to join you on this journey. It's not that I believe music is the only or strongest language in making the world a place worth living in. It's because music is the language which enables me to communicate and make a contribution to our society (6.2 N).

My final example from The Netherlands is taken from the testimony of Debora Patty who leads the Education team for Yo! Opera Festival and Laboratory in Utrecht. Debora has a dual passion – working in the creative arts and with young people (she is training to be a primary school teacher). She sees this relationship as part of a 'shared journey' that contains all aspects of life.

> I think art and creativity have a very important role because they touch your inside, your identity, your emotions and the way you look at things...(I love the freedom that art brings. It allows you to cross [unwritten] boundaries or barriers that are blocking your view or keeping you from 'playing'.) (...) At the centre of it all is 'relationship'. Your relationship with yourself, your relationship with others and the way you connect the two. I believe that honesty, openness and integrity are key words. This also counts for the way you work with people as an organisation (6.2 I).

Debora's commitment to certain fundamental values and to ways of seeing the world were also formed in early childhood. Her philosophy and beliefs are deeply rooted, although carried lightly in her work and in her relationships with people.

> For me it all starts where I was brought up – my family. I was born and raised in a Christian family. Faith still has a big role in my life. It tells me I have been made for a reason, that I have been given a set of principles and talents to enjoy life to the fullest and to help others to do the same. That is my responsibility. That is about the quality of life. That is why I am here (6.2 I).

I have left one narrative to the end: that of Sean Gregory, who was Head of Centre for Creative Practice at the Guildhall School of Music & Drama but who recently was appointed to the new position of Director of Creative Learning for the Barbican-Guildhall. This partnership, together with its organic links to the London Symphony Orchestra, now forms the basis of a Campus or Cultural Quarter that has enormous creative potential (see Appendix 6.2 C).

What stands out in Sean's testimony is the coherent thread, the sense of continuity that runs throughout his personal and professional journey – right from primary school to the Barbican. Sean's life has always been adventurous, displaying a passion for change and driven by a commitment to creativity, collaboration and community. In his words:

> The primary school I attended laid the perfect foundation for me. Looking back I think it was an example of 1960s/70s philosophy and values at its best; nurturing and intelligently child-centred, with a firm but fair line in discipline. Creativity, learning and working in groups was at the heart of all we did. I needed little encouragement in getting my own projects going, even at the age of 9 or 10, most of which involved drama and music-making. I was already taking and enjoying classical piano lessons out of school, and took particular pleasure in forming 'bands' with friends in order to play pop songs of the day. The funny thing is that these 'bands' consisted mainly of friends playing home-made percussion instruments (music enthusiasts who were not having music lessons), my brother on clarinet and myself on piano. We even composed our own pieces, which I suppose could represent my first experience of informal music-making.

> Central to my primary school experience, however, was a drama club (...) These after school workshops, full of improvisation, discussion, creative group exercises and ambitious school play productions had a huge impact on me. This is where I began to 'find my voice' as a young person; whilst it was too early to know what direction it was going to take me in, I already felt my identity emerging by contributing to processes that made things happen through creativity in the arts, particularly drama, writing and, to a lesser extent at that time, music.

Armed with this sound foundation from an enlightened primary school, Sean moved on to the more traditional Kingston Grammar School, where he took up the flute, whilst on Saturdays he studied at Trinity College Junior Music School. After the initial culture shock of leaving primary school, Sean says:

> I was now 'on track' again. I had a flourishing musical life at Kingston, with plenty of non-formal music-making in bands, and a trip to central London every Saturday, which I relished. Composing was becoming increasingly important to me, and I was openly encouraged to develop this interest at both Trinity and Kingston, despite the fact that composition did not feature in the curriculum at that time. What I was increasingly realising was that I loved the communal aspect of music-making; playing in ensembles with mixed line-ups, often by ear, exploring and improvising around a variety of styles and genres, coming up with our own ideas and then putting them into practice.

Sean was then faced with a dilemma confronting many young music students having to choose between a conservatoire route or that of a university – a very difficult decision for a versatile musician with eclectic musical tastes and broad cultural interests. Thanks to the care of his music teacher, Sean went to study at Bath College of Higher Education which ran a progressive Music Degree programme.

> The biggest revelation to me was the 'workshop' approach taken in the majority of classes and seminars, much of this being pioneered by the then Head of Composition and Music Education, George Odam. He and his departmental staff constantly encouraged us to be curious, to take risks and to think laterally as practitioners, engaging with as many approaches, styles and music-making as possible, as well as other arts disciplines and cultures. The funniest thing looking back is that during my undergraduate years of 1984-87 I was experiencing creative workshops led by one of our composition tutors, Nick Atkinson, who was picking up his ideas first hand from courses led by Peter Wiegold, who at that time was artistic leader for the MPCS pilot years at the Guildhall School.

On graduation Sean was again confronted with the question, 'what next?' "How on earth was I going to make sense of all these experiences and passions and translate them into some sort of meaningful and sustainable future professional pathway?" Sean was then shown details of the new postgraduate course in Performance and Communication Skills at the Guildhall and he decided to apply, as he felt that the course brought many of his interests in music and theatre together. This then became a critical moment in his life.

> If ever I was pushed to identify a seminal moment in my professional development it would have to be the audition experience I had for the PCS course at Guildhall. It was a revelation at this time to be asked as a musician competing for a place at an internationally renowned conservatoire not only to perform pieces on my principal instrument, but also to engage with a participatory workshop that involved musical and theatrical improvisation, as well as an interview exploring my own motivation for wanting to come on the course. This particular day, and the year that followed when on the course, quickly helped me to make sense of the many seemingly unconnected and even conflicting pathways I had taken up to that point. My primary passion felt genuinely able to reveal itself at this time; an uncompromising commitment to the power of creativity through collaboration amongst people, in artistic, community and educational settings (6.2 C).

These vignettes can only give a flavour of what motivates each individual in this enquiry. But it is clear that each person wants to make a difference in their own distinctive way. What is compelling is that they are all driven by very similar values and attitudes, although these manifest themselves in many different ways depending on their particular context. Their values and principles help to ground their self-evident 'passion'. Their search for knowledge, for new forms of practice and new ways of learning provides the backbone for their engagement and empowerment. Although in some senses they might see themselves as 'outsiders' (that is on the periphery of what most arts people see as 'core business'), in the current climate of change, their voices are increasingly being listened to. They now have to ensure that as their voices shift from the 'margins' to the 'centre', the strength and substance of their engagement is not diluted or weighed down by some leaden orthodoxy!

2.3   Personal motivation

During the interviewing process for this enquiry several people started challenging me about the source of my own motivation. As they were being asked personal life-shaping questions they felt that I should also say something about what has driven me over many years and perhaps most importantly, what continues to drive me. Without elaborating too much, the significant moments in this personal journey stand out pretty clearly.

As a child growing up in London during the War, my strongest memories all involve music. My mother had been a piano teacher and my father was an amateur 'cellist. Chamber music was their lifeline during those years of uncertainty. For me it was just part of the furniture. When I went away to school at the age of nine my main interest turned to singing and playing the violin. This growing passion quickly took over and during school holidays my enthusiasm was fired up further by singing in cathedral choirs and playing in the National Youth Orchestra. Little else mattered – I was rapidly creating my own small cultural bubble! I then sang my way into Cambridge as a Choral Scholar and embarked on a music degree. Not surprisingly, my life was dominated by performing music. I played in many different orchestras and formed a string quartet that was coached regularly by Colin Davis – a most inspirational experience.

But this seemingly cosy bubble was first pricked in 1956, when my political awakening began with news of the Hungarian Revolution and the Suez Crisis. This was the year when I also changed subjects to History. I had become disenchanted with a music course that seemed peculiarly disconnected from music-making and music performance. For me and for many other performers, it was arid and alienating. In contrast, the history course opened doors to a world that broadened my horizons and excited my curiosity about a life beyond music.

The three years after Cambridge were highly formative, as they took me into uncharted territory that provoked me to question many assumptions about my life that previously I had taken for granted. During National Service in the army I was posted to Singapore where I was responsible for a troop of British, Malay, Chinese, Indian and Singhalese soldiers – my first and enduring experience of multiculturalism. On return to England in 1959 I spent a year in industry, first as a management trainee and then as a sales representative.

During these three years I did very little music but my view of the world substantially shifted. I began to see that my privileged education and total immersion in music had distorted my perception and had protected me from a social reality that increasingly I was finding challenging and engaging. My growing anger with the social injustices embedded in the class system prompted me to go into teaching. In 1960 many people felt that education could play a significant role in changing the world, whereas today we might view such idealism as rather naïve! Anger, then, became a major force in my desire to generate change – and that has remained with me to the present day.

Whilst training to be a teacher at Oxford in 1960 a lot of attention was being given to World Refugee Year. Through the United Nations Association (UNA) students were going out to Austria to help build houses for the many refugees living in camps. Houses were obviously a basic need but I thought that live music might also be another way of enriching their lives. UNA was enthusiastic, the BBC gave me free access to their music library, whilst Ford Motor Company donated a vehicle for the trip. In the summer of 1961 I took 11 versatile musicians out to Austria for a month where we lived in the refugee camps in Linz, Graz, Salzburg and Vienna, giving daily concerts to children, parents and elderly people. The following year we repeated this with 22 musicians.

Out of the 60 concerts or so one particularly stands out. Whilst in Salzburg we took a string quartet to play to one elderly lady in her small room in a TB sanatorium. She was Hungarian and had been a professional violinist in Vienna before the War. For 15 years she had not heard any live music. We knew her background so we played Bartók, Kodályi and Haydn's 'Emperor' Quartet. In the middle of the slow movement of the Haydn, which is a set of variations on the theme of the Austrian national anthem, the atmosphere became highly emotional as it evoked so many memories for the elderly violinist. This deeply moving experience became **the** major transformative moment in my life. So much of what has happened since, hangs on the feelings and memories of that particular afternoon. Why?

One very simple point stands out – the potential power of music in people's lives, especially when heard in an 'ordinary' everyday setting. Of course, performances in a concert hall or theatre can be exciting, emotionally charged and highly illuminating. But the intimacy of a musical conversation in a more private space is something that can be very personal and compelling. This memory has remained alive within me and has inspired me to ensure that any performance or workshop has to connect to the social and cultural context of its audience or participants if it is to make any sense to them. For me this is central to the idea of engagement.

Two areas of my life have been most directly inspired by the refugee camp experience. Firstly, as Principal of the Yehudi Menuhin School from 1975 to 1984, I wanted to broaden the horizons of the talented young musicians by creating opportunities for them to perform in contexts outside the normal concert hall. We gradually built up and sustained relationships with a number of institutions and communities that could not have been more different from the Menuhin School – for example, hospices, psychiatric hospitals, homes for elderly people, centres for disabled people, young offenders' units and schools. One especially rewarding partnership was with the coal mining village of Thurcroft outside Rotherham in the north of England. Over a three-day visit students would perform in St. Luke's Hospice, Sheffield, in Thurcroft Church and in the local primary school. They also stayed with families in the village and went down the pit face in the colliery. Reciprocal visits were then made by Thurcroft children and parents to the Menuhin School. I would like to think that these experiences added another dimension to the way in which the young musicians saw the role that music can play in society.

On leaving the Menuhin School in 1984 I was invited by John Hosier, the then Principal of the Guildhall School of Music & Drama, to start a project which we called initially Music Performance and Communication Skills (MPCS). Again, the spirit of this initiative lies in the memories of making music in the refugee camps over 20 years previously. This is not the place to enter into the history of what later became PCS and then Guildhall Connect, but it is interesting to look at the kind of assumptions underlying the first proposal for MPCS (Renshaw, 1984). For example:

The belief that musicians should become more responsive to the musical challenges arising from our rapidly changing society.

The belief that musicians should recognise the role that music might play in a world of rising unemployment and enforced leisure.

The belief that music, along with the other arts, has a central role to play in the regeneration of society.

The belief that music not only has its own intrinsic value but that it can be therapeutic and help give meaning to people's lives in many different contexts.

The belief that musicians have a responsibility to help create new audiences for the future.

The belief that musicians should consider the possible danger of the egocentric and self-contained nature of their activities.

The belief that conservatoires should prepare their students more effectively with the skills, knowledge and insights necessary for communicating with audiences in different contexts.

The belief that the attitudes and preconceptions of young musicians need to be challenged by bringing more searching and fundamental approaches to their education and training.

In a letter of support for the idea of MPCS Yehudi Menuhin made the following observation:

> As far as the Guildhall students are concerned, there is no doubt that the experience of playing in various situations other than the normal concert hall, such as Broadmoor Prison and homes for terminal care etc., broadens the otherwise egocentric nature of musical careers. It is invaluable for the experience of the young performer because it enables him or her to relate self-expression to its valid reflection from the audience – in depth, revealing as might an X-ray photograph, the state of the audience. I have always felt that there is a very strong argument for introducing this relationship as early as possible into civilised society, which has strayed so far from that primitive recognition of the parallel between the very act of living and its musical and artistic expression in rhythm, melody and harmony.

It can be seen from this personal perspective that initially my main thrust was 'connecting to context' through performance. But right from the beginning, one of the strongest features of MPCS, which continues to lie at the heart of Guildhall Connect, was its commitment to developing different forms of creative collaboration and performance practice. Under the artistic direction of Peter Wiegold, supported by a team of composers and workshop leaders, the policy of the project took the following shape:

> The main aim of the Project has been to create and explore new artistic forms, modes of presentation and ways of working which encourage greater communication between performers, composers, conductors and audiences. This policy, together with its related community development programme, has been designed to break down social, musical and artistic barriers. It has been working towards a new kind of performer/composer who can make connections with artists from other disciplines, and who can also respond to a wide variety of community contexts (Guildhall Ensemble, 1989).

Looking back over the last 25 years it is gratifying to see the way in which PCS and Guildhall Connect have evolved thanks to a dedicated team under the leadership of Sean Gregory, now Director of Creative Learning for the new Barbican-Guildhall Campus, as mentioned earlier. The potential of this joint department for creative learning is enormous, especially as it will work closely with all art-form departments in the Barbican and with the London Symphony Orchestra. The shape and scope of this development is touched on by Sean towards the end of his testimony (see Appendix 6.2 C).

2.4   From passion to quality

There is little doubt that the Barbican-Guildhall initiative is a sign of the times and reflects one way in which a major multi-disciplinary arts complex, allied to its residential orchestra, the LSO, and further enriched by its associate and visiting artists, is responding to and helping to shape the changing cultural landscape. Together with its network of international, national and local partners, the whole complex can be seen as a creative hub, a laboratory that is at the cutting edge of arts practice.

The main emphasis in this chapter has been on exploring the passion, the source of motivation that drives people to do what they do. Similar values and drivers are also likely to underpin the spirit, energy and vision of the many artists, practitioners and cultural leaders who are committed to making the Barbican-Guildhall concept a living reality. This would be true of any vibrant cultural institution that harnesses the collective imagination and will of its artists and partners towards achieving a shared goal.

But as was stated unequivocally at the beginning of this chapter, passion by itself will not produce quality. That is equally true in the work of an international arts centre as it is in a school or any other community setting. The search for quality has now become one of the major critical issues confronting arts organisations and their practitioners as their work diversifies and extends into many different community contexts. The next three chapters address the complexity of determining what might count as quality and it is hoped that the arguments will contribute to the wider debate about quality and community engagement.

3

Partnerships and people

3.1 Connections, context and conversations

The quality of any community project is dependent largely on the effectiveness of all participants making meaningful connections, understanding and responding to each other's contexts and engaging in open conversations – guided at all times by the principle of 'respect for persons'. In other words, it is people – shaped by their intentions, values, beliefs, attitudes, perceptions, feelings, hopes, fears, uncertainties – that lie at the heart of any partnership. This spirit is expressed tellingly by Ninja Kors at the opening of her Personal Testimony. As Project Co-ordinator of the World Music & Dance Centre (WMDC) in Rotterdam, Ninja is well aware that at all times she has to be respectful of the many different voices contributing to the activities of the Centre.

> We are not alone... As people in this world we need to constantly find a balance between the big and the small. The local and the global. The 'me' and 'us'. It is a fascinating balance because it signifies how we need to be aware of both a sense of self, of who we are and where we belong, and of the notion that we are part of a bigger whole that gives us room to grow and challenges us to improve ourselves (6.2 G).

Maintaining this balance between our understanding of 'self' and 'other' is critical to creating and sustaining effective partnerships. As intimated in the last chapter, 'conversation' is a very powerful force in generating shared meaning and understanding because if it is to work, it has to respect differences, see commonalities and cross boundaries. It necessarily embodies such qualities as trust, openness, humility, integrity, empathy and active listening (see Renshaw, 2005a, p.100). Therefore, the health of any partnership depends on facilitating conversations that engage individual people and their organisations within the many contexts in which they work.

The transformational capacity of conversation within the context of partnership is highlighted by Theodore Zeldin in the Foreword to a publication, *Exploring the Impact of Creative Learning on Artists and Practitioners*, produced by Creative Partnerships London North (2007). Zeldin argues that "the key to a more adventurous kind of creativity requires not so much self-awareness as partnership" (p.5) – that is, strengthening our capacity to see ourselves and the world through other people's eyes.

> When two people learn from each other as equals, they are changing the world, because they are adding something to it that did not exist before, another particle of mutual understanding... So the question is no longer, 'Who am I?' but 'Who are you?' (CPLN, 2007, p.6).

This creative engagement with another person, through a meeting of minds, sharing experience, through reflective conversation, forms the bedrock of a successful partnership. Zeldin goes on:

> Conversation is a meeting of minds with different memories and habits. When minds meet, they don't just exchange facts: they transform them, draw different implications from them, engage in new trains of thought. Conversation doesn't just reshuffle the cards: it creates new cards (ibid. p.6).

The power of 'conversation', of critically reflective dialogue that connects to its context, has to be a fundamental principle in any successful partnership, as is evidenced in many of the case studies in this enquiry.

The Story Kitchen, Haarlem

In his Case Study of The Story Kitchen, situated in a multicultural working-class neighbourhood in the east of Haarlem, Eugene van Erven quotes an interview with Titia Bouwmeester, a visual artist and theatre maker whose ideas for The Story Kitchen grew out of her previous work in Delft in 2007. Titia makes clear some of the very real challenges that confront anyone aiming to create meaningful partnership in any community.

> Delft was one of the first times we worked in an actual neighbourhood. Before that, we worked in more enclosed environments, like a hospital, a prison (both with the site-specific performance group Dogtroep), a centre for asylum seekers, a psychiatric ward, a home for the elderly. In those places people already share a situation in common. Not in a neighbourhood, which is diffuse and where everyone wants something else. In Delft I discovered that you need to do more than turn people into documentary makers of their own lives. You also need to give people direct influence on their own existence. And because the people who live there are so diffuse, you also need much longer than the three months we had, to truly get to know the people, to generate local support for the work, to find out what they and what you want and what is possible, in short, before you can begin to make something together. (Interview between Eugene van Erven and Titia Bouwmeester, 28 October 2008) (6.3 A)

Building on this experience, Titia Bouwmeester ensured that as The Story Kitchen unfolded, the project drew on the support and creative energy of existing leaders in the neighbourhood – for example, two women who were the driving force of a new community centre for migrant women; an enterprising head teacher of a Broad School [1] that included a community centre, a primary school, a workshop for artists and a community kitchen. The artists then had the responsibility for developing the partnership.

---

1   A Broad School is a collaboration between partners involved with children and young people, with the aim of increasing opportunities for their development by initiating joint interconnected activities where education is the key. A Broad School is based on either a primary or secondary school but also includes sports, cultural activities, after-school care for children and social care.

Through their constructive, creative, and reliable participation in the planning meetings, the artists organically met and gained the trust of other stakeholders, such as the local representative of the public housing corporation 'PreWonen', politicians, social workers, the chairman of the informal neighbourhood council, and the editor of a local digital neighbourhood newspaper (6.3 A).

Building up any multi-faceted partnership is extremely demanding and as Titia Bouwmeester points out, "this work is continually searching for where the energy is and then to build on that and to place your personal ambitions as an artist on the backburner" (6.3 A).

The Brassband School, Rotterdam

Another example of harnessing the creative energy and interests of a local community can be found in Ninja Kors' Case Study on the development of the Brassband School (BBS) in the south of Rotterdam, which comprises a very culturally diverse neighbourhood.

The Antillean community is strongly social in the sense that social structures are defining in all areas, business and pleasure. The same goes for the Surinamese. In order to really reach the brass bands, one needs to be aware of how the social infrastructure fits together and how communication works within the community. The project leader of the Brassband School does not have an Antillean or Surinamese background but he is a community musician with an extensive network in many cultural groups. He has worked for several years in the communities of Rotterdam, of which the Antillean and Surinamese are a substantial part. He set up the BBS in Rotterdam South, a 'challenged' area where many Antillean people live. He did this by engaging brass bands in the development, and offering them rehearsal space in a building of the Rotterdam Music School (6.3 G).

The Operaflat, Yo! Opera Festival, Utrecht

Now, moving north from Rotterdam to Utrecht. In 2005 Anthony Heidweiller, Artistic Director of Yo! Opera Festival, initiated a new project, The Operaflat, as part of the Bi-annual Festival devoted to Community Opera. For the Festivals of 2005 and 2007 the project was placed under the guidance of Debora Patty and it continues to develop and strengthen its links with the residents of the flats in Overvecht. It would probably be fair to say that the project remains in the process of building up a mutually beneficial partnership between Yo!, schools, composers, singers and the residents. In her Case Study, Debora has been very honest about what has been learnt and continues to be learnt from The Operaflat. Again, people and relationships lie at the core of her observations:

I am amazed by the chemistry you get when you put different people together and introduce them to something totally new and crazy, like an Operaflat. They had to connect with people they would not normally meet. They had to find their position, they learned from each other and they were surprised by what they were capable of doing and what it meant for others.

But, with all these different groups of people, you have to be very clear about what you want from them. What do you want them to learn? What can they contribute to the process and the project? What are their qualities? What space do you give them? I think that we are now more and more conscious of the implications of this kind of project for our organisation – about our artistic goals, our social goals and our priorities (6.3 I).

For the 2009 Festival Yo! involved the residents of the flats more in the process of making an opera. The young people interviewed the residents as a starting point for writing a new opera. As Debora points out, "it is an experiment – a way of exploring the space that is available for people to join in, to really matter, to have an influence on the content and to have a voice". Debora feels adamant about this if the partnership is to be respectful of all participants:

Personally, I think that this is crucial – not just to put people in your project because you need them (or their door or a nice libretto), but to really think about the possible exchange. The learning goes both ways – to open the opera doors, to let people in, to start conversations and to leave them with a handful of new skills, new relationships, new experiences and new dreams (6.3 I).

dotComp training programme and the Royal Conservatoire, The Hague

Two of the Dutch musicians interviewed are especially concerned about the question of building up effective partnerships with schools and community groups: Renee Jonker, Director société Gavigniès, and Marga Wobma-Helmich, Director of Education, Participation and Programming at the National Ballet and Nederlandse Opera. Marga was former Head of Education at Het Concertgebouw, Amsterdam.

Renee started a training programme (dotComp) to enable professional musicians to develop and strengthen their skills in leading workshops and in setting up outreach activities. He has also initiated a course in Creative Music Making in the Classroom Music Teachers Department of the Royal Conservatoire in The Hague. In the light of this experience Renee raises several pertinent questions in his Case Study:

What has defined the limits of the dotComp programme so far?

What explanation can be given for failures in the programme?

How can 'quality' be defined for these kinds of activities?

What is this 'glass ceiling' that all parties involved experience, especially when they have put their full energy and enthusiasm into these activities?

What is missing in the formation of people leading and organising these programmes?

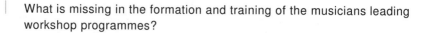

What is missing in the formation and training of the musicians leading workshop programmes?

How can one define the outlines for a partnership that is successful?

What are the specific conditions that make a successful partnership between an educational initiative (like the dotComp programme) or an educational institution (like the Royal Conservatoire)? (6.3 F)

Renee is well aware of the challenges arising from developing and sustaining meaningful partnerships within The Netherlands but his interest in investing in partnerships overseas, with their very different cultural contexts, is inevitably raising further questions and complexities.

> (The) need for evaluation has increased since new partnerships are to be developed by the société Gavigniès in the near future. These partnerships will expand the activities of the société Gavigniès abroad: the Melodi Music project in Pimville and Soweto (South Africa), the exchange programme of the Royal Conservatoire in The Hague with the University of Legon in Accra (Ghana) and with the Sarasvati School for Young Talent in Djakarta (Indonesia). All have applied for support from the société Gavigniès for developing outreach programmes. The challenges to invest in partnerships in a very different cultural context are enormous and it increases the demands on the quality of the dotComp programme substantially (6.3 F).

Education Programme, Het Concertgebouw, Amsterdam

Marga Wobma-Helmich is especially concerned by the effects of recent Dutch government initiatives to strengthen the capacity of schools and arts organisations to address a deficit in cultural learning in educational institutions.

> Our government has introduced some measures in order to stimulate schools to be more culturally active. It is seen as the responsibility of the schools as well as for the arts institutions. Instead of offering one-off projects, the arts institutions are expected to build up long-term relationships with schools and to help them develop an ongoing learning curve. Important ingredients are the three learning fields which are focused on the participation of the pupils in an active, receptive and reflective way. This role requires a major change in the way in which our programmes are constructed. But still, the main goal lies with musical outcomes. Another change of role is using the arts more for social goals than artistic: for example, using the arts to strengthen cohesion in society, to improve learning outcomes for pupils and so on.

> How can we as concert halls satisfy all these different roles? There are a lot of questions we ask ourselves. What elements are important in the music curriculum and how can we contribute to that as a concert hall? How can we make sure that we include all pupils from all different backgrounds? What can we offer as side effects of music education to our society and how can we bring this about? Who

are our partners? How can we train and who should be trained to do the actual job? (6.3 N).

Guildhall Connect and Globetown Education Action Zone, London

Through its Connect programme the Guildhall School of Music & Drama has been addressing some of the issues raised by Renee Jonker and Marga Wobma-Helmich over a number of years. In 2006 Rineke Smilde interviewed Sean Gregory (then Head of the Centre for Creative and Professional Practice at the Guildhall) about the factors that need to be considered when establishing sustained partnerships. Sean took as his example the work of Guildhall Connect with Globetown Education Action Zone in the London Borough of Tower Hamlets. The Guildhall began working in schools in this challenging neighbourhood of East London in the late 1980s and the Globetown partnership grew organically out of a number of its collaborations. Sean outlines the main features of the development.

> The Globetown Education Action Zone comprises a cluster of four primary schools and one secondary school. A Performing Arts Co-ordinator works for Globetown with an assistant in the secondary school. The schools agreed to have an annual performing arts project targeting top class primary school pupils (10/11 year olds) and instrumental learners from the secondary school (11-15 years). The first project took place in 1999 and it continues to grow each year.

> Education Action Zones were set up to in order to regenerate a particular area. Negotiation and liaison between organisations and individuals working within them are critical if this kind of partnership is to be successful. Creativity lies at the heart of the Globetown project. The point of departure is always the children's own ideas through music and words, facilitated by Guildhall postgraduate students (mostly on the music leadership masters programme) and the class teachers. With the experienced overview of a Guildhall tutor, the structure of the project piece starts to emerge, so that all participants feel a sense of ownership for the whole project...

> Since 2000 Paul Griffiths has been the Guildhall tutor leading the project. (More recently the leadership has been shared with Sigrun Saevarsdottir-Griffiths.) Paul's approach as a project leader and coach has been a crucial factor in building up a positive relationship with the Globetown schools and their teachers. He intuitively recognises and understands the strengths and weaknesses of the individuals and organisations involved. There is also a strong sense of trust and cooperation between the Globetown and Guildhall project management teams (R. Smilde interview with S. Gregory, February 2006 at GSMD).

February 2009 celebrated a 10-year partnership between Guildhall Connect and Globetown Education Action Zone. The collaboration between teachers, musicians, postgraduate students and management teams continues to strengthen the quality of work and has proved to be a good example of what can be achieved in a mutually enhancing relationship with clear shared aims.

Klangnetze Project, Vienna

Central to the success of the Connect/Globetown project is the growing working relationship between the teachers and music leaders. A similar observation about the importance of teacher-artist partnership is made by Christine Stöger (currently Professor and Head of Classroom Teachers' Training at the Hochschule für Musik, Cologne) in her Case Study of the Klangnetze Project in Vienna.

Klangnetze (1992 – 2000) was initiated by the Ministry of Art and Science in Vienna, especially to foster creativity and new music in the field of education. An expert in music education was selected to develop a concept and to carry it out. He first established a group of composers and musicians in the field of New Music for the project. Then teachers from primary and secondary schools were invited to participate with one of their classes.

The project phase started with a three-day workshop where teachers and artists came together to improvise and develop models of improvisation based on avant-garde sounds-noise and structures. Pairs of teachers and artists tried out their models in schools of the region and then reflected on the process.

After the workshop future partnerships were decided and the crucial phase started in selected schools. In a couple of workshops with the school classes, the classroom-teacher and artist team supported the pupils to create their own piece of music. Since most of the children did not play an instrument, they experimented with voice, body percussion and materials like paper, glass, etc. to create the music. The music pieces were finally performed in one of the large Viennese concert halls. All the participants and their families were invited. A person moderated the concert, which was especially necessary to prepare the audience for the unusual experimental and interdisciplinary creative products.

The most demanding point was how to build up a partnership between these two very different groups of people – teachers and artists. The project initiators worked against big prejudices with a long tradition. Some of the teams failed or in the worst case, just gave up. But most cases reported enriching experiences and an unforeseen musical development of their classes. Most progress was found in the area of co-operation because as the project was carried out over a number of years, a culture of partnership could be developed (6.3 L).

Music in Prisons, England and Wales

Moving into a very different environment, Sara Lee, Artistic Director of Music in Prisons, emphasises the importance of developing relationships and partnerships in her challenging work. Sara's view is strongly supported by a penetrating evaluation of her work in prisons (Cox and Gelsthorpe, 2008). For example:

The men regularly commented on how the process of creating, listening to, and collaborating on musical pieces impacted on their sense of self, their well-being, and their relationships to others (...) The men all commented on how music enhanced their mood, "broke barriers" between people, and made people "more full human beings" (p.14).

The evaluation report stressed that the collaborative music-making in groups strengthened the "men's relationships to each other as well as to individuals on the outside" (ibid, p.23). It maintains that:

> The importance of the experience of relatedness in this project cannot be understated. It was perhaps one of the more striking and surprising findings of this project, and may have important consequences for men's well-being and their ability to develop and cultivate empathy towards others (ibid, p.25).

But creating an environment that enables the inmates to build up effective relationships with each other, with prison staff and with the musicians is also largely dependent on the Music in Prisons team establishing strong working partnerships based on an informed mutual understanding. Sara Lee makes the point clearly in her Case Study.

> In any situation, good management is one of the keys to success and organising projects in prisons is no different. It is often as difficult to get into a prison as to get out of it and there are many hurdles to overcome before any kind of intervention can happen within them. Personal relationships and a keen understanding of what you are walking into are crucial at this stage as you are often dealing with people who have little or no understanding of the work. At this stage you *have* to understand their position and work closely with them to enable them to understand yours. If good relationships are built you will be welcome and you will succeed; if anything is taken for granted then the project will be in jeopardy (6.3 H).

In her conclusion Sara stresses the importance of bringing together all partners involved in any project so that they can share their reflections and views on the effectiveness of the preparation, process and product. This conversation helps to inform the development of any future project in prisons.

> In order to maintain the quality of the work over a long period of time, space for reflection on all aspects of the management and delivery is crucial. This allows the exchange of information, ideas and suggestions between prison staff, Music in Prison management, the project team and participants. It gives each party a chance to discuss and process all that has happened and therefore move forward with knowledge and confidence that attention to detail and musical quality will never be compromised (6.3 H).

Music Therapy, England

Although the relationships embedded in music therapy are especially intimate, Judith Webster, a former music therapist, emphasises the need for the therapist to work in close partnership with all the people involved with the client. These conversations help to contextualise the work of the therapist. In her Case Study Judith highlights certain key points that she would see as central to the work of any music therapist.

> It is clear that quality issues concern not only the interaction in the music therapy session itself, but the context within which it exists. Care needs to be taken to secure the right environment for the work. To do this, it is important to establish positive and collaborative relationships with the other professionals involved with the client, so that the work can be respected as playing its part in their development (6.3 M).

The music therapy process focuses on the personal development of the client – on their needs, on their perception of themselves and of their relationships with others – achieved through different forms of musical interaction and improvisation. Although the acquisition of new musical skills acts as "a barometer of the client's development", that is not the main aim of the therapy process. Judith maintains that:

> It is the contextualising of these 'skills' beyond the music therapy session which demonstrates lasting change in the client and the real meaning. Without this transfer of skills and ways of being to external contexts, it could be argued that the music therapy process has been ineffectual. In order to be able to assess this externalisation of the work and the progress of the client, it is important that the therapist interacts and collaborates with other 'communities' of professionals and carers who are involved with the client. It is through these interactions that they may have a fuller understanding of the client's context and the impact of their work, and that others may understand the contribution made by the music therapy.

> In my own experience as a therapist, I found it crucial to work collaboratively and saw it as part of my professional responsibility to enable co-workers and carers to share and witness their client's development in the sessions, so that we could identify how this translated into their every day life, or not. I made home visits to parents of children with special needs, sharing extracts of recordings or videos with them to help them understand the process, and indeed to understand their own child more fully. As a therapist, these visits were a source of support to me, as they enabled me to contextualise my experience of the work and celebrate changes and developments in a client which I might not otherwise have witnessed. The context beyond the therapy room gave further meaning to the work in the sessions (6.3 M).

Music for Life Wigmore Hall and for dementia, London

In 1993 Linda Rose founded the pioneering project, Music for Life, with the support of Jewish Care. After a very active history, 2009 saw its management transferred to the Wigmore Hall which recently formed a new partnership with the charity **for dementia**. Linda is now participating in the research project Healthy Ageing through Music and the Arts as part of the Research Group in Lifelong Learning in Music & the Arts.

In an article written for the launch of Music for Life Wigmore Hall and *for dementia*, Jude Sweeting (2009) makes explicit the significance of 'person-centred and relationship-centred care' and enumerates the wide range of live music activities that depend on creating different kinds of partnerships and collaborations – for example, "reminiscence groups, singing, choirs, music and movement, arts projects, music workshops, music therapy for individuals and groups, intergenerational projects, opera and live music concerts (p.9)". She also demonstrates how the different, yet inter-related, elements of Music for Life Wigmore Hall and *for dementia* – musicians, trainers, health and social care staff – require the sensitive development of partnerships. In the words of Jude Sweeting (2009):

> Music for Life, with its long-standing focus on learning about and supporting the development of dementia care, makes a unique contribution to the field. Specifically, it provides a model for personal and professional growth for all who participate in its projects, making a leading contribution to the training and development of health and social care staff, and to the development of vibrant care communities. It is an example of personalised support in action for all... Music and dementia have a lot in common. As experiences they both offer intensely personal expressions of life in an unpredictable universe. And they both profoundly alter us, moving us to see who we are beyond words, whilst prompting a myriad of new conversations (p.9).

Not surprisingly, for Linda Rose, 'conversation' is critical for the success of the many multi-layered partnerships she has developed over very many years. In her Case Study she describes in detail the care that needs to be taken when setting up and preparing for a project in a residential home.

Setting up the project

The location for a particular project is identified by the Music for Life project director or manager, together with the dementia care officer who has an overview of residents' needs in homes in the area. Prior to the start of the project, the manager and senior staff meet with project leaders to share information about the project and the care home. Here staff development needs are discussed as well as practical questions such as appropriate spaces to work in, staff rotas etc. The project makes significant organisational demands on a home or centre and so it is important to establish a trusting relationship early on where managers feel confident about the quality of the investment as well as leaving them excited about the potential of the project for improving the lives of residents.

Meeting the staff team

A second meeting is held to select the people with dementia who are to participate in the project. This meeting again involves senior managers together with any members of staff who might be interested and available to attend, and in particular the five staff identified to be on the project over the eight weeks. Here they meet the musician who is workshop leader for the project and the dementia care trainer with responsibility for spending time with the staff to reflect on their experiences of the workshops week by week. The focus of this meeting is to help the staff to select the residents to take part in the project and to introduce them to some of the people they will be working with. Again this is also about confidence building as staff are often particularly shy in the company of the musicians, commenting that they lack musical skill and fearful of being exposed in the workshops (6.3 K).

These excerpts from a number of case studies in this enquiry are intended to illustrate what is entailed in initiating, developing and sustaining any partnership between individual artists, cultural organisations, funding bodies and the communities with whom they are working. I think all the people interviewed would agree that partnership-building is always challenging but it is also an absolute precondition for effective engagement with any community. Further analysis of what is involved in developing partnerships will be examined in the next section. Observations are largely based on the interviews and case studies.

3.2 Factors necessary for developing effective partnerships

The illusion of 'partnership'

Without exception, all the interviewees are vigilant at being forced into collaborations that do little more than masquerade as 'partnerships'. As education and the arts have become increasingly politicised, schools and organisations in the community are frequently nudged into working together for quasi-political or funding reasons. In many such instances so-called 'partnerships' are driven by yet another government initiative or someone else's funding agenda that can hardly be resisted by an organisation desperate for extra financial support. Often the result can be summarised as 'one damn project after another' – with little attempt at achieving any form of development, sustainability or legacy. Over the last decade or so the managers of some organisations have become very adept at negotiating strong funding networks that help to position them strategically in relation to national priorities and their own futures. Their political antennae might be sharp, they may be connected to the 'right' people, they might be clever at playing the 'funding game' and their belief in the creative potential of partnerships might be made convincingly in any funding application. But how far is this often self-serving, cynical approach likely to generate long-term, mutually beneficial partnerships?

Relationships between individuals

Good partnerships are much like good relationships. They must be allowed to grow organically from existing relationships that have been built up between individual people over time. The interface between individuals is fundamental and as people learn to work together, the partnership potential unfolds and is gradually absorbed by each organisation. 'Learning through partnerships' then becomes a key principle underpinning the sharing of priorities and building up a shared vision. It brings with it an integrity of purpose based on fostering trust, mutual respect and listening to the voice of others. This is not only good for strengthening the relationships in any collaborative project but it often creates an enabling framework for devising funding proposals that reflect the shared values underlying the partnership. Basically, there is a unity and coherence between the partners, the funding bodies and the delivery of the project – partnership, project, process and product are seen to be working together towards the same end.

Shared perspective

As individuals and organisations build up their shared learning through partnerships, this can result in a qualitative shift in the ways the different partners view their practice. Any dynamic open partnership is unlikely to be afraid of extending its practice by taking risks, of being innovative and of fostering different forms of creative learning. The synergy arising from this kind of imaginative collaborative practice is further strengthened by all participants evolving a shared ethos, shared values, shared vision, shared aims and shared passions. But again, as with developing strong working relationships, achieving a shared perspective presents its own challenge and has to be guided by the qualities and principles raised earlier in this enquiry: for example, trust, mutual respect, integrity, empathy, tolerance, spirit of inclusion, equity of status, honesty, generosity, patience, authenticity, openness and curiosity. At first this might seem rather 'heavy' but most relationships begin to 'fly' when both partners are respectful of each other and share similar values and ways of seeing the world.

Shared engagement

Once a partnership begins to work from a shared perspective it has every chance of establishing the conditions that are necessary for deepening its sense of shared engagement and shared ownership – qualities that help to characterise a long-term partnership. As artists and practitioners in schools and the community begin working effectively together, as respective managements start developing a shared approach towards responsibility, each person gradually comes to understand and support each other's agendas, respecting possible differences and common ground. This becomes the basis of a healthy partnership that can be sustained, leaving behind a legacy of reflection and questioning that is central to a process of developmental learning.

Open communication

As was intimated at the beginning of this chapter, the success of any partnership depends partly on all participants having the competences to be able to engage in honest, open conversation that connects to the different contexts in which they may be working. Individuals and organisations have different histories, different aspirations, different professional identities and different ways of working. It goes without saying then, that if managers and practitioners are to work effectively together, their discussions would be enhanced by them having finely tuned communication skills – for example, being able to make meaningful connections, to ask appropriate questions, to listen actively, to respond and reflect, to monitor and evaluate. Communication may be verbal or non-verbal, but at all times it has to be clear, honest, open and direct. Communication in the context of a partnership is not about games-playing, scoring points or hiding behind status. It necessarily demands a respectful approach to relating and responding to people. Without an awareness of the significance and sensitivities of communication (and many people are trapped in a bubble of blindness and ego), partnerships are likely to flounder and may well not work.

Tension within partnerships
National initiatives

Many of the practitioners in this enquiry identified examples where partnerships were strained by sources of tension that block open communication and organic development within local communities and cultural organisations. One example at a national level is when major stakeholders are often driven by a funding imperative embedded in the latest government initiative. In England this has been marked by the influence of key strategic bodies such as the Department of Culture, Media and Sport, Department of Children, Schools and Families, Arts Council England, Creative Partnerships, Youth Music, and Museums, Libraries and Archives.

As was mentioned at the beginning of Section 1.4, in London some of the most recent funding stream is being redirected towards fulfilling the ambitions of the Cultural Olympiad in 2012. Major cultural venues such as the Barbican and the Southbank Centre have been encouraged to develop partnerships with the London Boroughs of Hackney, Islington, Lambeth, Newham, Southwark, Tower Hamlets and Waltham Forest. The main focus is on participation and engagement, especially with young people, but funding is dependent on the cultural organisations and Boroughs ensuring there will be a legacy of partnership. In principle this is a positive, forward-thinking policy, but developing and sustaining partnership can only work to an agenda defined and owned at the grassroots. It will fail if the rhetoric is not translated into practice at a local level.

Basically, partnerships have to be allowed to grow organically from within their local communities. They might then be enriched, inspired and nurtured by strategic alliances with bodies like the Barbican and the Southbank Centre – as long as the resulting activities are developmental, satisfying shared goals and aspirations, and do not degenerate into a potpourri of disconnected one-off projects aligned to one party's agenda. Considered attention from all contributory organisations needs to be given to devising systems and structures that will lead to effective delivery. Moreover, the collaborative thinking underpinning all long-term projects needs to be strategic and not territorial. There is no place for parochial vested interests in long-term planning.

Institutional initiatives

Partnerships at an institutional level are well exemplified by arts practitioners working in collaboration with teachers in classrooms. Without appropriate dialogue, negotiation and planning by management, teachers and artists, there will be little chance of any partnership working. It is critical that the roles and responsibilities of both teachers and arts practitioners are clearly defined and fully understood by everyone involved in the project or programme. The creative activities initiated by the artists have to be fully integrated into the school curriculum and pupils' patterns of learning, whilst the planning of activities has to take into account the progression and development of pupils' learning. In other words, partnerships cannot just be seen as a vehicle for facilitating activity per se. The aim has to be at enhancing the quality of learning, for both children and adults, and then the partnership has a chance to develop as a form of shared reflective practice. Without this shared understanding, achieved partly through appropriate professional support, there is a likelihood that some artists and teachers will feel dysfunctional and unable to operate according to their strengths.

For example, in England over the last decade or so, many teachers have become locked into a culture of accountability dominated by the delivery of targets and outcomes. This is especially so with those teachers who have trained most recently within a mechanistic system that has paid scant regard to ways of facilitating creative learning in schools. Unless teachers and artists are brought together on joint programmes of professional development there is little hope of building up a long-term partnership that can realise its joint creative potential. Such circumstances can be frustrating and counter-productive for both teachers and artists and this has to be taken into account during the early stages of planning and negotiation.

A similar dilemma is echoed in the Case Study of Marga Wobma-Helmich which is drawn from her work with Het Concertgebouw in schools in The Netherlands.

> One of the issues we were facing was a lack of time and a lack of musical skills by the school teachers in order to prepare their pupils for the concerts. In teacher training courses there is less and less time for arts subjects and teachers feel more and more insecure in teaching music. The music method books which teachers can use are expensive and require some basic music skills and understanding. But perhaps more importantly is the pressure on teachers to

spend as much time as possible on subjects like mathematics and language, which does not stimulate them to teach music on a regular basis (6.3 N).

Without the necessary background in music, these teachers are at considerable disadvantage when trying to collaborate with professional musicians from Het Concertgebouw. As there is little common language and experience to draw on, it is important that the teachers and musicians are given opportunities to work alongside each other in professional development programmes aimed at building up a shared skills and knowledge base. Without this, tensions and misunderstandings can easily arise.

The challenge of finding a common language that makes sense to the participants of complex projects in the community are well illustrated by the multi-faceted work of Eastfeast in East Anglia. For Clare Chacksfield, its Director, Eastfeast is a celebration of being human in a community with the main focus being on what one can bring to the table for the feast. The key participants are artists (all former teachers), headteachers, teachers, school governors, support staff, children, parents and gardeners. It is very community oriented and aims to work in close partnership with schools. The disciplines underpinning the project are also very diverse, including horticulture, permaculture (sustainability), ecosystems, science, poetry, ceramics, music, dance, visual arts, film and circus. Nothing could be more wide-ranging.

In order to pre-empt the flow of the project being constrained by unnecessary tensions and misunderstandings, all participants are encouraged to see themselves as learners on a shared transformational journey. Clare points out that in general the many different disciplines work well together and individuals are not especially territorial. But at times there can be tensions between the music practitioners and music teachers, and between the specialist gardeners and horticulturalists.

One of the strongest aspects of Eastfeast, and one that will help to ameliorate likely tensions and build up a legacy of partnership, is that it has developed a reflective culture that succeeds in deepening and extending shared learning for all participants. With its emphasis on collaborating and making connections, the project encourages critical reflection throughout the whole process. A professional development model (similar to that discussed in Section 5.3) has been created which highlights the importance of reflective journals, visual logs, reviews and dialogues in groups and in pairs. This may well lead to setting up a mentoring and co-mentoring programme which will further strengthen the different partnerships.

Finally, in the light of her experience of initiating partnerships between teachers and professional musicians in Vienna and Cologne, Christine Stöger (Professor and Head of Classroom Teachers' Training at the

Hochschule für Musik, Cologne) considers that the following points are crucial if partnerships are to enable teams of teachers and musicians to function fully according to their strengths.

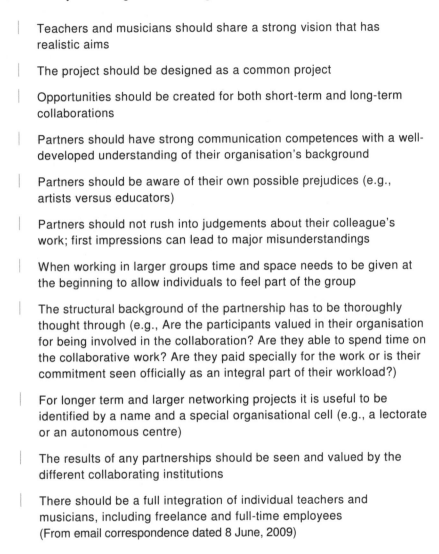

- Teachers and musicians should share a strong vision that has realistic aims

- The project should be designed as a common project

- Opportunities should be created for both short-term and long-term collaborations

- Partners should have strong communication competences with a well-developed understanding of their organisation's background

- Partners should be aware of their own possible prejudices (e.g., artists versus educators)

- Partners should not rush into judgements about their colleague's work; first impressions can lead to major misunderstandings

- When working in larger groups time and space needs to be given at the beginning to allow individuals to feel part of the group

- The structural background of the partnership has to be thoroughly thought through (e.g., Are the participants valued in their organisation for being involved in the collaboration? Are they able to spend time on the collaborative work? Are they paid specially for the work or is their commitment seen officially as an integral part of their workload?)

- For longer term and larger networking projects it is useful to be identified by a name and a special organisational cell (e.g., a lectorate or an autonomous centre)

- The results of any partnerships should be seen and valued by the different collaborating institutions

- There should be a full integration of individual teachers and musicians, including freelance and full-time employees
(From email correspondence dated 8 June, 2009)

It can be seen from these observations drawn from many different kinds of organisations that when partnerships work well, they provide a rich source of learning for all participants. But without exception, they are complex and challenging. Deepening the understanding of all partners is probably best achieved by creating opportunities for participants from their respective organisations to work together in professional development programmes that are underpinned by a culture of critical reflection. Further support could be provided by a co-mentoring programme designed to strengthen individual and collaborative forms of learning. The possibilities for this kind of development are examined in Section 5.2.

4

Quality of project

4.1   Aims

Guiding principles

This enquiry is premised on the view that there are two over-riding principles for determining the quality of a project:

  fitness for purpose

  relevance to context

On this account artistic activities can only be judged fairly by considering the appropriateness of their aims and the way in which they make meaningful connections to their particular context (Renshaw, 2007, pp.37-40). As Eugene van Erven indicates in his Case Study, "the quality of (community art) projects cannot be judged by assessing a single performance alone with criteria borrowed from a mainstream arts discourse" (6.3 A). In his interview Eugene raised the challenge of making appropriate judgements. He asks the question, "how do we look at 'new' art arising from different contexts?" He urges us to look at art criticism in new ways, always taking into account the contextual variables embedded in complex community projects. It is essential to have a comprehensive understanding of the total project and to see the ways in which it relates to the background and experience of the participants.

For example, in the following cases it would be wholly valid to make qualitatively different judgements according to a wide spectrum of criteria:

  a music therapist working with an autistic child in a special language unit

  a violinist performing a concerto in a concert hall

  a master drummer leading a drumming workshop in a community context

  a collaborative arts workshop in a young offenders' unit

  an open-access ensemble performing a genre-free collaborative composition in a club for young people

  a cross-arts project working in a multi-ethnic neighbourhood

  the experimental work of a sound and image lab for young musicians, visual artists, singers, DJs and programmers

Although there may be similarities when judging quality at the level of the form of various artistic experiences, significant differences have to be taken into account when regarding the aim, content and context of any particular activity. For instance, the criteria used for evaluating a creative project in a non-formal setting are determined as much by the workshop/performance context (e.g. school classroom, hospital ward, prison, youth club, neighbourhood) as by the shared values and expectations of the participants and their leader (Renshaw, 2007, p. 38). As Sean Gregory (2004) points out, "even conventional terms such as playing (or singing) 'in tune' or 'in time', have different connotations according to the physical and human resources at hand" (p.44).

Connecting to context

The integrity and honesty embedded in community engagement necessarily ensures that the aims of a successful project have to grow out of the specific context in which it is located. Its social and cultural parameters have to be taken into account if the artistic experience is to resonate with all participants. In a sense, full justice can only be done to these complex projects if a multi-perspective conversation is generated involving all stakeholders. Therefore, 'connecting to context' has to be seen as a fundamental principle underpinning the genesis, development, delivery, assessment and legacy of any project.

Within this enquiry there are many examples of projects striking a balance between their artistic and social aims. In most cases these respective aims feed each other. Music-making, for instance, is developed within a social-cultural context – it is located in its own natural habitat which helps to define the artistic aims and illuminates the quality of the artistic experience. The need for this balance between the artistic and the social is made explicit by Ninja Kors in her Case Study of the Brassband School in Rotterdam.

> The World Music and Dance Centre and its partners may be primarily concerned with musical development but most brass bands in The Netherlands that currently come into existence, start because of social aims. Antillean youth are regarded as a risk group in Dutch society and many initiatives by social workers and youth organisations include starting up a brass band to 'keep the youth off the street' (...) Some of the political interest in the Brassband School comes from the same corner; and not without reason. The brass band leaders deal not only with musical and didactic matters but also need to concern themselves with other social issues of the band members such as social and economic deprivation and for example, teenage pregnancies.
>
> The effects a brass band can have on young people on the edge of society are undeniable. The Brassband School has developed into a hub of this activity and has the potential to be an important access point to many issues that face this group. But we need to be careful with this. The first priority is the bands! New music is composed and arranged, new musical concepts to the participants (such

as polyphony) are introduced into the performances, brass players and teachers are trained to a higher level. The first target, after all, is the music. In order to target the music, we need to be aware of and take care of the social environment. And in turn, the development of the music feeds into the social climate as the bands improve and the music is picked up and taken seriously by a wider audience – including other musicians (6.3 G).

Ninja, then, argues for maintaining a balance between artistic and social aims, but in her testimony she adds an important rider in her search for a clarity and integrity that ensures these two aims are not conflated:

> If you want to set up a project to improve purely musical quality, let it be about purely musical excellence. If you want to improve living standards in a certain area or group, let it be about that. Activities can have more than one aim but it is difficult to combine several aims in one when choices need to be made. There is a real danger of compromising *everything* (6.2 G).

The World Music and Dance Centre (WMDC) has a clear raison d'être that recognises the synergy between the artistic and the social. Culturally the Centre is very diverse offering a wide range of music, and through its engagement with its local community it is constantly exploring new channels for making music. Both the social and cultural aspects of the WMDC are enhanced by the integrity of its space which is very open, welcoming and draws people in. It is designed as a village square concept so that the space embodies a way of life – it is not just bricks and mortar. The space is located in a real community in the 'real' world. It is seen as a cultural space that allows an organic social context to develop. This concept of the WMDC helps to illuminate Ninja's view of the relationship between the artistic and social aims of its projects.

> (Music) takes place within a context of society, culture, community. In short: music is people. In order to work on one aim, one needs to take into account the context in which music thrives. For example, many of the projects of the WMDC in Rotterdam deal with cultural groups and social development. Because music is a social activity and because WMDC is in the middle of a large multicultural (and multi-generational, and multi-social, and ...) urban community, WMDC concerns itself with music projects that carry within them a strong social component. This is true on many levels of music-making.

> All this does not make WMDC a social institution. Our aim is not to keep young people out of trouble, or to relieve the elderly immigrants of loneliness, or to provide a platform for political debate, or even to provide young people with career opportunities. Our aim is to facilitate the development of music (and to some degree dance and other arts) and to make that development visible. In order to reach that aim, we need to care for other things as well (6.2 G).

Other projects in this enquiry are also equally aware of their dual commitment to an artistic/musical aim and a social/personal aim. Sara Lee made this very clear in her interview about her work in prisons. For Music in

Prisons the over-riding aim is to create music of quality. Music is fundamental to the musician's engagement with the participants, but this artistic aim has to work within the setting of the particular prison. The musical activities have to be appropriate to the context: for example, the content of the lyrics has to arise from and relate to the specific context. Each prison has its own clear rules and regulations, and the aim of the musicians is to achieve quality within these boundaries. But the work of Music in Prisons also has a social aim – basically, to stop people re-offending. Music is then seen as a vehicle for achieving social ends – but the music leader is not an artistic 'social worker' or therapist.

In her capacity as a music therapist, Judith Webster emphasises that connecting to the context of a client's life is fundamental if the therapeutic process is to work. Aims can never be purely musical as they have to include the personal, psychological, social and physiological. The main aim is to choreograph a musical journey together through a musical framework, but the context in which this musical conversation takes place is critical for determining what happens during the therapeutic process. As Judith points out in her Case Study:

> The key element in the music therapy process is to quickly establish a therapeutic relationship, as opposed to simply improvising or making music with the client. Whilst making music is worthwhile for its own sake, it is not the intent in this context. To establish this relationship, the therapist must 'play the client's music'. This involves improvising precisely what is communicated by the client in order to gradually heighten their awareness of themselves, and then of the therapeutic relationship. To do this, the therapist must focus completely on them – how they move, feel, look, vocalise, breathe etc. and play that music, the music of the client through clinically directed improvisation (6.3 M).

Similarly with Music for Life, the project created by Linda Rose for musicians to work with people with dementia and those who care for them. Although music is the core of each workshop, the aims are as multi-faceted as the processes are subtle and varied. In the words of Linda:

> (Music for Life) aims to re-build confidence and trust for people who have become isolated and disempowered through their condition. Central to the work are the music workshops in which three musicians encourage communication and connection through the music they improvise together. Both the musical and the interpersonal skills of the musicians are crucial in this work. With support from the senior management of the setting, the musicians work to develop a cohesive group where each participant, whether a person with dementia or a member of staff becomes responsive and open to the possibilities for relating to any other in the group on an equal basis. The workshop space becomes a place for all kinds of exploration, experiences ranging from the most joyful and celebratory to the gently amusing and teasing to the saddest sharing. Both the music and the quiet spaces between the music in the sessions are created and owned by individuals in the group, and responded to in different ways by everyone in the group (6.3 K).

It is clear from all these cases that an informed, empathetic response to any community context has to be built on trust – trust between the artists, between the artists and clients, between the artists and staff of the institution, between the artists and the community they are working with. In an important sense the aims have to grow organically out of this web of relationships. Clare Chacksfield describes this well in her testimony, drawing on her experience of working with Eastfeast.

> Each school and community we work with brings with it different challenges. Often we as practitioners enter the (school) staff room amidst a sea of expectations, judgements and protocols. Being the outsider at first gives us a privileged fresh perspective. As a team we are all profoundly aware that the first task we have to focus on is about earning trust from the community we aspire to work with. Quality for me therefore is about the quality of relationships and learning in the work that I do. The quality will be different for all the different people we work with, but having high expectations and ambitions for what we can achieve together is absolutely fundamental to making our projects work in practice. Time to build this trust is an essential ingredient in making the process of engagement work (6.2 A).

From these few examples it can be seen that in an ideal scenario there has to be a synergy and flow between the people's aims, vision and context. Although aims have to be honest and have integrity, they cannot be too idealistic. The concept, the idea underlying a project has to work in practice, so the aims have to be achievable and realistic. They have to arise out of and relate to a specific context. Little good comes from 'dressing up' a concept in rhetoric that might be politically expedient and attractive to funding bodies, but which in practice is unrealisable. Eugene van Erven offers a word of warning from his wide experience of community art:

> Over the years, I have come across many projects that label themselves as 'community arts'. In the worst cases these are concept-driven, autonomously created site-specific works in which a working-class or immigrant location is used as exotic backdrop and some locals are fitted in as token participants. The cultural parameters that shape the style and form of such projects are alien to such places and to the people who live there. Audiences and critical acclaim are recruited downtown. In the best cases I know, however, an entire neighbourhood is permanently infected with the arts activities, which are sustained well after the professional artists, who have propelled it in the first place, have left (6.3 A).

Quality of space

Although the success of a project is largely dependent on people – on practitioners, participants and partners – the integrity of space is an especially important aspect of a project's response to its context. The nature of the space, the form and function of the space, the status of the space, how the space is perceived and valued – all these aspects of space are fundamental to the quality of a project. Yet, only too frequently quality is undermined by a physical environment that is neither appropriate nor fit for purpose. This can be equally true in traditional performance venues, educational institutions and community settings.

We saw earlier how the artistic and social aims of the World Music and Dance Centre in Rotterdam have a good chance of being realised partly because of the quality and location of its space. This is reiterated by Ninja Kors in her testimony.

> The WMDC is lucky. In its development phase it was decided to keep the core of the building, the performance space, central. An open space was created that has good acoustic qualities, many uses (although not enough) and more importantly a good feel to it. Many groups feel at home in the WMDC, and the space facilitates easy mixture of groups and people. It is a professional performance place where people are also at home during the daytime when they are eating lunch, practising etudes or waiting for other people. It is relatively easy for musicians, all kinds, to claim the space as their own, something that happens frequently and almost always with success (6.2 G).

A similar commitment to the quality of space can be seen in Eugene van Erven's account of the Story Kitchen in Haarlem. After the success of the pilot phase of the project, the artists of the company, 5th Quarter, were invited by the main stakeholders of the community to collaborate in the design of the Broad School (see Section 3.1), which would form the centre of most activities in that particular community. "The tangible result of this partnership was the inclusion of two workshop spaces for art, a large kitchen operated by the Mother Centre, and a spacious central area with tables and chairs that could easily be converted into a performance space" (6.3 A). As with the WMDC in Rotterdam, the social, cultural and artistic aims can be valued and realised in a quality space which is seen to matter and is owned by the people in its neighbourhood.

Space is critical in any project but it is of absolute importance in those environments where relationships are especially sensitive and intimate. The therapeutic relationship in music therapy can only develop fruitfully within a safe physical space for the client. Each session is confidential, so it has to be conducted in surroundings that are private with no interruptions. Similarly, in the case of Music for Life great care is taken to provide a secure, predictable space in which musicians, residents and care staff can feel comfortable. As Linda Rose points out in her Case Study:

> On the morning of the workshop, the project room is set up, the circle of chairs carefully set out, the observers chairs carefully placed. The range of percussion instruments is laid out in the centre of the circle, taking account of sightlines, accessibility and interest in the shape of the layout, often with a 'centre piece' maybe a djembe to look inviting and aesthetically pleasing (6.3 K).

How projects are perceived and valued are reflected in the quality of space provided. If possible it is preferable for projects to be rooted in a space where practitioners have contributed to the design, as in the case of the WMDC and the Broad School. Both these spaces 'work' as they have been conceived in relation to the aims of their engagement with their respective communities. Therefore, integrity of space matters but in practice, time and again lack of space, inappropriate space, limitations of space, sub-standard space undermine the realisation of the aims of many projects. This is not necessarily a funding problem for it generally reflects the attitudes and priorities of those organisations that only pay lip-service to community engagement.

4.2   Quality of arts practitioners

Introduction

It seems artificial to separate out the many diverse qualities of those arts practitioners (e.g. performers, improvisers, composers, choreographers, visual artists, DJs, workshop leaders, curators and creative producers) who deliver high quality work in schools and the wider community. In many ways their artistic, professional and personal qualities are all closely interconnected. A highly skilled, yet narrowly focused performer, for example, is unlikely to be able to rise to the multi-faceted challenges of a community context without having the necessary creative, personal, interpersonal, leadership and communication skills.

For this enquiry I intend to focus on the four domains that the interviewees regarded as central to the success and quality of a project: the personal, artistic, leadership and management. Most of the examples are taken from the domain of music and they draw partly from the Guildhall Artist Programme in Leadership and in its professional development course in Creative Music Workshop Leading (Guildhall School of Music & Drama, 2009).

Personal qualities

At the beginning of Section 2.2 an emphasis was placed on the commitment of all the interviewees to the qualities, values and attitudes implicit in the principle of 'respect for persons as ends in themselves'. Each person felt that their engagement with the community is premised on their passion for creating quality artistic experience – but most importantly, one that respects and listens to the voices of the people they are working with, without tolerating any anti-social actions that might arise. Certain human qualities and skills, then, form the bedrock of this quality artistic experience. For example:

Values

Respect; tolerance; honesty; compassion; integrity; sincerity; authenticity

Interpersonal skills

Ability to relate to other people; empathy; trust; openness; responsiveness; listening to and acting on other points of view; ability to work collaboratively in a team with interchangeable roles; having the confidence to share ones vulnerability; ability to facilitate and sustain working partnerships with teachers and community leaders

Communication skills

Ability to use language flexibly so that it resonates within its context; framing appropriate questions; active listening (respecting silence; reading body language; reframing and reinforcing the substance of a conversation); being open and non-judgemental; engaging in non-verbal dialogue through, for example, a musical conversation or a shared visual log

Personal skills

Personal organisation; time-management; reliability; problem-solving; decision-making; dealing with conflict; managing ones own health; managing stress; coping with success and failure

Artistic qualities

In his address, *What is Excellence in Higher Music Education?* Einar Solbu (2007), Vice President of the International Music Council, recognising the links between the artistic, professional and personal, makes a general statement about the importance of artistic skills.

> Every musician must have artistic skills, must have something to tell others through music, must have the ability to convince a listener, musically. There are many ways in which a performer of an instrument for instance, can show artistic skills, and we should appreciate artistic diversity. But we should not accept artistic short cuts or impressive instrumental or vocal surfaces without anything beneath. Artistic skills in the real sense are reflected through such characteristics as musical refinement, originality and reflection (p.3).

In the context of community engagement a range of artistic and creative skills are necessary including:

Performance skills

- Technical skills on instrument or voice (e.g., facility, co-ordination, control)

- Musical versatility and flexible approaches to performance

- Vocal skills

- Body and percussion skills

Quality of listening and sensitivity to sound (e.g., tone, timbre, intonation, ensemble)

Speed of reaction and response to music

Ability to communicate music to an audience or to workshop participants (e.g., quality of engagement, commitment, conviction, urgency, inner energy, daring to take risks)

Creative skills

Creative responsiveness – ability to respond creatively to musical ideas of participants (e.g., to listen; to make musical sense of a lyric provided by participants; to translate a musical idea and make it into music; to be able to shift from a blank piece of paper to an idea and then to make it work in musical terms)

Fluency in improvisation; composing and arranging skills

Understanding elements of composition (e.g., compositional starting points; organising musical material; techniques for developing material and extending ideas; working with modes; group developmental processes; approaches to working with structure and form)

Musical, social and psychological responsiveness (e.g., making musical sense in relation to human and psychological needs of participants; establishing connections between musical and human responses)

Understanding different approaches to arts practice (e.g., non-European and folk-based; cross-arts and cross-cultural collaborations; creative and repertoire-linked projects)

Leadership skills

Leadership skills in the context of community engagement are complex and inevitably are partly dependent on the personal and artistic qualities identified earlier in this section. The present discussion is based on an analysis of 'musical leadership' arising from the work of Guildhall Connect (Renshaw, 2005b, pp.18-20).

Artistic leadership skills

Having the skill and judgement to create and frame a project that will work (e.g., making artistic decisions about the musical language and structure of the project; delineation of roles and responsibilities; managing people within a collaborative context)

Knowing how to enable the participants to hear, see, feel and understand the connections that are integral to the creative process. Encouraging people to get on the inside of musical experience. Engaging their aural, bodily and emotional memory in order to internalise sound, rhythm and musical structure

Establishing a sense of high expectation for the group and individual participants, by presenting a clear indication of the musical quality that might be achieved

Creating a balance of 'pace' that allows time and space for artistic development and creative momentum

Generic leadership skills

Creating an inspiring, enabling environment that encourages participants to build on their strengths and acquire the confidence and skills to explore new challenges and extend their musical skills

Having the capacity to respect, listen to and act on other points of view. Although leadership needs to be strong and clear, there is no place for inflexible assertiveness within collaborative ways of working. It is important to have the openness and generosity to go with the flow of the musical material being generated by the whole group

Having the interpersonal and organisational skills to be able to work collaboratively with various teams and project managers, on the basis of equality, playing to individual strengths and acknowledging different roles and responsibilities

Knowing how to choreograph leadership in a group, creating opportunities for devolved leadership. This entails ensuring that the ego of the leader is not allowed to inhibit the creative process

Leadership and tacit ways of knowing

Tacit knowledge – implicit or latent knowledge that cannot be put into words is central to the process of coming to know experientially. Echoing Michael Polanyi (1966, pp.4-5), the creative energy or spirit embedded in tacit knowledge can only be caught and not taught. In effective workshop practice the leader creates space in which all the musicians become totally engaged in the spirit of the music in the moment. This is caught through the act of doing and it remains unspoken. Depending on the context this might be felt most deeply through a silence and stillness that has a resonance for each person.

Although Polanyi is not writing in the context of music and the performing arts, he observes that in the area of tacit knowing "we incorporate it in our body – or extend our body to include it – so that we come to dwell in it" (p.16). A sense of 'place' is created which holds people in that moment and helps them to feel secure in themselves. This enriched feeling of tacit knowledge can strengthen a person's sense of connection to their creative source.

Experienced music leaders are well aware that they have to create a music environment that is conducive to fostering tacit forms of learning. Leading by example between people at all levels of experience becomes critical in an effective learning process. Learning will then take place through watching, listening, imitating, responding, absorbing, reflecting and connecting within that particular musical context.

Management skills

Project managers and curators have to work closely with arts practitioners if projects are to be successful. Whereas project management is very hands-on, a curator or creative producer helps the artistic director give shape to the end-product. The distinctive roles of project management and curator need to be respected and understood by all participants in a project. For example:

Project management

Knowing how to create appropriate practical conditions for enabling projects to be effective

Selecting and managing the physical space and aural environment

Having a realistic timescale that will allow for developmental work

Being pragmatic about logistical challenges

Ensuring the availability and reliability of musical instruments and technical equipment

Managing an experienced team of workshop leaders and supporting musicians

Creating opportunities for presenting high quality performances, events and recordings

Ensuring sustained funding for future projects

Helping to build up and nurture appropriate partnerships

Role of curator

Responsible for shaping the flow of the final event or performance

Responsible for choreographing and programming the end-product

- Responsibility for curating the event in terms of number of groups performing, sectors involved, contributory art forms etc.

- The curator's role is a second order position – that of a 'spectator' who makes connections. This presents a challenge when working with different music genres, art forms and ensembles

- Working closely with the artistic director and arts practitioners, the curator's role has an important artistic dimension to it. The aim is to ensure that a presentation has integrity and coherence and is not just celebratory and superficial. Imaginative presentation will always reflect where participants come from and how they relate to the stage

Supporting evidence from case studies and interviews

The ways in which the success of a project is largely dependent on the artistic, professional and personal qualities of its arts practitioners, managers and curators are clearly illustrated in many of the case studies, as can be seen from the following examples. For Sara Lee, the quality of the work of Music in Prisons lies in the wide-ranging musical skills supported by the human qualities and pragmatism of her team, who have been working together for many years.

> Many factors are crucial in achieving and maintaining this quality and it is how these things combine that make the work so effective. The project team is one of the most important factors in its success. First and foremost they are all amazing musicians but very importantly, each of them has the specific social skills needed to work with sometimes challenging prisoners and the patience to deal appropriately with the vagaries of the prison system. The core team has been working together regularly for many years and because of this, has been able to develop an enviable working relationship built on trust, support and a strong musical understanding.

> The project team works effectively because the musicians possess not only a deep understanding of the context but have a personal authenticity and an absolute integrity and respect for the work and the people participating in it. It is a skill to be able to assess individuals quickly and accurately and to gauge the right time for each of them to make the next big step both musically and personally. The team instinctively knows how far to push people, when to leave them alone and when to coax something out of them. It is about having an innate understanding of people and very importantly an innate understanding of oneself. Any form of musical or personal ego does not work in the prison environment as the work is solely about what the participants can achieve with the team's support (6.3 H).

Similarly in Music for Life, where Linda Rose states unequivocally that the quality of music-making and the personal qualities of her musicians go hand in hand.

At all times, the quality of their music-making is paramount. For their music to communicate they need to be at the height of their musical skill. Their playing must matter and mean every bit as much as any public performance on the concert platform. The musicians often comment that it matters more to them and has greater meaning, as the integrity and quality of their playing directly affects the extent to which they will connect with the person with dementia. The demands are great, as they also need to be aware of more than one response or initiative from the circle at any one time and be responsive to each other, sometimes relinquishing a long awaited opportunity to work with a resident as another interaction has already begun. Sometimes the skill involves moulding two pieces together whilst giving a sense of personal attention to each resident (...) The work requires '360 degree radar' according to one musician. The musicians need to keep everyone in the group safe enough to cope with unpredictability, risk, trying something new. They need to be prepared to be out of their own comfort zone whilst at the same time inspiring confidence in the group (6.3 K).

Another example comes from the field of music and disability. The organisation Drake Music works primarily with people who have severe physical impairments, using assistive technology to explore, create and perform music. It also collaborates with a much wider range of musicians, including people with cognitive and sensory impairments. In discussion with Carien Meijer, Chief Executive of Drake Music, it was clear that working with disabled people raises further challenges for the arts practitioners and project managers responsible for the success of their projects. The composers, performers and music leaders, both disabled and non-disabled, working for Drake Music are expected to be good musicians who are also skilled in the use of assistive music technology and new technologies. It is crucial that these musicians are able to relate musically both to the technology and to all participants, as the main aim is to use technology as a means for exploring, creating and performing music. To this end, the musical identity of the leader is of paramount importance. Workshop 'facilitators' who rely on recipes and formulaic-led creativity are not seen as ideal leaders for Drake Music projects. This echoes the view of each organisation involved in this enquiry. The primary driver is always artistic but each project has to respond creatively to the social, cultural, psychological and physiological needs of its particular context.

The final example is taken from community-based theatre, drawing on the work of Stut Theatre in Utrecht and the Rotterdam Neighbourhood Theatre, both of which devise plays with working-class and immigrant residents in urban areas that are culturally and artistically under-serviced. Again, in his Case Study Eugene van Erven emphasises the importance of the artists involved in these projects being of high quality as well as having the necessary human qualities for relating to the residents of these particular communities.

We know that this kind of theatre works in community settings, as long as the professionals involved (who direct, write and produce) are very flexible indeed, are unambitious when it comes to mainstream status, can quickly establish trust and confidence through a gregarious and genuinely caring attitude, and can muster deep-felt concern for the often complicated lives of the people they work with. They must be high calibre artists who possess the ability to shape that material that comes from the participants into exciting and meaningful products that those actively involved can be proud of and that contain local cultural parameters so that they communicate with a public for which they are primarily intended (6.3 A).

4.3 Quality of process

Complexity, clarity and context

We have already identified many of the key factors that are fundamental to the success of any collaborative project but right at the heart lies the quality of the process used to facilitate creative learning and generate an end-product that is felt to have integrity and authenticity by all participants. Time and again interviewees expressed their concern that the people they worked with were placed in situations where their voices were not heard and valued. Yet most people, if given the opportunity, are only too keen to extend their learning, develop their creativity, make new connections and broaden their perspective. Therefore, the way in which processes are choreographed in particular contexts is absolutely critical to the quality of a project.

Clare Chacksfield, Director of Eastfeast, sees an urgent need to ensure that people of all ages are given the chance to engage in creative, artistic processes.

> Working in a society and education system where there are less and less opportunities for children to be 'free range' in their learning adventures, it feels of paramount importance to us to create opportunities where children can work beyond their normal boundaries. Defining a focus for all these different relationships is about making a quality experience for those who are involved in this creative process (...) It is important to me that the art process can create a window upon reflection that can often be missing from the day-to-day grind of everyday life. Something about making art or artistry alone or with others seems to fuel our ability to question ourselves and the things that happen around us. If we can ask ourselves questions then we can learn and grow, get to understand ourselves better, be more self-aware (6.2 A).

Clare and her team work in 18 schools in very different contexts: for example, in rural and urban secondary schools, small rural primary schools, a multicultural inner city school in Norwich, a pupil referral unit and in a large urban area by the sea at Clacton. All these contexts present different ways of seeing the world but using food and the arts to create a Feast has helped to establish a 'community of purpose' and a 'community of learning'. Clare sees this process of shared learning as transformational. All participants are on a shared journey that is continually deepening their awareness and extending their learning.

Perhaps shared learning is at the core of any process that is seen to 'work' by leaders and participants. But whatever the challenges raised by a project, the first few minutes into the process are critical. At all times they have to be carefully orchestrated, always being alert to the strengths, vulnerabilities and emotional temperature of the individuals in the group. The complexity of each context stands out and this has to be responded to with clear goals, clear procedures and clear means of delivery – that is, with clarity.

Within Music for Life contexts, for example, the initial process is extremely subtle with the musicians knowing they have to pay attention to possible unexpected cues.

> From the moment that staff bring residents into the room, the workshop begins. Aware of the vulnerability of those in the group, every moment is important, from the warmth of the initial greeting and welcome to both staff and residents, to the care of inviting people to join the circle. Musicians respect the need for space to settle for some people and for others, the wish to engage in social interaction. For residents, this initial connection may involve conversation or hand-holding or for others, quietly 'being' beside someone as they absorb their new environment, the circle of people, the chairs, the instruments. The musicians' interest in them and their care staff, and responsiveness to them all impacts on the confidence any participant may have to even be in the room (6.3 K).

Setting the scene, then, establishing a safe, welcoming, respectful space are essential preconditions for entering the musical relationship that will grow out of this opening. The initial emphasis is on the residents and the care staff.

A similar attitude is taken by the musicians working for Music in Prisons, where the process grows out of a response to the participants in the group. The leaders must have the capacity to get on the 'inside' of other people quickly. They cannot allow ego to block the flow and pace of the workshop. Each person needs to feel they are acknowledged and safe enough to express their fear, as they are often fragile and broken human beings. Sara Lee describes some of the factors that help participants to feel valued.

> From the outset we show the people we work with that we are coming in on a high level. If they see us taking pride in our work then the likelihood is that they will also take pride. It is clear to all of them – and they have said it on many occasions – that we are people who know and care about what both we and they are doing. We bring in great instruments for them to play and great musicians for them to work with. This shows an immediate investment in them, something too few of them have experienced in their lives before. Many feel blown away by this and the effort that has gone in to it, but everyone responds. At the outset, some shy away from it, some feel immediately anxious about failing, others just dive in. All these feelings must be accepted and worked with; it can be a delicate balance

between understanding someone's feelings and at the same time instilling in them the confidence they can do it (6.3 H).

The complexities of this process can be seen in an account of a project in HMP Full Sutton, Yorkshire, where the inmates are serving very long sentences.

> As the project began, it was clear the seven participants in the group were all extremely excited about participating in the music-making. They were also vulnerable and at times challenging. Some were very afraid of making mistakes, and would be endlessly critical towards other band members. Others were difficult to engage, tending to get diverted very easily, to experience extreme mood swings, or to get caught up in conflicts within the group.

> As the team noted in their project diary, "There are layers of complexity to the personalities in the group. Negotiating through these layers takes careful consideration and calm so as not to get tangled amongst the confusing dynamics".

> As the week progressed, the participants worked incredibly hard, with a few in particular bringing a level of sensitivity, musicality and application to the process which inspired and galvanised the rest of the group. In spite of the difficulties they had experienced, the band rose magnificently to the challenge and performed to rapturous applause on the final day of the project (Music in Prisons, 2009, p.2).

Complexity and quality of learning

Further observations drawn from the interviews illustrate the need for arts practitioners to have the flexibility, knowledge and understanding to foster quality learning and personal development within the complex conditions of their particular context. Without exception, each situation demands high levels of skill. Three different areas will be taken as examples – music therapy, assistive technology with disabled people and cross-arts collaborations.

As a music therapist Judith Webster outlines the way in which she might approach working with a child:

> Firstly, the therapist has to connect to the child through creating a musical context which directly reflects what the child communicates about themselves and their world as they enter the therapy room. The therapist creates a shared musical experience that makes sense to the child. Making this connection in music is fundamental to the therapeutic process, and to the learning and development that is possible as a result. It establishes key foundations, communicating to the child that they are being listened to, empathised with, understood, and respected. It is only through the therapist explicitly taking the lead from the child initially, 'making' their interaction a conscious musical dialogue, that a meaningful connection is made, trust is established, and the therapist is able to take the musical lead.

The connection made is *in* the music – not *with* the music. The therapist tries to reach the child through building up an implicit understanding. Meeting **in** the music involves the clinically directed use of such tools as pitch, tempo, rhythm, form, shape, structure, timbre and tonality. Given that we are all inherently musical beings, the therapist will 'translate' the child's movements (voluntary and involuntary), their energy, their breathing, their vocal sounds for example, through improvisation – sometimes mirroring them directly, sometimes improvising music to communicate what (the emotion that ...) they are picking up from the child. In this way, the child is immediately able to join the therapist in a musical environment, entering a shared experience where the leadership transfers from child to therapist and vice versa according to the needs of the child, in the therapist's judgement, and the stage in the therapy.

The therapist creates a musical metaphor through an improvised musical 'conversation'. Through this the therapist guides the child through different musical, and therefore emotional experiences of themselves and how they relate to the world, opening up new possibilities for them, and aiming to extend behaviour rather than reinforce existing patterns and limitations. Through music, the therapist is able to connect with the healthy part of the child and offer them the opportunity to be different. This is an effective way of getting to know a child through musical interaction – for example, whether they are stuck or flexible, quiet or noisy.

The musical metaphors are clear. For example, do they repeat the same rhythmic patterns obsessively or can they be encouraged to follow the therapist's change in tempo and metre? Do they overpower by playing loudly and without listening to the therapist or can they join in something more lyrical? How do they respond to something angular and constantly unpredictable? Is their own music chaotic or bare? Are they willing to use their voice and what is the quality of their vocal sounds and singing?

This is primarily a challenging personal development process in which the music is not seen as an end in itself, but specific musical goals provide the stepping stones and are an integral part of the child's psychological journey. Non-musical outcomes are the evidence of the success of the therapeutic process.

Similarly, with Drake Music, Carien Meijer emphasises the complexity of the learning process when using assistive music technology with disabled people. The process is very subtle as each participant interacts with the technology in their own distinctive way in order to produce the sound they want to hear. There is a point in the process where the sound is created and controlled by the participant. This gives them a strong sense of ownership and it is important for both the leader and the participants to see that what they have achieved is the result of their own actions. Personalising technology presents a challenge to the music leader as the process has to relate to the diverse individual needs of the participants. Identifying what works for each person takes time, patience, care and skill. This process cannot be rushed if one is striving for a quality response.

Different kinds of challenges arise from cross-arts collaborations which are inevitably complex and demanding. Such projects are popular with many young people who do not perceive the world in discrete compartments. For them, the interconnections between the arts – between music, dance, theatre, visual arts and technology – are an integral part of their experience and they are keen to engage in this creative challenge. During his interview, Horst Rickels, a creative artist working with students and young people in The Hague, drew attention to some of the issues that need to be considered if cross-arts processes are to work:

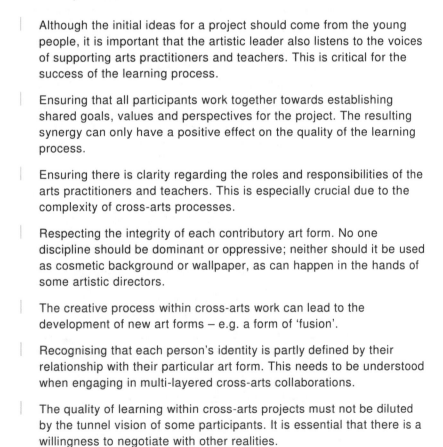

Although the initial ideas for a project should come from the young people, it is important that the artistic leader also listens to the voices of supporting arts practitioners and teachers. This is critical for the success of the learning process.

Ensuring that all participants work together towards establishing shared goals, values and perspectives for the project. The resulting synergy can only have a positive effect on the quality of the learning process.

Ensuring there is clarity regarding the roles and responsibilities of the arts practitioners and teachers. This is especially crucial due to the complexity of cross-arts processes.

Respecting the integrity of each contributory art form. No one discipline should be dominant or oppressive; neither should it be used as cosmetic background or wallpaper, as can happen in the hands of some artistic directors.

The creative process within cross-arts work can lead to the development of new art forms – e.g. a form of 'fusion'.

Recognising that each person's identity is partly defined by their relationship with their particular art form. This needs to be understood when engaging in multi-layered cross-arts collaborations.

The quality of learning within cross-arts projects must not be diluted by the tunnel vision of some participants. It is essential that there is a willingness to negotiate with other realities.

Creating a learning environment in which each person is encouraged to be open to the unknown - to explore new possibilities, new ways of seeing and making new connections – the ultimate challenge in cross-arts work.

One approach towards facilitating a quality process

In Section 1.4 reference was made to the project Musical Futures as an influential model of music education for secondary schools in the UK. As part of the project I wrote a research and development report on Guildhall Connect (Renshaw, 2005b) and will now to draw on some of this material (see pp.11-15) to illustrate one way of engaging young people in a quality learning process. One of the strongest features of Connect is that it is committed to making music in a collaborative way – an approach, a creative process that excites young people and professionals alike. Its various ensembles embrace a wide range of participants including Guildhall tutors, supporting artists, students, teachers and young people from different London boroughs. Perhaps Connect's approach to learning can be summed up in this way:

> Although the musical context is non-formal and the approach to learning informal, the way in which the music is created, shaped and performed is both organised and goal-directed (ibid, p.11).

As was stressed in Section 4.2, the effectiveness of the learning process within each ensemble is largely dependent on the quality of the music leaders. From the beginning of the process the challenge for the leaders is:

to know how to allocate roles within the ensemble at the appropriate level of skill

to know how to 'read' the participants' musical interests

to know how to respond creatively to these musical interests

to know at what point to extend each individual's musical experience

to know how to structure and shape the musical material so that it resonates with the whole ensemble

to create the opportunity for all the young musicians to share in the responsibility for solving problems, making decisions and taking risks

to enable the group to build up a collective sense of musical expectation and aspiration (ibid, p.11).

Central to Connect is the use of oral and aural processes that enable young people to have a voice in shaping their own living culture. Within this spirit of vernacular music-making, Connect has created a climate of openness, experimentation and interchange that has acted as a catalyst for producing authentic original work.

Fundamental to this process is that each group starts by making a piece through working with raw, basic musical material. Because of the broad musical interests of the leaders, none of the ensembles is locked into any one particular music genre. The young musicians are exposed to many different kinds of music in their lives and do not wish to be pigeonholed in any way. Therefore, within each Connect ensemble different musical voices are given the space to be heard and the musical material reflects the shared interests of the leaders and the participants. As one young musician commented:

> (Tutors) make an effort to take at least one aspect of each music genre that they can think of and put it all together so that everyone can hear part of the music that they want. They can hear how it isn't that different from other music and how it all really works together – in the end, that it is all music (ibid, p.15).

What stands out is that each group builds up its own musical identity. If this is to have any validity for the young people, they must feel that the sound world being created is authentic – that it is 'theirs' and they can enjoy a collective ownership of the music that can strengthen the quality of engagement in performance (ibid, p.12). To achieve this, the music leaders have to be flexible and open-minded, as was instanced by another young musician:

> If you don't like something, you can ask if you can change it. They won't really mind because from the way the music is structured there can be so many different things you could do instead. It would give the piece a different feel but it would still sound good, so they don't actually mind if you want to change something or mess around with some notes because it is what they are really encouraging you to do (ibid, p.14).

The processes used in Connect are firmly rooted in aural-based learning. In the words of Paul Griffiths, one of the most experienced leaders in Connect:

> The importance of aural-based learning is that it makes music feel alive. It is 'real' music. It instantly grabs you by its immediacy, power and strength. If you are trying to play and replicate something by reading (notation), you have to work very hard to capture that authenticity, power and magic. It (aural learning) endows it with that pretty much straight away. That is its main strength (ibid, p.12).

Within Connect the whole approach to learning has a rigour that comes from the many different forms of musical material generated through the compositional process. Complex musical structures are created and shaped by the young musicians working with the Connect team. An example of this complexity was cited by Guy Wood, one of the Connect musicians:

> Have you ever done a gig with 30 kids, where they play the A section in 6/8, a B section in 5/4, with a ridiculously high pitched melody screaming over the top and four of them improvising together, whilst all of this is going on? This is quite a feat for any group of musicians, never mind the fact that these players are all 10 and 11 year olds (ibid, p.12).

At no time is this aural approach allowed to invalidate the use of notation, but direct engagement with the music through improvisation and other creative processes helps to sharpen up the listening of the musicians and extends their musical vocabulary and sound world.

One major aspect of Connect arises from the musicians' commitment to a holistic approach to music-making. They believe that it is partly through aural processes that we come to see and feel some of the fundamental connections in the creation and performance of music. For example:

  | between spontaneity, freedom and structure

  | between ears, eyes and body

  | between physical, mental and emotional memory

Our aural memory enables us to remember such reference points as sounds, structures, forms and rhythms. Our bodily or physical memory helps us to respond to the beat, pulse, groove and rhythmic feel, whilst our emotional memory embraces those feelings, moods and emotions that enable us to capture the spirit of the music. These interconnections are central to Connect learning processes and they result in a strong sense of hearing, feeling and knowing that is absorbed, held and remembered by the musicians (ibid, pp.12-13).

Through this approach Connect aims to create a new kind of musician – one who is rounded as a creative musician and not circumscribed by notation and instrumental technique. Connect is more interested in developing a resourceful musician, whose musical personality displays itself in different ways through creative processes that use a range of instruments and technology appropriate to the particular musical needs of their ensemble (ibid, p.13). This approach is challenging for all participants but it is one that has succeeded in generating quality learning in many different forms.

4.4   Quality of end-product

Diversity of end-product and appropriateness of judgements

The preceding analysis has tried to look honestly at the complexity of what is entailed in describing and making judgements about the quality of any project in the community. It must be clear that many diverse factors have to be taken into account if the judgement is to do full justice to all the practitioners and participants involved in the planning, preparation and delivery of the project. Where does this leave the end-product?

End-products are as diverse as the processes leading up to them. For example, they can include a performance, event, exhibition, recording, website, participation on line, blog, film, visual log, community meal with performance. They can be multi-media, cross-over, cross-arts, cross-cultural, drawing on the richness of a particular neighbourhood.

On the other hand, in some contexts the notion of an end-product is not even appropriate. In music therapy, for example, one is not working towards an end-product in the normally accepted sense of the term. Certainly there may well be a moment of celebration as part of the process, but this is seen as a self-validating process where only the therapist is the audience. Similarly with Music for Life, the product is the process. The final 'closing piece' will include the whole group and it will arise organically towards the end of the process. It will be especially sensitive to the needs of the residents but in no way could it be described as an end-product. In the words of Linda Rose:

> The session ends with the 'closing piece', a repeat of the opening improvisation, which emerges from a piece already being played. This often requires subtle key changes, changes of mood, reorientation in many ways to bring the session to a predictable close. The ending is as important as the opening and supports the transition that is about to happen – saying goodbye, moving from chairs, changing to another environment again, all of which can cause confusion and upset to a person with dementia (6.3 K).

But in most cases the end-product is seen as a natural arrival point – a valid reflection of the participants and their voice, both individually and collectively. The aim is to achieve a true expression of the group in the most appropriate way possible. As indicated above, end-products can take many shapes and forms, and can be equally challenging for participants and audiences alike.

For example, with Eastfeast their 'finale' in each village or town can include a feast, a performance, a picnic, an exhibition, a tea party with clowns and jugglers, costumes and site development (e.g. allotments, growing site, river mosaic, willow tunnel) – a rich medley of imagination, creativity, experiment, risk-taking, skills and disciplines.

A similar richness can be seen in Eugene van Erven's description of the process leading up to an end-product in The Story Kitchen in Haarlem.

> Between October and December (2008), visual artists went into the classrooms to work with children on six-week project cycles, not as teachers but as artists with a great deal of freedom to experiment. Another visual artist was put in charge of a

workshop to artistically shape tablecloths of recycled fabric and family album photographs printed on textile. Bouwmeester and van Leeuwen started to film portraits of women preparing (and talking about) their favourite dish. Sometimes by zooming in on hands only, this allowed them also to include Muslim women who otherwise might not have participated. From 10 through 13 December all of these activities culminated in eight public neighbourhood meals (lunch and dinner), which were sold out.

Seated in De Hamelink's central meeting area at tables covered with the most fantastic table cloths (some of which even included pieces of original wedding dresses), visitors were treated to a screening of the elaborate preparation of a Moroccan appetizer accompanied by two musicians playing live music. Towards the end of the 5-minute documentary the actual smells of the dish being prepared on the screen began to emerge from the kitchen. When the film ended, the kitchen doors opened and the dish in question was brought out in sufficient quantities to serve everyone. The main course (Kurdish) and desert (traditional Dutch) were offered in a similar combination of film, music, smell and taste. Simple, effective, and very meticulously produced with substantial local involvement, it provided once again artistically-shaped dialogic space that mobilised all the senses, generating conversations that would not have happened otherwise (6.3 A).

In both these examples the nature of each project demanded a multi-faceted approach to achieving quality. The boundaries of the contributory art forms were extended with the intention of producing work of quality – that is, demonstrating originality, imagination, inspiration and quality of engagement, at all times celebrating the voice of each participant and acknowledging the importance of their authenticity, commitment, motivation, passion, energy, honesty, integrity, self-esteem, growing confidence and feeling of achievement. Qualities that were nurtured throughout the creative process and that become the life-blood of an end-product that 'works'. This sense of connection and coherence between process and product is critical to the quality of any project.

But establishing this connection and coherence cannot be taken for granted. So much depends on the circumstances and the context. When writing about the *Percossa* project (a percussion ensemble) in Het Concertgebouw in Amsterdam, Marga Wobma-Helmich points out some of the challenges confronting the musicians and the teachers. The particular situation helped to shape how the quality of the end-product could be viewed.

> We (had) a project for these pupils (from pre-vocational secondary schools) before we started with the *Percossa* project. This was a success for schools outside Amsterdam but not for those in Amsterdam. During one of the concerts in our Main Hall the pupils of two schools started to tease each other and it ended in a fight with knives at the Central Station. The schools involved decided not to go outside the school with their pupils anymore and not to attend any cultural activities in the future.

This was the starting point for the *Percossa* project. Together with these schools we had long sessions and developed different workshops leading to a concert at the Concertgebouw given by the pupils, presented by the pupils. The scenery, the costumes, the cakes during the coffee break, the publicity – all were realised by the pupils themselves. Only one school at a time is involved in order to avoid problems between schools. And there is strong involvement of the teachers and the musicians of the ensemble who know how to communicate and work with the pupils. Their professionalism, the way in which they keep challenging the pupils, keep them concentrating and winning their trust was of great value for both the teachers and pupils involved.

During the concert, with parents and friends present, the pupils performed to a very high level. For some of them, they could finally feel proud of themselves, standing on the stage and receiving the appreciation that they deserved. After one of the concerts I congratulated the director of the school with his pupils. He pointed out that for him the greatest value was for his teachers. The project gave a quality impulse on working with the pupils on a project basis, which he had been trying to introduce for several years but had not succeeded. He saw his teachers change and he realised the school could benefit from this in many different ways (6.3 N).

Again, for Music in Prison projects, the final performance together with a recording is a strong form of validation of the work that has gone on. For the participants quality is seen in terms of the great songs created, which everyone feels good performing. This instils a feeling of excellence in terms of desire, motivation, sound, integrity, commitment and passion. As Sara Lee said in her interview, "the performance might have rough edges but that does not detract from the quality of the experience". The inmates practice hard so that they don't get it wrong – there is a strong sense of shared responsibility. In her Case Study Sara describes how she views the quality of this performing experience.

There is a big focus on the performance at the end of a project as it is a great mark of achievement and allows individuals to get immediate praise and appreciation for what they have done. It takes a huge amount of confidence to take part in a project which has the potential to open you up in ways you may not have been before and it takes an even bigger effort to present your work in the final gig. Many people have never started *and* finished something in their lives so this is a massive step into often uncharted and frightening territory.

Time and effort is put into mixing and designing the project CDs as this is another very important aspect of the whole process. To have something tangible that you can be really proud of and to have the opportunity to let family and friends hear what you have achieved is a wonderful and positive link back to life outside (6.3 H).

Sara's sensitive, yet grounded observations demonstrate clearly that any judgements made about a culminating performance in a prison context have to include social and psychological factors along with artistic criteria. Without this balanced perspective a judgement could well be invalid – it just fails to understand the complexity of the situation. Criteria of judgement have to be rooted in a context of reality – this is what illuminates the meaning for the participants, the music leaders and the audience.

But this is equally true when working and performing in any community context and understanding the relevant variables should provide the frame of reference for making appropriate judgements about an end-product that is connected to its context and creative process.

We have now come back full circle to the comments made by Eugene van Erven at the beginning of this chapter: "the quality of (community art) projects cannot be judged by assessing a single performance alone with criteria borrowed from a mainstream arts discourse" (6.3 A). And yet this is what happens so frequently when funding bodies, arts councils, arts cognoscente, Board members, senior management in arts organisations, and higher arts education teachers view performances and end-products. In general, their judgements are mono-dimensional and inappropriate. They fail to understand the multiplicity of aims of the project; they fail to connect what they are seeing and hearing to the realities of the context; and they fail to grasp the complexity of the process leading up to the end-product. Basically, their judgements are limited by a single-track frame of reference, a narrow aesthetic that fails to reflect what is entailed in community engagement. It is hardly surprising then, that much work rooted in the community remains in the margins of arts organisations, where it has to compete with the intransigence of so-called 'core business'. Things are beginning to shift in the more enlightened organisations but the process of change remains sluggish in those individuals and institutions that fail to connect to where the world is moving. The need for cultural change in institutions and the realignment of their priorities will be examined in Section 5.4.

5

Impact of community engagement

5.1 Learning and development

Guiding principles

The aim of this final chapter is to explore the implications of the preceding discussion for the development of musicians and artists working in schools and the wider community. It will focus partly on those ways of learning most likely to prepare and support practitioners for the challenges arising from different forms of community engagement. It will also reinforce the key point that for any such learning and development programme to work, it has to be rooted in an organisational culture that subscribes to similar values and ways of seeing the world. In practice this might well entail the organisation making a fundamental shift in perspective resulting in a re-ordering of its priorities.

As was intimated at the beginning of Chapter 3, the quality of community engagement depends largely on the effectiveness of all participants making meaningful connections, understanding and responding to each other's contexts and engaging in those open conversations that lie at the heart of any successful partnership. In brief, 'engagement' necessarily entails:

connecting to different contexts

connecting conversations between individuals and organisations

learning through partnerships

In addition to the range of quality issues discussed in Chapter 4, the above three principles must be seen as central to shaping any learning and development programme aimed at fostering community engagement. Examples of different approaches to learning and development will be drawn from the Case Studies, Personal Testimonies and interviews.

Approaches to learning and development

Kunstenaars&CO, Amsterdam

One of the Dutch organisations interviewed for this enquiry, Kunstenaars&CO (Artists, Culture and Entrepreneurship), is a national training, research and development agency whose mission is very much grounded in the needs of the market place. In his Case Study Joost Heinsius, Manager of Knowledge and Innovation, emphasises the importance of providing opportunities for artists to learn how to connect and engage with the many possible different contexts within the community. Joost states that:

> Kunstenaars&CO sees itself as a builder of bridges, both within the arts sector as a promoter of continuing education, but also connecting the arts with the world

out there where there is a lot to gain, not only as new sources of income but also strengthening the position of art within society as a whole, to show that art can really contribute, can be of real value to real people (6.3 D).

For Kunstenaars&CO there is a symbiotic relationship between the development of art forms, the development of artists and their interaction with different communities, cultures and sectors. Artists have to continually innovate in order to make sense of and respond to the challenges arising from different contexts. Being contextually aware is now a necessary condition of being an effective arts practitioner. Joost makes the point well in his Case Study:

> We are convinced that there is much to be gained from working outside the art sector as an artist. Responding to different contexts requires artists to redefine their own skills, testing them with professionals from other fields and developing new kinds of art. Working in communities, in business, within health care, within other public sector organisations helps artists to redefine their art, to develop new forms of art which are just as valid on these new 'stages' as traditional art is on its own particular stage (6.3 D).

From this perspective it is self-evident that individual and collaborative learning and development has to hang like a thread throughout the working life of any artist who is trying to engage with the demands of the contemporary world. For example, Kunstenaars&CO has devised a programme of training workshops, counselling, mentoring, coaching and work experience aimed at developing the skills and attitudes of artists so that they can function more effectively in the constantly changing workplace. It also recognises the importance of strengthening their sense of entrepreneurship and understanding of how to be economically independent. In his Case Study Joost makes a clear statement about the skills required by an artist today:

> In the firm belief that independence is a necessary condition for a professional working life, we see the artist as a professional who is able to put his or her competences into the work he or she is committed to. Those competences are not only about being artistic or being creative, but also comprise general competences such as being able to influence others, to lead a process, to negotiate, to network, to be able to translate his or her unique contribution meaningfully into contexts other than only the art sector (...) Since the majority of artists are small entrepreneurs (whether by choice or by necessity), they also have to be capable of finding work opportunities, of managing themselves well and managing the different sources from which they draw their income (6.3 D).

Kunstenaars&CO fears that the training and development of artists in Higher Arts Education institutions has yet to fully engage with the question of what arts practice is likely to look like in 2020. There is reluctance from many teachers and students to broaden their perspective and to redefine their role and practice. Echoing the research of Rineke Smilde (2009a) on *Musicians as Lifelong Learners*, Joost Heinsius makes explicit the importance of lifelong learning for all artists:

> Most of art education concentrates only on the artistic side and does not prepare artists for the working life that is ahead of them. Nor are there many opportunities after finishing their education to systematically reflect on these challenges together with fellow artists. Lifelong education for artists is very necessary, but certainly is not offered within the world of most artists (6.3 D).

Joost then poses several fundamental questions that need to be addressed by Higher Arts Education institutions if they are going to do full justice to their students in the future:

> The working practice of the future artist is much more varied and context sensitive than it was in the past. How can artistic quality be maintained whilst at the same time training students to be prepared for a working life that has never been experienced by their present teachers and directors? How can we find new didactic models that respond to the situations of real life after school? How can we transfer a new image of the artist of the future when the present image is still dominant within many parts of the arts sector itself? (6.3 D).

Guildhall School of Music & Drama, London

A similar point of view to that held by Kunstenaars&CO was clearly articulated by a music student about to graduate from the Guildhall School of Music & Drama in 2001. Whilst preparing a vision statement for the School, I interviewed Chris Branch who made the following perceptive comment on conservatoire training:

> The highly competitive nature of the world's top conservatoires results in extreme conservatism due to fear of losing their traditions and elitist position. The closed cultural perspective of many professional musicians and students could lead to the destruction of the Music Conservatoire in the future. The danger is that they are producing huge numbers of incredibly skilled players who have little idea how to connect with the rest of the world, and who are struggling to understand the place of music within a post-modern culture (Renshaw, 2001, p. 4).

Despite significant changes in recent years, conservatoires and other Higher Arts Education institutions still need to move on and radically reappraise the main thrust of their provision. New frameworks are necessary in order to enable students and arts practitioners to move convincingly through the changing cultural landscape. The words of the eminent historian Eric Hobsbawm (1997) help to give a sense of perspective to our understanding of both the present and the future.

> At the end of this century it has for the first time become possible to see what a world may be like in which the past, including the past in the present, has lost its role, in which the old maps and charts which guided human beings, singly and collectively, through life no longer represent the landscape through which we move (p.16).

If we project forwards into the Noughties – or "a decade that changed the world" (Footman, 2009) – Hobsbawm's observations are especially pertinent. Events in the last ten years strongly reinforce his position. The need for new maps is now absolutely critical if we are to make sense of the new world.

In the context of Higher Arts Education we need new maps to chart a cultural topography that is far more inclusive and less self-referential. In conservatoires, for example, the main focus continues to lie in conserving 'classical' traditions. There is no doubting that the integrity and transformative power of these traditions will always be seen as of central importance, but the urgency of change also necessitates a shift of perspective. As is clear throughout this enquiry, musicians and arts practitioners now need to develop the skills, attitudes and outlook that will enable them to connect to different contexts and changing cultural values. All learning and development programmes need to take these changes into account. The resonance of new ideas, innovation and entrepreneurship arising from the necessity of change, has to act as a catalyst for action that has artistic, social and cultural relevance.

Joint Music Master for New Audiences and Innovative Practice

New approaches to learning and development have been built into the Joint Music Master for New Audiences and Innovative Practice (2008), which was initiated by the Lectorate Lifelong Learning in Music. It was developed and piloted between 2005 and 2009 by Prince Claus Conservatoire, Groningen; the Royal Conservatoire, The Hague; Guildhall School of Music & Drama, London; Iceland Academy of the Arts, Reykjavik; and Jyväskylä University of Applied Sciences, Finland. Currently it is in the process of implementation. The substance of this new degree very much reflects changing practice within the workplace. For example, it recognises that:

> In today's changing world careers in music are more flexible and international in scope than ever before. Consequently, in addition to performance skills, today's musicians must be capable of working within diverse contexts and situations that are ever changing.
> (www.jointmusicmaster.org)

At the core of the two-year degree lie four compulsory modules in:

Action Research

Leading and Guiding

Performance and Communication

Project Management and Entrepreneurship

Improvisation, technology and leadership in different contexts underpin each of the areas of specialisation – i.e., Ensembles, Collaborative Practice and Cross-sector Settings. Perhaps most important, throughout the programme students are supported by reflective forms of mentoring aimed at helping them to identify and develop their personal pathway into their professional career.

Guildhall Connect

Many of the principles underlying the Joint Music Master degree were originally developed and implemented by Guildhall Connect since its inception in 2002. Sean Gregory traces some of this development in his Personal Testimony.

> My priority for Connect over recent years has been for the creation of an efficient, workable and sustainable model that embraces both the formal and non-formal sectors. An ongoing and obvious challenge along the way has been that the music generated by Connect participants is often embedded in a contemporary, vernacular culture that does not necessarily resonate with the core business of a conservatoire. In order to assist the evolution of its profile and position, the gradual consolidation of a broader administrative infrastructure took place to support the activity and to enable its ongoing development. As well as continuing to run access and inclusion workshops/projects, satellite Connect Ensembles (local, national and international), apprenticeship schemes and continuing professional development for teachers and leaders, a more ambitious progression route – a type of 'golden thread' – has begun to emerge through the programme:

> A new 'non-formal' curriculum for young participants that offers genuine opportunities for sustained and personalised musical learning alongside a robust mentoring circle of co-participants, students, teachers, parents and Connect tutors.

> A new Connect undergraduate programme set up for 'creative portfolio practitioners' who break down the boundaries between musical genres, art disciplines, 'specialists' and 'non-specialists'.

> A postgraduate programme/research forum (particularly through an MMus in Leadership and the proposed Collaborative Masters in New Audiences and Innovative Practice) for the training and development of contemporary practitioners who collaborate, create and perform as artistic leaders, cultural producers and curators in a variety of contexts.

> A continuing professional development programme offering lifelong learning to performing artists, teachers, project managers and creative producers.

> (...) Crucial to Connect is its role as a laboratory, particularly in relation to the developmental work around creative and collaborative practice, leadership and the role of the musician as a 'portfolio practitioner' in society (6.2 C).

Project Connect in Brazil

The principles underlying Connect also formed the foundation of Project Connect at the Music School of the Federal University of Minas Gerais (EMUFMG) in Brazil, which instigated an optional course in 'Music Education and Social Projects'. The course had three related aims:

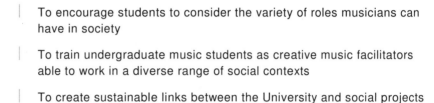

   To encourage students to consider the variety of roles musicians can have in society

   To train undergraduate music students as creative music facilitators able to work in a diverse range of social contexts

   To create sustainable links between the University and social projects

Heloisa Feichas and Robert Wells describe and analyse this project in Minas Gerais in their joint Case Study. The Brazilian context raises some especially interesting issues which the leaders had to take into account. For example:

> The idea of bringing this project to a Brazilian reality came from our questioning of the gaps in undergraduate music student's learning. The music school at EMUFMG is based on the European Conservatoire model, a system which is both chronologically and culturally displaced within modern Brazil. The 'master/apprentice' hierarchy, which can encourage reliant behaviour in students, is pervasive. The study of performance, composition and conducting is decontextualised; rooted in the European classical tradition, students explore only a fraction of the diverse musical life of Brazil. There are scarce opportunities for students, including those studying Music Education, to engage practically with the wider society. Collectively these issues frequently prevent students from developing into conscious, self-aware, creative musicians who can positively add to the society of which they are a part. We felt it essential to develop new opportunities for students so that they could explore the connections between their musical interests and the social and cultural landscape of contemporary Brazil (6.3 B).

Heloisa and Robert chose Guildhall Connect as their model because they wanted to focus on collaborative forms of learning, on group composition and on collective ways of creating and performing music. In their Case Study they identify some of the challenges arising from this kind of approach in Brazil.

> As students gain a practical and theoretical understanding of Connect's processes there is a natural development of their leadership skills. These skills are transferable to a number of musical, educational and social contexts. This is particularly relevant in Brazil where there has been a steady increase in the number of Brazilian NGOs supporting social projects involving music. These projects frequently engage communities through musical activities, however in many cases the pedagogical approaches are based on old models, frequently involving the reproduction of existing music. We hoped that engaging students in

this project would make them re-consider the role of a leader/teacher within both the formal and non-formal educational environment (6.3 B).

During the programme several key issues had to be addressed by the students – issues that are not unique to Project Connect in Brazil. For example:

- Making decisions and finding consensus within group work

- Understanding how to balance individual autonomy and shared responsibility when working in a group

- Learning how to communicate effectively and productively in group problem-solving

- Strengthening interpersonal skills

- Structuring ideas and developing musical material in group composition sessions

- Reconciling different approaches to music-making – between classically trained students and those from a popular music background

- Redefining the role of leader and teacher in a music and educational context

The students' responses to this project will be discussed later in this chapter.

Royal Philharmonic Orchestra, Community and Education Department, London

One area of learning and development that has been especially significant over the last 25 years has been the training of orchestral musicians to work in schools and the wider community. One very important outcome of this redefinition of the role of an orchestra was the recognition that as the players began to extend and deepen their skills, it was also essential for training programmes to focus on their personal, artistic and creative development. As early as 1992 I made the following observation, arising from the work of the Guildhall School's Department of Performance and Communication Skills, under the artistic leadership of Peter Wiegold. The initial development work was carried out with groups of players from the City of London Sinfonia and the London Symphony Orchestra.

> Engaging in different kinds of performance practice has widened the opportunity for players to become more responsible for their musical actions. They have been encouraged to make artistic, social and educational decisions of their own, rather than merely be efficient cogs in a high-precision machine, energised by a

charismatic conductor. As one principal player in the London Symphony Orchestra put it – "I now feel a musician again, rather than an instrumental operative".

For some people, then, the debate has shifted from serving the community to serving the players. At last the artistic health of the individual player is on the agenda. It is now recognised that each musician needs to be confronted by an internal creative challenge as a necessary precondition for working in the community. Responding to this growing emphasis on the rediscovery of the orchestral player as an individual, several orchestras have initiated ambitious training schemes which place their players at the centre of a rigorous research and development programme. Those enlightened managements who care about the survival of the orchestra have begun to see that individual change lies at the heart of institutional change, and that training is the main vehicle for changing the professional culture (Renshaw, 1992, p.62).

One orchestra that responded creatively to this challenge was the Royal Philharmonic Orchestra (RPO). In 1993 Judith Webster was appointed to lead its new Community and Education Department. As was discussed in Chapter 2.2, Judith came to the orchestral world from a background in music therapy. Her understanding of improvisation and creative music-making, together with her insight into questions of motivation, identity and personal development helped to inform her approach to the learning and development of the players in the orchestra. In her Personal Testimony Judith outlines some of the main elements of her approach:

On arrival at the RPO, the first decision I made was to provide professional development to the orchestral musicians who chose to be involved in community and education work for the first time. Rather than teach them how to be a teacher or workshop leader, and provide them with lots of tricks and clapping games which they could use in workshops, I decided to focus on their own musical skills – giving them opportunities to learn to improvise, to work without notation, creatively, flexibly and freely with other musicians from different traditions. Remembering my own fear of improvisation when first training as a music therapist, I considered it vital to support them through this process by doing it with them. I was more familiar with improvisation than they were, albeit a less skilled player. I felt instinctively that I needed to make a relationship with each of them in music as they would relate to me differently than if our relationship was one of 'management and player'.

This was one of the most important decisions I made, and enabled me to gain their respect, and to challenge entrenched views about management and what to expect from me. It also allowed them to realise that I understood the implications of what I was asking of them, understood their fears and demons. As a result, they respected me and we began our journey of discovery together. As an orchestral musician myself, I gave a great deal of thought to the roles they play within the orchestra, how the psychology of, for example, a rank and file violinist might differ from that of a principal trombonist and how these might affect their responses to an improvisation workshop with colleagues. An important influence on my approach to setting up this new work was therefore my own awareness of personal identity, how it was expressed in music and how to work with this creatively (6.2 L).

One key point stands out in Judith Webster's approach to her work with the RPO – that is her awareness of the importance of making connections. For example:

| Ensuring that the learning processes in the development programme made meaningful connections with the individual players

| Enabling each player to make connections between their personal, artistic, creative and professional development

| Unlocking the motivation of the players so that they might re-connect with their initial reasons for becoming a musician

| Understanding the culture of the Orchestra so that the learning and development programme would connect to its DNA

| Making connections with those community contexts that resonated with the psychological and social character of the Orchestra

| Building up and sustaining external partnerships that connected to the Community and Education mission of the Orchestra

Further excerpts from Judith's Testimony illustrate the strengths of her holistic approach to the development of the players and their work in the community.

The other key decision I made was that I should understand the core identity of the Orchestra itself – its DNA, its essence, what made it tick and how that showed in its playing, how it collectively expressed itself. In my judgement, it was this that would determine the kind of work we should initiate in a community setting. It would guide me in setting up projects – who with, what we would do well, how we would approach the work. Once again, this proved to be a crucial decision which affected the type of challenges I offered the musicians through their evolving community engagement and context.

I used my music therapist's insight to steer their individual and collective professional and personal development. Through continually reassessing this, I was able to unlock high levels of motivation and watch them grow into new creative roles, with a sense of achievement and pride in their work. They re-connected with the reasons they took up music in the first place, sought out musical and social challenges and faced new situations with relish and commitment. This was the opposite of what I had been told to expect from them.

(...) Once I had tuned into the DNA of the Orchestra, I then needed to create appropriate and developmental opportunities for the players to work in. In my assessment, the Orchestra was earthy, uncompromising, gutsy, passionate, and possessing huge warmth and compassion. So I sought out challenging social contexts where our work could question the status quo and make a difference. The Orchestra proved to work best when working with offenders, young homeless people, children with special needs and their families, and in tough youth club settings. They were fantastic at working with underdogs – and could relate to the psychology of their situation in their own way.

(...) My music therapy background also informed my approach to setting up external partnerships. It was imperative that the community partners, just like the orchestral musicians, had a clear and honest understanding of what we were trying to achieve together, what we could not achieve and how we might expect to reach our shared goals. Key to this was ensuring that the musicians and partners all understood their different roles, and respected their own skills as well as those of the partners (6.2 L).

The effectiveness of the model devised by Judith Webster and the RPO can be put down to three interconnected forms of development: player development, organisational development and partnership development. To be successful each strand needs to be integrated into a holistic learning and development programme that is fully engaged with the continually evolving changes in the wider world.

Music for Life Wigmore Hall and for dementia, England

The final example of the pivotal place of learning and development in fostering quality community engagement is taken from the work of Linda Rose with Music for Life. As can be seen from her Case Study, quality of outcome is largely dependent on the quality of the musicians' development, care staff development and trainers' development. The work of Music for Life is exemplary in the way in which it puts the three key procedural principles into practice. That is:

connecting to context

connecting conversations between individuals and organisations

learning through partnerships

Linda explains how after each workshop an hour-long debriefing session is designed to strengthen the learning and reflection of the musicians and the staff. It is an opportunity to learn from each other and to deepen the partnership.

Changes in behaviour and mood are noticed by staff and discussed with the dementia care trainer in the debriefing. Individual staff members are encouraged to share in the discussion, their own vulnerabilities are sensitively drawn out and gradually they may risk talking about their relationships with each other within the workshop or within their teams outside the sessions. Often, tensions are revealed, overlooked promotions discussed, poor teamwork addressed. Also compliments are paid, laughter shared, warmth and trust developed.

The impact of the work on themselves is as important as for those they care for. Valuing feeling responses, reaching staff at an emotional level, raising their confidence and self-worth has a direct impact on the residents. The trainer needs to work with the same level of integrity and sensitivity as the musicians, recognising that he too needs to improvise, working from the personal experience of each member of staff rather than arriving with a body of knowledge about dementia that needs to be transmitted. In encouraging questioning and discussion in this way, the trainer is laying new foundations for learning and the quality of life improves for the care staff too.

The musicians need a period of debriefing too. It is not easy for them to withdraw from the session and look at it objectively as they too need a time of transition to surface back to life outside the intensity of this experience. A facilitator who has also observed the session helps the transition and leads the discussion: talking about the detail of the session, the effectiveness of their planning, exploring the ways they have worked together and the affect on each resident. The detail of this discussion will influence the subsequent session and often raises issues which will need further thought and conversations over the next week. Support for the team is vital, just as it is for staff as they cope with the emotional rigours of the work and face the occasions when connections are not made, as well as celebrating the progress of individuals (6.3 K).

In terms of fostering quality of experience and integrity of engagement, the work of Music for Life clearly demonstrates the necessity of thorough preparation, understanding the context, grounded practice, effective communication and collaboration, and quality of shared reflection and assessment. This is a challenge to the learning and development programme of any organisation.

5.2 The place of mentoring and co-mentoring in learning and development

The scope of mentoring for arts practitioners

Increasingly, those organisations committed to community engagement are beginning to see that mentoring offers a strong form of support that underpins the learning and development of their arts practitioners, as is evidenced in the Case Studies of this enquiry. This is hardly surprising as collaborative ways of working within community settings draw on those forms of learning that are integral to reflective practice – experiential learning, context-based learning, work-based learning and action learning. In each case, face-to-face mentoring, co-mentoring and group mentoring circles can be used to address specific personal, professional and artistic challenges.

The following scenarios might help to illustrate the challenges confronting musicians and artists as they extend and deepen the quality of their community engagement. The success of such multi-layered projects depends in part on all participants having a clear vision, realistic goals, meticulous planning and shared preparation. There has to be a mutual understanding of different ways of working arising from different traditions and perspectives. Performing artists, visual artists, creative writers, IT specialists, teachers, care workers, and staff from different community contexts have to learn how to work together, to explore new possibilities and to make new connections. There has to be a willingness to negotiate with team members who might hold different views, but whose identity, integrity and skills need to be respected. On occasions, collaborative work can very easily lead to misunderstandings, role confusion, frustration, tension, apprehension, fear, vulnerability, breakdown of trust, and feelings of inadequacy and dysfunction.

Different approaches can be used to heighten awareness and address such complex issues. For example, opportunities for shared learning and development, shared preparation, monitoring and evaluation are critical to making such projects work, but the mentoring of individuals and groups can also provide informed support that will strengthen personal and professional understanding.

Scenarios:

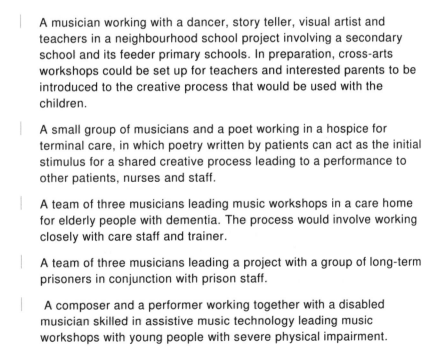

A musician working with a dancer, story teller, visual artist and teachers in a neighbourhood school project involving a secondary school and its feeder primary schools. In preparation, cross-arts workshops could be set up for teachers and interested parents to be introduced to the creative process that would be used with the children.

A small group of musicians and a poet working in a hospice for terminal care, in which poetry written by patients can act as the initial stimulus for a shared creative process leading to a performance to other patients, nurses and staff.

A team of three musicians leading music workshops in a care home for elderly people with dementia. The process would involve working closely with care staff and trainer.

A team of three musicians leading a project with a group of long-term prisoners in conjunction with prison staff.

A composer and a performer working together with a disabled musician skilled in assistive music technology leading music workshops with young people with severe physical impairment.

- A multi-disciplinary community project involving artists, teachers, governors, support staff, children, parents and other specialists (e.g. crafts people, cooks, gardeners, horticulturalists) in the neighbourhood.

- An experimental community project in a sound and image lab for young musicians, visual artists, singers, DJs and programmers.

Mentoring, then, is just one way of helping arts practitioners, teachers and staff in community organisations to work more effectively together and to enhance the quality of their projects. But the mentoring process can also play a critical role in supporting individuals in their response to the wider challenges of the workplace.

As was indicated in Chapter 1, musicians and artists are now having to diversify, to extend their roles and work more flexibly within a portfolio career. To reiterate, the implications of these developments for musicians are made explicit by Rineke Smilde in her PhD dissertation, *Musicians as Lifelong Learners: Discovery through Biography* (Smilde, 2009a, pp.1-2):

- Changes in the social-cultural landscape are helping to shape a very different workplace for musicians

- Flexible portfolio careers require finely tuned transferable skills and a more entrepreneurial attitude towards work

- Musicians now have to perform different roles as they are expected to respond creatively to cultural and educational contexts that go beyond the concert hall

- Increasingly musicians have to work collaboratively with professionals in other fields – in cross-arts, cross-cultural and cross-sector contexts

All these changes are having a significant impact on arts practitioners and mentoring can be an effective way of supporting their development throughout their careers. But there are three critical stages when mentoring can play a particularly active role – at college, on entry into the profession and during periods of career transition. Here are examples of ways in which mentoring can foster development at these stages:

Students at college

- enabling students to shape and reflect on their personal pathway from the beginning of college right into the profession (building up a sense of progression through college and beyond)

- helping them to identify and reflect on key aspects of their development – e.g. personal, emotional, professional (as a learner and collaborator), technical, artistic, critical perspective on being an artist

- strengthening their sense of artistic identity in a world of changing practice

- inviting them to reflect critically on their professional practice in performance and artistic learning

- making meaningful connections through professional integration in different cultural and social contexts

- developing a strong entrepreneurial attitude

- learning to work effectively in collaborative teams

- deepening their understanding of documenting the reflective process – for example, writing a reflective log and self-reflective account of their development

Entry into the profession

- confronting the practicalities of the workplace (e.g. funding, budgeting, networking, negotiating, initiating projects, creating and seizing opportunities, self-management)

- managing a balanced work portfolio within a diversified career

- managing work-life balance

- understanding and coping with performance anxiety

- responding to the challenges arising from working in different community contexts

Career transition

- clarifying possible future direction

- re-kindling motivation

- shifting from performing and teaching to management

- developing new roles

- building up leadership skills

- extending repertoire of skills

- deepening and broadening perspective and awareness

A framework for mentoring

In both her own research and that of the Research Group in Lifelong Learning in Music and the Arts, Rineke Smilde (2009a, pp.92-93) takes the view that if lifelong learning is to become a dynamic and relevant force in the lives of musicians and artists, a process of mentoring must be pivotal at those critical stages of an individual's personal, artistic and professional development. The questions raised in the research are now being addressed by many institutions across Europe with the support of networks like the Association of European Conservatoires (AEC) including the ERASMUS Thematic Network for Music 'Polifonia' (also see CUREE, 2005a, 2005b, 2007).

In 2005 Rineke Smilde invited me to conduct a study of mentoring within the context of lifelong learning for musicians. I produced a Framework for Mentoring which has subsequently been modified in the light of my role as evaluator of REFLECT, the Creative Partnerships National Co-mentoring Programme for creative practitioners and teachers. This programme was led by The Sage Gateshead (see Renshaw, 2009, pp.94-102; Renshaw & Smith, 2008).

The Framework for Mentoring draws on those forms of learning that are central to reflective practice in the areas of continuing professional development, informal learning and adult education. The principles that helped to shape the study are rooted in a body of knowledge that is shared by such disparate areas of professional practice as nursing, general practice, social work, education and the visual and performing arts.

Such a shared philosophy of practice can only strengthen the work of those conservatoires, Higher Arts Education and training organisations that are beginning to realign their priorities within a culture of reflection and responsiveness. Within this context of renewal and development, mentoring is just one of several processes that can be used to help arts practitioners to engage in their own lifelong learning.

The core of the Framework rests on the following areas:

- Definitions of coaching, mentoring and co-mentoring

- Principles underlying a mentoring process

- Relationship between mentor and mentee

- Relationship between reflection and reflexivity in the mentoring process

- Characteristics of effective mentors

Definitions

Coaching

Coaching is an enabling process aimed at enhancing learning and development with the intention of improving performance in a specific aspect of practice. It has a short-term focus with an emphasis on immediate micro issues (e.g., How can I improve my performance in this particular area? How can I strengthen my workshop practice? What are the most appropriate ways of making my team work together more effectively?).

Mentoring

Mentoring is a more developmental process, including elements of coaching, facilitating and counselling, aimed at sharing knowledge, and encouraging individual development. It has a longer-term focus designed to foster personal growth and to help an individual place their artistic, creative, personal and professional development in a wider cultural, social and educational context (e.g., Why am I doing what I do? How do I perceive my identity? In what ways does this impact on my professional life and work? Where am I going? What determines my long-term goals?).

Co-mentoring

Co-mentoring entails a collaborative learning process in which both partners (possibly in a cross-arts or cross-sector context) engage in an equal exchange of knowledge, skills and experience in relation to a clearly defined shared focus. It constitutes a form of peer-learning.

Principles underlying a mentoring process

- Developing a non-judgemental, non-threatening working relationship based on empathy, trust and mutual respect

- Establishing a safe, supportive learning environment

- Creating conditions that encourage openness, honesty, informality and risk-taking

- Defining boundaries and ground rules before commencing the process, by drawing up a mentoring or learning agreement

- Building rapport and a clear understanding of who does what and why

- Allowing the person being mentored (the mentee) to determine their own agenda, to select their shared focus and shape their process of learning

Relationship between mentor and mentee

- A one-to-one relationship in which the mentor has the knowledge and skills to empathise and understand the position of their mentee

When mentoring arts practitioners it might be more appropriate to include non-verbal dialogue or exchange. Most artists have chosen their art form as their primary means of communication. In general, they connect with each other through making music together or engaging in shared creative practice, rather than through verbal, analytical, reflective processes. This can affect the dynamics of a mentoring relationship

A reciprocal relationship in which the mentor respects their mentee's potential for personal and professional development, and acknowledges their motivation for engaging in critical self-review and further learning rooted in practice-based evidence and experience

An effective relationship depends in part on the strength and integrity of a working partnership that is bound by a mentoring or learning agreement in which mutual roles, responsibilities and expectations are made explicit

A mentoring relationship should be time-based with a beginning and an end. It should not be ongoing as compared with peer professional relationships or peer mentoring

Relationship between reflection and reflexivity in the mentoring process

This section on reflective and reflexive practice draws on the seminal work of Donald Schön (1987, pp.26-31) and Anthony Giddens (1984, p.1). *Reflective practice* or *'reflection-on-action'* entails adopting a critical perspective about the reasons and consequences of what we do in different contexts. By focusing on the why rather than the how, this process of self-observation and self-review, rooted in evidence and experience drawn from their practice, enables a person to evaluate their starting point and to redefine their future actions. A reflective conversation helps a person to shift their perspective, change their behaviour and develop a sense of responsibility and ownership of their professional practice in a wide range of social and cultural contexts.

The main elements of a reflective conversation include:

Making connections – asking open questions – active listening – absorbing – rephrasing – reflecting – mirroring back – responding by leading and challenging mentee in a non-directive way

Using different levels of conversation by moving between social, personal, analytic, what-if, strategic and integrative questions

Deepening the mentee's awareness and conviction in what they are doing by fostering a greater understanding of context and place

- Empowering the mentee by asking neutral, open questions that encourage critical self-reflection, curiosity and a sense of enquiry

- Strengthening the mentee's ability to challenge their preconceived views, to take risks, to make new connections and to shift their perspective

Reflexive practice or *'reflection-in-action'* focuses on how the quality of a person's inner listening, attention and awareness can help them clarify their purpose and motivation. Using empathy and being reflexive in a conversation can strengthen a person's sense of identity, deepen their self-awareness and enable them to understand how their personal motivation, values and emotions can affect their professional practice and learning. Being able to connect ones own inner listening to that of others is central to a sensitive mentoring relationship.

The main elements of a reflexive conversation include:

- Helping the mentee to clarify their motivation and to identify their core purpose

- Enabling the mentee to find their own voice and to deepen their understanding of who they are

- Encouraging the mentee to explore and verbally articulate the emotional interconnections between their identity, motivation and professional practice

- Assisting the mentee to develop an understanding of their relationship with their own creative learning (e.g., What does it mean for you? Why do you do what you do? What do you care about in your creative learning?)

- Helping the mentee to connect their self-awareness and sense of identity to their outer world – i.e., to the context in which they work and live

- Encouraging the mentee to reflect on their own story, their own biography, as a means of clarifying and deepening their understanding of themselves, their history and their personal and professional journey

- Connecting the mentee's tacit or implicit understanding with their explicit knowledge of their particular situation

- Creating the possibility for the mentee to engage with their emotional intelligence by:

- becoming emotionally self-aware
- developing the ability to manage their emotions and feelings
- understanding how to use emotions for the benefit of their self-motivation
- recognising and responding to emotions in others through the use of empathy
- strengthening their interpersonal skills and understanding

The importance of reflection and reflexivity in mentoring

Effective mentoring conversations have to take into account the importance of the dynamic relationship between reflection and reflexivity, between the outer and inner thought processes of the person being mentored. By drawing out the interconnections between the mentee's artistic, creative, personal and professional development, fundamental questions regarding identity, motivation, meaning and personal creativity become the heart of a continuing reflective and reflexive dialogue (Renshaw, 2009, p.101).

Characteristics of effective mentors

Being willing to let go of ego, status and authority in order to understand the work of your mentee and to adopt a listening, supportive role.

Using empathy and interpersonal skills in order to ask appropriate questions regarding the personal development of your mentee.

Having the skills and insight to act as a sounding board for your mentee. This is central to any learning or developmental process aimed at enabling a person to clarify their sense of direction, to identify their strengths and realise their potential.

Aiming to develop a flexible range of language registers in order to frame appropriate questions, respond to different personal narratives and communicate meaningfully, understanding where your mentee is coming from.

Learning to listen actively, including respecting silence, reading body language, focusing on the substance of the conversation and, where necessary, reframing and reinforcing what has been said.

Developing the ability to be self-reflective and self-aware in order to nurture these qualities in others (e.g., questioning motivation; separating out professional from personal issues).

Being open and non-judgemental in relation to your mentee's individual and professional context.

The place of co-mentoring in collaborative work

The REFLECT Creative Partnerships National Co-mentoring Programme

Throughout this enquiry it is clear that most arts projects within the community involve collaborations between different sectors and sometimes between different disciplines. The Case Studies have demonstrated that such collaborations can act as a creative crucible for shared learning and development for all participants. Nevertheless, as discussed earlier in this section, the complexity and richness of these multi-layered projects can generate issues for the practitioners who can then benefit from mentoring support. But due to the collaborative nature of these projects, further support can also be provided through co-mentoring between practitioners from the contributory sectors – for example, between artists and partners in schools, health care, prisons, social work, youth clubs, hospices and psychiatric hospitals.

In England special attention has been given to the relationships between education and the cultural sector. The most extensive work in co-mentoring can be found in the REFLECT pilot programme led by The Sage Gateshead as mentioned earlier in this section (see Renshaw, 2008). The main aim of REFLECT was 'to provide one-to-one structured co-mentoring support for emerging leaders from schools and creative and cultural organisations and businesses to develop more innovative partnership practice and enhance creativity at the heart of their organisations'. The objectives of the programme were:

To strengthen and develop innovative and sustainable partnerships between schools and the creative and cultural sector

To build the capacity of the education sector to work effectively with the creative and cultural sector through inter-organisational learning and reflective practice

To give emerging leaders the opportunity to develop innovative partnership practice through the process of one-to-one co-mentoring

To offer opportunities for collaborative professional development for the co-mentors

To promote the effectiveness of mentoring in developing co-learning and reflective practice within and across organisations

To enhance the importance of creativity and innovation at the heart of schools, organisations and businesses
(The Sage Gateshead, 2007, p.33; also Renshaw, 2008, pp.23-24)

The purpose of the programme for the participants was clearly articulated at the beginning of the REFLECT Handbook (The Sage Gateshead, 2007). This helps to demonstrate what might be achieved in other co-mentoring programmes.

> REFLECT will enable you to engage in an equal exchange of knowledge, skills and experience aimed at sustaining innovative partnership practice and embedding creativity and creative learning at the heart of your organisation or your business. Your co-mentoring relationship will be centred around a self-identified focus based on your needs and those of your organisation. Through a series of creative conversations you will engage in a dynamic, collaborative learning process giving you space to think and reflect on your own practice. You will have the opportunity to share your learning with colleagues in your organisation and beyond and to consider what impact that might have on children and young people (p.1).

The legacy of REFLECT in the development of partnerships

The REFLECT programme not only helped to strengthen understanding about co-mentoring but it also raised crucial questions about the creation and sustainability of partnerships between organisations in different sectors. The Evaluation Report was clear about the legacy of the programme.

> The legacy of REFLECT is that it has developed an interactive model of reflective learning between practitioners who wish to extend their horizons by engaging in cross-sector collaborative dialogue. The strength of the co-mentoring process described and examined in this Report lies in the capacity of creative conversation to transform personal and professional practice. It is underpinned by a framework of principles and procedures whose main purpose is to guide but not to impose. Moreover, the cross-sector aspect of this process has been enriching because it has opened new doors, shifted perspectives and resulted in some unexpected outcomes (Renshaw, 2008, p.78).

Four themes kept recurring during REFLECT and they could well inform the planning of future projects and development programmes between other partnership organisations:

> What are the necessary conditions for ensuring an effective co-mentoring relationship?

> What are the necessary conditions for enabling cross-sector co-mentoring conversations to facilitate personal and professional learning?

> What are the necessary conditions for strengthening creative learning through cross-sector co-mentoring?

> What are the necessary conditions for using the process of cross-sector co-mentoring as a vehicle for organisational change? (ibid, p.78)

The interactive process developed by REFLECT is a creative challenge to any organisation but the outcomes of the programme demonstrate the transformational potential of cross-sector engagement. In a global world increasingly aiming to develop interdependent and interconnected ways of working, the need to create effective models of co-mentoring is becoming critical across the whole workforce. The arts and cultural sector is no exception.

5.3   Reflective learning, evaluation and assessment

Reflective learning and context-based evaluation

Reflective learning or reflective practice lies at the core of Rineke Smilde's research on Lifelong Learning (see Smilde, 2009a, p.51). In my study of mentoring (Renshaw, 2009, pp.16-30) I outlined those modes of learning that are most closely connected to reflective practice – for example, experiential learning; action learning; situated learning, context-based learning; work-based learning; problem-based learning; collaborative learning; transformative learning; learning through self-assessment; learning through reflective conversation, learning within communities of practice, reflexive learning and tacit knowledge (see Tavistock Institute, 2002). All these processes generate a strong form of engagement and understanding because the learning arises from and is connected to the context and experience of the participants.

In its discussion of context-based learning, the Tavistock Institute Report (2002) highlights the importance of situated learning, which is rooted in the notion that "the context in which learning takes place is an integral part of what is learned (p.126)". This implies that because the knowledge, understanding, insight, skills and attitudes are acquired from engaging in a particular context, in a collaborative setting, it follows that such joint ways of working generate a shared sense of belonging and knowing within that particular context. In such situations meaning is socially constructed with learning arising from active engagement in a 'community of practice' (see Lave and Wenger, 1991; and Wenger, 1998).

The theoretical perspective developed by Lave and Wenger provides strong foundations for understanding the fundamental principle of connecting to context in a practice of collaborative learning. It helps to broaden traditional notions of 'apprenticeship' from a master/student or mentor/mentee relationship to one of "changing participation and identity transformation in a community of practice (Wenger, 1998, p.11)". Instead of seeing knowledge as an object to be handed down from one generation to another through apprenticeship, collaborative practice is rooted in a history of shared learning in which there is a coherent connection between knowing and learning, and between the ways in which knowledge is acquired, shared and developed. By positioning learning and knowing in the context of active participation in social communities, arts practitioners are far more likely to deepen their understanding, engagement and commitment to what they are doing. But at all times their growing practical awareness of what it is to be socially engaged has to be underpinned by reflective conversation and critical dialogue within a shared process of collaborative learning. By exposing all practitioners to different contexts and perspectives, this enables them to make new connections, and opens them up to new challenges and a wider range of possibilities in their practice.

It is these factors that have to be taken into account in any evaluation process. Reflecting critically on the quality of engagement, on the quality of collaborative learning in a community context, is the bread and butter of informed evaluation. In his Case Study Joost Heinsius emphasises the importance of artists developing the skills of self-reflection and self-management, along with an active outgoing attitude. For Joost "learning by doing and reflecting on their practice afterwards are essential professional competences for artists when they go out and engage in the world" (6.3 D).

An example of students being encouraged to develop the skills of reflective evaluation is provided by the work of Heloisa Feichas with her music students at the Federal University of Minas Gerais in Brazil. With the guidance of Robert Wells, the principles underlying Guildhall Connect were introduced into a course called Music Education and Social Projects. The first phase of the programme culminated in an afternoon project with children from *Projeto Cariúnas,* followed by a performance of the students' compositions. Heloisa and Robert then led an evaluation process in which the students were asked to divide into three groups and create mind maps focusing on what they felt they had learnt during the whole course. The main categories that came up from the analysis included: composition, leadership, group working, group feeling, teaching and informal learning. The student evaluation was very perceptive and spelt out the following comprehensive points:

> Within the *Composition* category there were sub-categories such as creativity, originality, connection of ideas, innovation, adapting musically (acceptance of unusual/unexpected material), sense of collective, detaching from your own ideas, language adaptation, contextualisation. Improvisation was also mentioned as an important area that had been developed.

> When discussing *leadership* students pointed out the importance of learning about humility, patience, sharing, making mistakes, knowing when to be passive and active, being ready to act, developing commitment, listening to others, knowing the limits of leading and being led.

When talking about *group working* students considered all the stages of the process including warming-up, collaborative composition and performance. They learned about the importance of humility, of getting on well with each other, having a good atmosphere, compromising, having responsibility towards the group, coping with adversity, trusting and respecting each other, being comprehensive, tolerant and sensitive to the group, having the ability to listen, knowing the limits of ones action, having positive attitudes and a sense of unity, putting yourself in somebody else's place, having a sense of commitment, developing a sense of the group (group feeling), and having an understanding of musical and technical issues. Students also mentioned the pleasure and satisfaction of working in a group.

Other issues mentioned as important in their learning included concentration, teaching strategies, an awareness of their learning processes, body consciousness and music. They also pointed out some characteristics from informal learning practices such as playing by ear, improvisation, sense of liberty and spontaneity (6.3 B).

Engaging in this kind of reflective analysis was a very new experience for these students. It focused largely on the development of new roles and responsibilities, on the acquisition of creative skills and on the quality of interaction within the group. But as one of the main aims of the project is 'to train undergraduate music students as creative music facilitators able to work in a diverse range of social contexts' it is intended that in future projects with the Social Project *Cariúnas*, for example, there would be more emphasis on evaluating the quality of engagement with the community – that is, it would be more context-based. This aim is made explicit at the end of Heloisa Feichas and Robert Wells' Case Study:

During the second semester programme it is hoped that students will engage in longer placements increasing their skills and creating further links between the young people in the projects and the University. There are also increasing opportunities for leaders from social projects to meet and share their practices due to this work, creating a more interconnected community of music leaders across Belo Horzonte (6.3 B).

This statement of intent demonstrates that for context-based evaluation to be effective, it has to arise from and feed back into an interconnected community of practice. In this particular case the reflective analysis would necessarily involve students, tutors, professional musicians, teachers, young people and community leaders. Fostering this kind of reflective learning within such a diverse group of experience and interests requires skilful and sensitive facilitation from the project leader: for example, making contextual connections that resonate within the group; asking questions that foster the development of a critical perspective about the quality of practice; exploring key issues arising from the project; drawing all participants into a conversation that analyses the quality of the collaborative learning process; broadening perspectives and deepening understanding of reflective practice. Such honest reflection that acknowledges the validity of different points of view, different perceptions and responses lies at the heart of context-based evaluation. It is critical to the quality of community engagement and would aim to explore the many quality issues raised in Chapter 4.

Reflective learning and assessment

For the last decade or more arts practitioners, along with people working in such sectors as education, health, welfare and criminal justice, have increasingly been subjected to the demands of public accountability through benchmarks, targets and performance indicators embedded in Quality Assurance. These mechanistic approaches to controlling and managing knowledge may have succeeded in erecting a model for assuring Quality systems are in operation, but at worst, they effectively fail to *ensure* that quality outcomes are evident in arts practice. It is partly with this in view that this enquiry has focused on examining what might count as 'quality' in many different community contexts.

Time and time again the case studies and testimonies have emphasised the central role of critical reflection in initiatives designed to assess the quality of projects, processes and end-products. Different forms of reflective learning are seen as the bedrock of all aspects of development – personal, artistic, creative, professional – and it is incumbent on arts practitioners to begin devising forms of assessment that have a coherence and connection with a reflective approach to arts practice.

The 'measurement' of any development process arising from reflective learning presents a challenge, because it does not constitute a mechanistic target- or outcome-driven activity. Quantitative data about project, process and product can readily be collected, collated and analysed but the significant outcomes are qualitative in kind. Therefore serious questions have to be addressed in the search for identifying ways of 'assessing' rather than 'measuring' quality. For example:

What is the evidence of gain from a reflective learning process?

What is the nature of the evidence?

How do we assess the gain?

How do we generate testimony of gain that goes beyond what is measurable?

A final quotation from Music for Life illustrates the need to retain a delicate balance between measurement and assessment. Linda Rose points out that:

> Quantifying changes and outcomes is not easy. This level of engagement aims to encourage less isolation, a sense of being part of something, of being recognised and respected. Staff often report significant changes in behaviour. A lady who

would spend all day every day in bed now gets up and comes out of her room each day to join others. A man who would bark out single words and walk out of the company of others, even frightening staff, now speaks in sentences and allows staff to touch him so he is able to receive hand massage and be led into the garden. Changes may reveal themselves slowly, sometimes noticed after the project has left. They are small and sometimes seen only in the absence of certain patterns, may be a person has less need to search or wander around constantly, for example. There may simply be moments of connection in a workshop, which for that individual is a momentous event.

The project is about endeavour, intention and process. Music for Life is a tool for learning, a place to experience immediacy, to be respected and to give respect. The outcomes of the project are reciprocal; the beneficiaries are not only the person with dementia but the staff and the musicians too. Their personal and professional lives are affected by their relationships with each other, by the challenges they face through those relationships and by the skills they learn together. The interplay between the three promotes change, affects the communities they live and work in and enhances the lives of them all (6.3 K).

The learning outcomes of the staff, musicians and the residents instanced by Linda, together with the subtle yet significant changes in behaviour of the people with dementia, provide clear examples of what might count as evidence that can be assessed. The notion of measurement in such contexts seems highly inappropriate. On the other hand, different forms of assessment can be used where the evidence of gain arises from evidence-based reflective learning that will help to inform future practice.

The place of reflective logs, diaries, journals and testimonies in assessment

As organisations become more receptive and open towards facilitating a culture of reflective practice, they are beginning to introduce assessment procedures that use different approaches to observing, recording, analysing and reflecting on the quality of projects, processes and end-products. Special consideration is increasingly being given to the use of reflective logs, diaries and journals as a way of documenting, reflecting, extending learning, deepening awareness and making connections. A reflective account can then be used as the basis of a personal testimony that can form an integral part of the evidence of a person's reflective learning (as can be seen from the testimonies in this enquiry).

This evidence can be assessed in different ways – through self-assessment, peer assessment and group-based assessment (see Smilde, 2009a, p.89), but it is difficult to see how it can be 'measured' with a grade. For example, how far can fundamental aspects of personal, emotional and artistic development be seen as outcomes that can be measured? How far can the 'tacit', implicit elements of artistic and creative development be given a mark? (i.e., such qualities as inner awareness, inner stillness and the creative spirit are 'caught' in the moment through the act of doing and are likely to remain unspoken.)

One example will be given to illustrate how reflective learning can be fostered through a mentoring process leading to 'self-assessment'. This took place between a mentor and the tutor responsible for instrumental teacher training in a European conservatoire from September 2008 to June 2009. The approach taken included:

- Face-to-face mentoring conversations that were recorded (each session about 3 hours in length)
- Follow-up telephone conversations
- Reflections on progress via email correspondence
- The tutor kept a reflective diary comprising:
  - an outline of particular personal and professional issues
  - a personal impression of factors arising from the issues
  - the challenge of how to respond to the issues in the future
- The mentor responded to the reflections in the diary by asking further questions both in writing and verbally
- The tutor wrote a Mentoring Review comprising:
  - starting situation
  - contact and working method
  - key challenges arising from the mentoring process:
    personal development
    professional development (leadership; teaching and learning; research)
  - outcomes of the mentoring process
    personal development
    professional development (leadership; teaching and learning; research)
  - new goals for the future (personal and professional)
- The Mentoring Review was fully discussed in a mentoring session followed by a written response from the mentor. Both documents were passed to the appropriate authorities in the tutor's institution – that is, they were placed in the public domain serving as evidence of reflective learning through the mentoring process.
- The reflective process embedded in both the diary and the Mentoring Review can be seen as a personal testimony, a reflective narrative that acted as a form of 'self-assessment'. This was not graded but the outcomes served as sufficient evidence of quality reflective learning.

A framework for self-assessment

In addition to reflective logs, diaries and journals, practitioners can be encouraged to keep self-assessment profiles that reflect the purpose and processes of their particular course, programme or project. These profiles can contribute to strong forms of reflective learning that are not graded, but which enhance the quality of individual and collaborative practice and directly inform subsequent action – for example, course development, shifting priorities within a programme, devising new processes and deepening understanding of future projects.

As an example I intend to describe the main features of a self-assessment profile that was designed in 1988-89 for full-time postgraduate students studying Performance and Communication Skills (PCS) at the Guildhall School of Music & Drama. Initially this was developed with the assistance of the Centre for Applied Research in Education (CARE) at the University of East Anglia, and it was further modified when the course changed into the Guildhall Ensemble and later into a modular Continuing Professional Development programme. (Details of the self-assessment profile can be found in Renshaw, 2005b, pp.22-23; Renshaw, 2007, pp.41-42; and Smilde, 2009a, pp.89-90).

One of the basic premises underlying the approach to assessment taken by the PCS course was that any professional practitioner is constantly making judgements in action – judgements that can benefit from greater clarification, monitoring, evaluation and critical reflection. One of the main aims in evolving a system of self-assessment was to establish a procedure that supported and invited students to develop a more reflective approach to all their activities. Central to this process was the belief that assessment is concerned with improving the quality of learning for both students and tutors, rather than working towards achieving a final grade. With self-reflection at the heart of the course, it was decided that the assessment process should be continuous and collaborative, including elements of recording, evaluation, peer assessment and negotiation with tutors. Self-assessment, then, became an integral part of the curriculum thus reflecting the aims of the course. There were sound logical, psychological and educational reasons for pursuing a system of student self-assessment.

The core elements of a self-assessment profile

The following categories could act as a basic frame of reference for a self-assessment profile focusing on the learning and development of practitioners engaged in creative, collaborative projects in a community setting. The priority placed on different elements within each category would vary depending on the aim and context of the project or programme. For example:

  quality of project, process and end-product

  quality of leadership skills

| quality of communication skills

| quality of interpersonal skills

| quality of management skills

| quality of creative skills

| quality of performing skills

| quality of evaluation skills

| quality of reflective learning

| quality of personal development

As discussed earlier in this section, an extensive self-assessment profile, further informed by logs, diaries, journals and testimonies, can only strengthen the quality of reflective learning for all participants – students, tutors, mentors, professional practitioners, co-workers, project leaders and managers, for example. Such a comprehensive combined assessment portfolio constitutes the backbone of reflective practice.

5.4 Shifting the culture of organisations

Towards a culture of reflective practice

The main focus of this chapter has been to identify those modes of learning, evaluation and assessment most likely to strengthen the quality of community engagement – always connecting to different contexts, sectors, cultures, organisations and partnerships. But the quality of this engagement is also dependent on creating a climate committed to fostering reflective learning – that is, building up a culture of reflective practice within partnership organisations. As was stated at the beginning of the chapter, a successful learning and development programme has to be rooted in an organisational culture that subscribes to similar values and ways of seeing the world. An important rider was added: "(...)this might well entail the organisation making a fundamental shift in perspective resulting in a re-ordering of its priorities" – for example, making new maps and frameworks that respond to the needs of the changing cultural landscape; to create new ideas, forms of innovation and entrepreneurship that resonate with artistic, social, educational and technological change.

Making such a significant paradigm shift can be threatening to any organisation because at one level it is touching the values, meaning, history and philosophy of that organisation. The following observation regarding Google could be seen as relevant to any sector or business:

> We believe that Google and other Clever Collectives face a number of distinct organisational challenges. The first is that the very source of organisational strength – their mission – can become a cultural straitjacket. Over time, organisations need space to adapt to their changing circumstances. The worry for an organisation like Google is that the beliefs of the founding fathers can easily become a cult. Over time, what started out as a simple philosophy can become a rigid doctrine or ideology that is resistant to new ideas and ways of looking at the world. This can lead to cultural and organisational sclerosis. In the end, insiders may become hostile to anyone from outside who challenges the beliefs of the cult. What began as intellectual curiosity and good intentions can easily become dogma (Goffee & Jones, 2009, p.143).

Although the most enlightened arts organisations have become more critically aware and alert to their widening artistic, social and cultural responsibilities, there remains a significant rump of intransigence – exhibiting 'cultural and organisational sclerosis' – that is stubbornly resistant to change. This is especially the case within the world of conservatoires and Higher Arts Education, despite the extensive initiatives of the Association of European Conservatoires (AEC), the European League of Institutes of the Arts (ELIA) and other international organisations.

In conservatoires, for example, innovation and development rooted in community engagement finds itself positioned in the margins, whilst to a large extent so-called 'core business' continues to remain aloof from changes in the outside world. The seriousness of this situation was flagged up clearly by Rineke Smilde in her PhD dissertation:

> A dynamic synergy between the conservatoire and the outside world is clearly needed. Often conservatoires still act in an isolated way, but could instead be part of a wider network of professional training and development, challenged to build up a more informed perspective which impinges upon developments in the profession, including cross-arts, music technology and the cross-cultural and cross-sectoral world.
>
> (...) The conservatoire needs to constantly fine tune and adjust itself to the needs of the profession, and vice versa. This requires a reorientation by the conservatoire, where a shift in culture has to be accompanied by a reappraisal of what actually counts in today's world. Portfolio careers are the result of the big changes in the music profession and should not remain on the periphery of the conservatoire, but instead become part of core business (Smilde, 2009a, pp.251-252).

As early as 1993 in a Gresham Lecture I voiced my concern about conservatoires remaining entrenched within the norms and values of a performance tradition that is hermetically sealed from the changes taking place in the outside world. I felt and still feel that many staff and students suffer from a tunnel vision that cuts them off from the creativity, flexibility and breadth of outlook that are necessary for music to be a vibrant force in society (see Renshaw, 1993, p.13). Responsiveness to change and innovation, underpinned by critical reflection and practice-based research, has to lie at the heart of cultural renewal. But as indicated in the Gresham Lecture:

> (...) In conservatoires there is no such resonance because, historically, critical reflection has never played a significant part in their organisational culture. If many staff fail to question the validity of what they are doing and why they are doing it, it is little wonder that students remain culturally and psychologically adrift, often lacking any sense of connectedness, social responsibility or wider contextual perspective (ibid, p.13).

Although in 2010 the context is very different from that of the early 1990s, response to change (or rather lack of response) continues to pose a challenge for many conservatoires. Perhaps the following observation continues to have some relevance today:

> Change can be bedevilled by the constraints of organisational structures, traditional allegiances and individual attitudes which are closed and ideologically ossified. Continuity with the past has its place in any institution, but when it results in ostrich-like behaviour, some discontinuity is necessary to galvanise it into action (ibid, p.15).

Many conservatoires will now claim that they offer students a diversified portfolio of possibilities underpinned by opportunities for critical reflection. In the Preface to a volume of papers prepared by teachers from the Guildhall School of Music & Drama – *The Reflective Conservatoire* – its Principal, Barry Ife, states that "since the early 1980s, the Guildhall School has been leading moves to develop the classic conservatoire model to meet the rapidly changing needs of the performing arts industries (see Odam & Bannan [eds], 2005, p.5)". The emphasis throughout the volume is on the Guildhall School seeing itself as a crucible for critical reflection and this thrust has led to the creation of the two bi-annual international conferences on the Reflective Conservatoire.

The fundamental question is how far is this spirit of reflection embedded in the whole of the Guildhall School or in any other conservatoire, for that matter? Also how far does it underpin the quality of its engagement within the wider community? It is questionable whether the many initiatives that have taken root within the community, the partnerships that have been developed and sustained over time have had much impact on the core business of the School.

But the future is now looking decidedly more positive with the creation of the Guildhall School and Barbican Centre campus, working in close conjunction with the London Symphony Orchestra. What is most exciting is that learning and engagement, learning and participation, linked to artistic development and changes in performance practice, are now firmly on the agenda. With this shift in culture, with new directions, new maps and new partnerships, old assumptions are now being questioned as staff and students begin to move forwards into a creative future in which community engagement is a key pillar.

Some aspects of this shared creative future reflect the shift in priorities articulated in the vision statement – *A Continuing Journey* – prepared for the Guildhall School in 2001. It was suggested that existing priorities should be reappraised and realigned in relation to artistic and educational developments that are responsive to different contexts. For example:

- encouraging innovatory approaches to performance which open up access to artistic experiences and engage audiences from broad, diverse backgrounds

- developing new work, new art forms and artistic languages which resonate with different audiences

- exploring the value and contribution of the vernacular within contemporary culture

- using participatory processes to foster the development of creativity in different contexts

- creating new performance environments and spaces which attract new audiences

- extending artistic practice through exploring the interconnections between new technologies and different art forms

- developing the School as a flexible resource for the professional arts community, the education community and the wider community (Renshaw, 2001, pp.5-6)

Cultural change and connecting conversations

The recent developments at the Guildhall School provide just one example of how the culture of an organisation can gradually become more responsive to change and begin to extend its horizons and make new connections. But a cultural shift of this kind presents a challenge to any organisation. It raises several key questions that need to be addressed. For instance: what are the most effective ways of enabling an organisation to adapt to change? How can an institution and its partners be helped to understand and manage change and uncertainty within a shared vision for the future? What conditions need to be created that will enable new structures, new practices and new styles of management to evolve organically within newly aligned priorities? What form of leadership might best bring about this transformation?

As was mentioned towards the beginning of Chapter 3, at the heart of this complex process lies the central role of 'conversation'. It is partly through sustained critically reflective dialogue that cultural change evolves in an organisation. Through respecting and listening to different points of view, people should gradually let go of cherished assumptions and begin to see themselves and their world differently. They might begin to tell a different story. For this process to work there has to be a sensitive awareness of the different levels of language used by groups when describing their experience and shaping their stories. Discussions also have to be grounded in where people perceive themselves coming from. The psychological climate in which these conversations take place is absolutely crucial to any likely shift in future action.

The key to ensuring that honest conversation takes place throughout any organisation is in adopting a style of leadership that is genuinely open and facilitatory. This involves drawing on the skills and attitudes at the core of a mentoring process (see section 5.2) – the ability to make connections, to let go, to ask appropriate questions, to engage in active listening and to use empathy. Through the process of collaborative reflective dialogue an organisation can be challenged to reappraise its distribution of knowledge and control – to consider the shift from mechanistic management structures to greater opportunities for shared leadership and responsibility. Effectively, processes and procedures become more accountable and transparent, and all staff and students have a voice in shaping their own future. This can only be healthy for the life and work of any organisation (see Renshaw, 2005a, pp.114-115).

Final reflection

Enabling all arts practitioners 'to have a voice in shaping their own future' matters, but each voice has to engage with the world as it is, not as it was. All arts organisations have a responsibility to ensure that they are not locked in a bubble that is culturally and educationally adrift. Community engagement can no longer be seen as an 'optional extra'. It needs to be brought in from the margins and allowed to establish its place as a key player in all future developments. Many professional arts organisations not only see the point of this cultural imperative, but they are also acting on it with imagination and a keen sense of connection. One significant area that needs to reconsider and re-order its priorities lies in the training sector of Higher Arts Education – unfortunately many staff and students continue to remain impervious to changing circumstances in the workplace.

In recent years many commentators have observed how the arts are seen to matter more and more in our present turbulent world. It therefore behoves all people working in the arts to ensure that their engagement resonates with the diversity of needs found in the many different arenas in which they work. As has been argued throughout this book, engagement must always have integrity and quality at its heart. A commitment to people and to art goes hand in hand. This is the basic dual passion that drives all the practitioners in this enquiry.

A similar philosophy was articulated recently by Jude Kelly, Artistic Director of the Southbank Centre. "My ethical beliefs underpin everything I do. What I believe, wholeheartedly, is that we still live in an unequal society, and that art is a fundamental right of every human being. That is, and has always been, my guiding principle (Kelly, 2010, p.2).

This principle of entitlement is fundamental to how the arts should be conceived, funded, managed, delivered and evaluated. It should also serve as a guiding principle underlying the quality of community engagement. In practice, entitlement only has teeth if there is a collective commitment to connecting to context, community, collaboration and creativity through conversation. To achieve this remains a major challenge for both individuals and institutions, but it has an urgency that cannot be put on hold. The voices heard throughout this book illustrate what can be achieved when vision, values and motivation connect to creative engagement with the wider community. Perhaps their example will serve as a catalyst for other practitioners wishing to extend and deepen their own community engagement.

6

Appendices

6.1   Structure of the enquiry process

The backbone of the enquiry comprises 16 interviews, 14 personal testimonies and 14 case studies from experienced arts practitioners, managers, project co-ordinators, teachers and evaluators involved in cross-arts and cross-sector work within community contexts.

Interviews

The enquiry commenced with 16 in-depth interviews (15 face-to-face and 1 e-mail): 7 from The Netherlands; 8 from UK; 1 from Germany

Interview questions

What criteria do you use when assessing 'quality' in different cross-arts and cross-sector contexts, focusing especially on three interconnected areas:

- quality of the project
- quality of the process – for participants and creative/artistic leaders
- quality of the end-product (e.g., performance, event, exhibition, recording, website, visual log) – for participants and creative/artistic leaders?

What factors do you consider essential for creating effective partnerships in any collaborative community project?

How far do you consider the principles of 'appropriateness of aim' and 'connecting to context' as fundamental to determining quality?

What are the significant contextual variables you take into account when assessing the quality of community engagement in your collaborative work?

In what ways does your view of 'quality' impact on the following areas:

- the learning and development of arts practitioners engaged in collaborative projects
- assessment processes within a culture of reflective practice
- the culture of your organisation and that of your partners?

Personal testimonies

14 testimonies describing the personal responses of interviewees to the challenge of facilitating quality in their work – raising questions connected to personal motivation, commitment, values, attitudes, vision and quality of

engagement: 5 from The Netherlands; 7 from UK; 1 from Brazil; 1 from Sweden (2 testimonies incorporated into their case studies)

Case studies

14 case studies providing a narrative to illustrate the context and work of the interviewees: 6 from The Netherlands; 4 from UK; 2 from Brazil; 1 from Sweden; 1 from Austria

6.2 Personal testimonies

6.2 A Clare Chacksfield

Director, Eastfeast, East Anglia

Eastfeast is a multidisciplinary project drawing on the arts, horticulture, permaculture and education, bringing together artists, teachers, school governors, parents, children and gardeners in order to create a feast as a celebration in different communities in East Anglia.

I have never been a very good specialist. It seems to be a recurring theme for me. Maybe it's some kind of short attention span, which means I end up hopping between different disciplines, or is it that I am just interested in the places where the edges of artforms blur? Or maybe this creative purpose is itself a specialism? Either way, it's why I ended up doing theatre design as a student – a chance to try everything out and see what happens when musicians, actors, technicians, makers, writers and dancers come together for a common purpose.

I can remember my first experience of a captivated audience of young faces, cheering in unison as they watched my first devised piece of theatre in education unfold before our eyes. 100 children all whooping to generate enough noise that would coax out the character of the 'strawberry plant' from its hiding place, where an actor wearing a strawberry laden wig waited inside the 5ft box I had made for her, accompanied by 'Jack' our handmade life-sized puppet.

We had made the performance using ideas generated through workshops with the children, alongside the skills of an experienced writer and a multi-disciplinary team of fantastic people. I can still remember how hard we worked coupled with the feeling of satisfaction I have, knowing how I had collaborated with a new team of people to make something that those children had never seen before.

The inclusive way of drawing out ideas from the children that I experimented with on this first theatre project have become more and more important to me as my career has evolved. I needed to engage a new group of young children in that first show back in Nottingham. Including their contributions was pivotal to its success and their resulting ownership of the experience. These principles still remain fundamental to my work up to the present day. The project sparked an interest in the magic that can come from collaboration and fair exchange, all part of the process of working together for a common purpose. Whether enticing groups of disengaged boys in the valleys of Pontypridd to sew puppets made from tights or getting a group of parents who hated school to come and teach the teachers in a garden project, there is something about the challenge of getting people engaged in something 'new' and purposeful that fuels my enthusiasm.

To put on 'the show' bringing whatever talents you can to the team and working together to achieve something bigger – there is something about this idea that still gives me a buzz. It was this kind of buzz which attracted me to Eastfeast - the idea of lots of people getting together to celebrate and eat what they have grown whilst working with people from different worlds and different walks of life along the way.

This buzz, an interest in inclusion and facilitating children's imaginations led me to become a teacher and facilitator myself and has been a reoccurring thread in my career over the past 15 years. My practice is fuelled by a desire to learn something new, often as part of a collective or shared experience. It is important to me to have opportunities to immerse myself in something that challenges me creatively and constructively. Each school and community we work with brings with it different challenges. Often we as practitioners enter the staff room amidst a sea of expectations, judgements and protocols. Being the outsider at first gives us a privileged fresh perspective. As a team we are all profoundly aware that the first task we have to focus on is about earning trust from the community we aspire to work with. Quality for me therefore is about the quality of relationships and learning in the work that I do. The quality will be different for all the different people we work with, but having high expectations and ambitions for what we can achieve together is absolutely fundamental to making our projects work in practice. Time to build this trust is an essential ingredient in making the process of engagement work.

I am invariably inspired by the change demonstrated in the physical growth process you can see in the planting, growth and production of homegrown food and handmade artefacts. Seeing a bare patch of ground become a pathway of sunflowers and fruit canes before your eyes in a series of months has a touch of magic to it. The fact it isn't instant is good for an impatient person like me. It reminds us the pace of life has a course to run and has a cycle to it that is bigger than ourselves. There is something profoundly satisfying about working with a group of children who are fully absorbed in the process of digging in muddy earth - its simplicity and the fun it generates makes it memorable for them. Visualising the journey from the unknown seed of an idea to something you can see, touch and smell does something which fuels transformation in the individuals we work with and in ourselves. It is deeply nurturing on a level, which as in many artforms and disciplines is difficult to put into words. The metaphor of growing articulates part of a learning journey, which embodies the heart of the Eastfeast process that excites me. The framework of combining the arts with horticulture proves to be endlessly diverse according to the community who are inspired by the concept of a shared Feast.

Working with Eastfeast has enabled me to start learning about the principles of permaculture, caring for the earth we live on, the people we work with and sharing the resources we have available. There is something that continues to captivate me about this work as it embraces all the things that feed me – metaphorically, spiritually and literally. The importance of sustainability as part of our way of life goes beyond the parameters of the day job and is a part of our mission, to enable young people to have authentic contact with the real and tangible outside world so they can protect it for future generations to enjoy. The layers to our work go beyond the notion of being about 'growing vegetables' or 'working an allotment'. They permeate the challenge of creating meaningful connections for people through experience with different art forms. We see horticulture as a creative discipline in itself here which is what makes an interesting interdisciplinary focus to the work.

I am captivated by the transformational potential that a nexus of relationships between the arts, horticulture and education seems to have. Back to that buzz from collaborating again, which at times can also be hard work and difficult to establish in practice. My daily work reminds me of the meaningful and therefore potentially therapeutic effect on people's wellbeing that this alchemy of artforms can create. As a team we take a subversive interest in being an organisation that is a catalyst for change, and part of the changes we see come about as a result of the combination of disciplines. Working in a society and education system where there are less and less opportunities for children to be 'free range' in their learning adventures it feels of paramount importance to us to create opportunities where children can work beyond their normal boundaries. Defining a focus for all these different relationships is about making a quality experience for those who are involved in this creative process.

I see the work we do as helping people to realise their potential in new and unexpected way. When people join us on Eastfeast projects there is a way to interweave their talent or particular specialism which in turn helps the project respond and grow in a new direction.

It is important to me that the art process can create a window upon reflection that can often be missing from the day-to-day grind of everyday life. Something about making art or artistry alone or with others seems to fuel our ability to question ourselves and the things that happen around us. If we can ask ourselves questions then we can learn and grow, get to understand ourselves better, be more self-aware. Seeking of this kind fuels my continual interest in professional development, training and education projects. Professional development is integral to all our work and is vital in recharging both our own batteries and those of the people with whom we work. A profound interest in this kind of learning underpins my work for Eastfeast. I believe I learn more from areas that are outside my own parameter of study or background, which provides a source of new perspectives and ideas to sustain my interest.

As a leader and Director of Eastfeast, a new and evolving charity, my constant challenging and changing role offers many opportunities for development and diversity which is both motivating and at times exhausting. Most importantly though, I am supported by a highly motivated, passionate and trustworthy team who bring me great joy and friendship. Eastfeast is important to me because of this team; the shared common purpose we have evolved together and the values to which we are committed. As a team, its significant that we are all part-time working mothers with a mission in mind! It is a privilege to operate with such a high level of trust and openness. I thrive on this high quality of trust. It enables us as a team to influence and shape artwork that feeds our own passions about the world in which we live.

6.2 B   Heloisa Feichas

Professor Adjunto, School of Music, Federal University of Minas Gerais, Brazil

The aim of Heloisa Feichas is to transform the way music is perceived and learnt in the School of Music in the Federal University of Minas Gerais. She is in the process of strengthening links between the university and its wider community which suffers from major social problems, inequality, poverty and poor quality education.

I am a musician and a music teacher. From an early age I knew that I would be a music teacher and that Music would always be part of my life. I was born into a very musical family. My father is a great musician with lots of musical skills as well as my grandfather and my great-grandmother. Therefore I grew up surrounded by music – recorded music – and lots of jam sessions with my family and family friends – all great musicians. Since I was very little I used to pick up instruments and play by ear. When I was nearly 4 years old I started having piano lessons and never stopped making music. I can say that my learning process was based on two modes: informal because of my family and formal with a traditional piano teacher who taught me music notation. Therefore I developed skills from both sides, which I recognised later was extremely helpful for my career but was also quite rare.

I am grateful to both my family and my old teachers for giving me a great opportunity to open doors to so many ways of making music. Also I always had an enormous passion for music making.

I started teaching music, both piano and music in groups, when I was 16. I was also very inspired by a vocal group I was in during my adolescent years. This totally transformed my view about music, life, collective, collaborative and creative work. I was one of the leaders of the choral group and from a young age developed a sense of responsibility and seriousness in the work. This was one of the most special experiences in my life. 'Quality' was always present in the work. The 'quality' had to do with happiness in being together (we all were good friends), along with a high level of motivation in making music. This led us to strive for excellence in terms of developing our musicality and trying to reach a 'perfect' result in our performances. We used to rehearse a lot until we could perform the music without making mistakes and feel comfortable on stage. So 'quality' was also connected with lots of practice! We almost became a professional group as we were seen as having great potential and success in Brazil. Our work lasted 7 years (starting when I was 14 until I turned 21 years old).

After that experience I went to university to do a Bachelor in Music – Piano course. However I nearly left because I never found the same 'quality' I used to have in all my earlier years of singing, playing, organizing and leading my choir. I felt no motivation in the Music School and experienced lots of blockages to making music. The conservatoire system failed in encouraging and developing my music career. I was about to leave the Music School when I met some friends in the same situation as mine and we decided to start a group in order to practice our creative skills since they had been killed by the conservatoire system. Therefore we started a quartet with a quite unusual instrumentation: piano, cello, flute and guitar. This was not a conventional quartet at Music School, and obviously there was nothing written for that combination. The aim was not to play written music but rather to create our own arrangements of the music we loved and to try out new musical ideas. This was the anchor that held me at school and strengthened me to finish my degree in music. Fortunately, at that point I had a very open-minded piano teacher, who agreed with my decision and allowed me to play the repertoire of my quartet together with the piano programme established by the Music School. This was a second important musical experience that has continued to influence the way I make music. Again, as well as with my old choir, the 'quality' in the work of my Quartet had to do with the motivation, happiness, the level of creativity involved, the freedom to choose music we loved, and the joy of making music together with friends. We learned at a high level how to work collaboratively, and how to explore and develop our skills. We used to pick up music by ear, copy artists we loved, and then transform the music in our own way, creating new possibilities and new arrangements. It was a great learning process. This was done in a mode of total cooperation.

Both experiences – the choir and the Quartet – were a turning point in my life and even now continue to underpin the way I teach music. Since I started teaching at university I have been trying to pay attention to the students' needs, listening to their voices, allowing them to create their own space and to discover who they are and what they want to do in their musical lives. I try to give them autonomy to choose, to think about their own process in a way that raises their consciousness about themselves, both musically and as human beings as part of society. I am only a facilitator. Having had the experiences I mentioned earlier was crucial for developing my pedagogical view which has subsequently been enhanced by studies in the field of music education. The PhD studies with Lucy Green in London were the theoretical turning point in which I developed other types of intellectual skills through lots of reading and writing. It was a big challenge for the totally practical musician and intuitive teacher I used to be. After the PhD I realised with much greater clarity all the musical processes I had gained in my life and I now have much more confidence in carrying out my pedagogy of integration for all the students who come to my class. My thesis is related to my own musical history since it showed possible ways of integrating students from totally different backgrounds when studying together in a traditional music school.

Now I have reached a point in which I want to establish links between the university and the community in a clearer and more effective way. I live in a country – Brazil – with lots of social problems due to a complex historical background. The differences between the social classes are huge. There are a large number of poor people living in bad conditions experiencing very low quality education. Finding a way of inspiring students (from the Music School) to be active in the world has been my target: working with a pedagogy that allows the students to discover about themselves; helping them to unlock different doors according to their needs and their consciousness; also provoking them to look at the world outside the Music School and to understand its needs and what we as artists can do to transform it. With this aim in mind I have started a partnership with Robert Wells from the Guildhall School of Music & Drama in order to introduce Connect principles to 20 undergraduate students, organising possibilities for them to go into the field to engage in social projects and work with poor kids from favelas.

To sum up:
All this work is important for me because I want to make a difference to the world in which I live. The motivation for me to be involved in all my educational projects is to influence people (students) to be critical and conscious in the world. I believe we can change things through passion,

through commitment and developing our knowledge and skills. This means engaging in a constant process of learning and searching, always using our sense of curiosity and creativity. It is fascinating to think about expanding a community of musicians that are also learners, thinkers and creative artists.

'Quality' is achieved through a combination of motivation, passion, pleasure and joy in what you do, together with commitment, constant expansion of knowledge and skills (towards mastering certain types of knowledge and skills), coherence and consistency and the capacity for self-assessment. 'Quality' in working in groups demands the capacity to hear all the voices of the members of the group, allowing them to develop their own capacities through questioning about their needs. 'Quality' would be determined by ongoing forms of assessment that involve constant questioning, in which awareness of who you are and what you do is continuously challenged in order to strengthen and enhance quality. The artistic and social criteria for judging the effectiveness of my musical work has to do with the level of happiness, motivation, joy and pleasure in doing it, which will consequently affect other peoples' feelings – also in the pleasure of attaining new knowledge and expanding it.

6.2 C Sean Gregory

Director of Creative Learning, Barbican Centre and Guildhall School of Music & Drama

Sean Gregory has been at the centre of all initiatives at the Guildhall School of Music & Drama designed to develop different forms of arts practice that engage with the wider community. With his special interest in cross-arts, cross-cultural and cross-sector work, his experience includes a teaching and managing role in the Department of Performance and Communication Skills, directing Connect, Head of Centre for Creative and Professional Practice and now Director of Creative Learning in the new Barbican-Guildhall campus.

> When driving along the motorway once with a colleague, on the way to a teacher-training workshop we were due to lead, a discussion started between us about signs and adverts on the sides of lorries. It was one of those jokey, spontaneous dialogues one often has when passing time on a long journey. Then, out of the blue, this colleague turned to me and said quite seriously: "I know what the slogan would be on the side of your lorry Sean – the letters Y-E-S – we could then have hundreds of lorries driving around the country that just say a Sean YES." It took me by surprise at that time, though thinking about it now I realise there is probably much in this that is true; what has always motivated and inspired me is being able to offer people - as well as to receive from them - a sense of permission, as individuals and collectively.

I was born in 1966 - a time I am certain when people felt they could make a difference. Whilst I am too young to remember the decade itself, I do feel I have been fortunate enough to benefit from its legacy, particularly in relation to the people I have worked with for over the past twenty years or so. Many of those people were student-graduates during the sixties, and were part of an international movement of young people from all walks of life who, for better or for worse, made sure that seemingly unchallengeable assumptions about life, politics, culture, gender, race etc. could no longer hold ground with the post World War II generation. The spirit, passion and vision that these people carry from that decade still resonates strongly today; what comes across so clearly from this particular generation is the sense of 'can do'; a belief that things can change for the better, for everyone rather than just the chosen few.

My formative years were spent in the south west suburbs of London: suburbia (for me) in the worse sense of the word – it wasn't even 'leafy' suburbia, just a sprawl of residential streets, interspersed with the odd, uninspiring shopping parades that represented a no-man's land between the better known urban and rural features of England. However, due to the people around me, I was fortunate enough to grow up in an essentially creative, enabling environment that helped me to commence the journey I am currently on.

The primary school I attended laid the perfect foundation for me. Looking back I think it was an example of 1960s/70s philosophy and values at its best; nurturing and intelligently child-centred, with a firm but fair line in discipline. Creativity, learning and working in groups was at the heart of all we did. I needed little encouragement in getting my own projects going, even at the age of 9 or 10, most of which involved drama and music-making. I was already taking and enjoying classical piano lessons out of school, and took particular pleasure in forming 'bands' with friends in order to play pop songs of the day. The funny thing is that these 'bands' consisted mainly of friends playing home-made percussion instruments (music enthusiasts who were not having music lessons), my brother on clarinet and myself on piano. We even composed our own pieces, which I suppose could represent my first experience of informal music-making.

Central to all my primary school experience, however, was a drama club set up by a young and dynamic teacher called Lorraine Bell. These after school workshops, full of improvisation, discussion, creative group exercises and ambitious school play productions had a huge impact on me. This is where I began to 'find my voice' as a young person; whilst it was too early to know what direction it was going to take me in, I already felt my identity emerging by contributing to processes that made things happen through creativity in the arts, particularly drama, writing and, to a lesser extent at that time, music. As I write this now I have suddenly remembered a poster stuck on my bedroom wall (bought by Mum) for many years saying 'Ideas don't work unless we do'. This has, I think, remained a subconscious mantra for me ever since; ideas, values and beliefs only have meaning and impact when realised through concerted individual and collective effort.

My parents offered an ideal balance for my development, my mother on the nurturing, creative side and my father on the pragmatic 'no nonsense' side. I was never a high academic achiever; I generally plodded through my work and sat around the 'pass-merit' area. More often than not I shone when able to work 'outside the box', to start something from nothing and produce a result that could surprise and even make a difference. The opportunity to do this was critical for me – an opportunity to explore, take risks and to synthesise different experiences. My father meanwhile ensured I passed my 11+ by tirelessly coaching me through verbal reasoning tests, which consequently got me to a grammar school and a totally different type of educational experience.

I struggled greatly during my first year at Kingston Grammar School. The culture shock after primary school was immense; I was now in an all boys establishment still firmly set in the 1950s, where teaching was didactic and the focus was on passing exams and excelling in sport, with music and drama barely to be seen in the curriculum. In fact music for my first two years consisted of hymn singing only, taught by a man who had been there for thirty years and was also the RE teacher. I quickly learnt to play 'the game' in this 'old boy' environment, but at the same time was in danger of losing the creative spirit I had found over the previous few years.

Two things happened to ensure this was not the case. A new, young music teacher took over at Kingston Grammar and quickly changed things for the better. Instrumental lessons were introduced, I took up the flute as a second instrument, choirs and orchestras were started and we were openly encouraged to get our own bands going. The second development was, following a disastrous musicianship test with a 'talent expert' that left me in tears and ready to give up music for good, my mother (quietly determined as ever) took me to auditions for Junior Music School scholarships at all the London colleges. I got a full scholarship at Trinity thanks to an extraordinary interview process where I was asked to improvise (for the first time ever) on the piano, the result of which was a revelation to both the panel and myself!

I was now 'on track' again. I had a flourishing musical life at Kingston, with plenty of non-formal music-making in bands, and a trip to central London every Saturday, which I relished. Composing was becoming increasingly important to me, and I was openly encouraged to develop this interest at both Trinity and Kingston, despite the fact that composition did not feature in the curriculum at that time. What I was increasingly realising was that I loved the communal aspect of music-making; playing in ensembles with mixed line-ups, often by ear, exploring and improvising around a variety of styles and genres, coming up with our own ideas and then putting them into practice.

Whilst there was little drama activity on offer at my secondary school, I had become very involved with the school debating society (which I eventually led), introducing me to a whole new world of dialogue, discussion and public speaking on issues that mattered to us at the time. My interest in community continued to grow through my membership of the Scout movement, which I had joined at the age of eight and worked my way up to being a 'Senior Patrol Leader'. This entailed me organising all sorts of events, from weekend camps and hiking expeditions out of London to social and entertainment events for the elderly in local community halls. An absolute highlight for me at this time was to represent South-West London at the World Scout Jamboree in Banff, Canada in 1983, with over 100 countries from around the globe in attendance. This experience had a huge impact on me, in terms of its scale, the diversity of cultures, and the overall sense of unity and friendships made.

Towards the end of my school days it felt as if I had two parallel pathways ahead of me; one could be seen as a slightly more conventional academic route, the other slightly less obvious. The first would be to take modern history (a subject I loved) at university and to seek a career, on the advice of several teachers, in politics. Combined with a compulsion from an early age of wanting to change the world for the better, I had a genuine fascination of how political parties, governments and Westminster worked. Often was the time that Mum stood and sat by me patiently as we observed debates from the House of Parliament's public gallery or I browsed for books with toe-curling titles such as 'So you want to be Prime Minister'.

The alternative for me was to take music, though the pathway at that time seemed unclear. In the 1980s, music study at Higher Education level had fairly stark choices, and none of them particularly appealed. Whilst I was thoroughly enjoying my time at Trinity I had seen enough of conservatoire culture to know it would not serve me well in the long term. I was never going to be a concert pianist and sitting in orchestras and wind bands playing second or third flute bored me senseless. Universities meanwhile offered very little practical music-making opportunities, and focused almost entirely on academic work. My music teacher, Roger Askew, was a critical influence for me at this time. He had already forged an 'O' and 'A' Level route especially for me (music had never been offered at this level by the school before) and he persisted in encouraging me to pursue music. I can now vividly picture sitting with Roger at his desk, pouring over prospectus after prospectus trying to find the right type of course. The sense of implicit empowerment one receives through this type of investment in time and energy from a teacher (or parent or mentor or leader or anyone) is immeasurable and something I feel that everyone should have access to when required at critical points such as this.

Through Roger's support (as well as a tip off from a Trinity friend already there) I ended up on a progressive Music Degree programme at Bath College of Higher Education, enabling me to engage with performance and composition, as well as academia. The biggest revelation to me was the 'workshop' approach taken in the majority of classes and seminars, much of this being pioneered by the then Head of Composition and Music Education, George Odam. He and his departmental staff constantly encouraged us to be curious, to take risks and to think laterally as practitioners, engaging with as many approaches, styles and genres of music-making as possible, as well as other arts disciplines and cultures. The funniest thing looking back is that during my undergraduate years of 1984-87 I was experiencing creative workshops led by one of our composition tutors, Nick Atkinson, who was picking up his ideas first hand from courses led by Peter Wiegold, who at that time was artistic leader for the MPCS pilot years at the Guildhall School.

It was the enabling environment at Bath College, the innate sense of permission (fuelled no doubt by living away from home for the first time), which encouraged me to go further than ever before. I composed individually and collaboratively, led workshops in schools, listened to a vast array of music, took up drums and guitar, played in rock, jazz and free improvisation bands and got back into acting and producing in theatre. My only self-imposed challenge, as through all of my school life, was having too many things on at the same time, to the potential detriment of my formal studies.

It was also to be my challenge when I graduated; how on earth was I going to make sense of all these experiences and passions and translate them into some sort of meaningful and sustainable future professional pathway? I was never going to 'make it' as a performer or composer in the more established sense, yet I knew that I wanted to be making music in as many contexts and styles, and with as many disciplines, as possible. School and community settings resonated with me in particular, but I also knew that I didn't want to take the teacher training route either.

I spent another happy year in Bath playing, teaching, composing when possible and selling art cards part-time around the UK and Europe for a company called Prime Arts – my one flirtation with 'industry'. What I realised increasingly was that I couldn't drift for too long – somehow I had to find a way of making sense of all these disparate interests. I made half-hearted applications for Masters in Composition and production assistant jobs for the BBC and other recording companies just as a way of moving things on.

Then one day a friend who was still a student at Bath College showed me a leaflet that George Odam had handed out advertising a new postgraduate diploma course in Performance and Communication Skills at the Guildhall School of Music & Drama. The essence of the text offered musicians, and even performing artists from other disciplines, the opportunity to explore their role in society. The leaflet went on to describe a programme of activities and a range of contexts that was a mirror to what I had been doing over the previous few years; what particularly struck me was that these activities, many of them long-standing interests of mine, were being presented as something central, rather than peripheral to the diploma's content. In the words of my former Head of Faculty, who wrote one of the references for my application, the course looked somewhat unrealistic in what it set out to achieve but at the same time completely up my street in terms of what it stood for and covered.

If ever I was pushed to identify a seminal moment in my professional development it would have to be the audition experience I had for the Performance and Communication Skills course at Guildhall. It was a revelation at this time to be asked as a musician competing for a place at an internationally renowned conservatoire not only to perform pieces on my principal instrument, but also to engage with a participatory workshop that involved musical and theatrical improvisation, as well as an interview exploring my own motivation for wanting to come on the course. This particular day, and the year that followed when on the course, quickly helped me to make sense of the many seemingly unconnected and even conflicting pathways I had taken up to that point. My primary passion felt genuinely able to reveal itself at this time; an uncompromising commitment to the power of creativity through collaboration amongst people, in artistic, community and educational settings.

I was extremely fortunate to begin my professional life at a time when so much was beginning to change in the arts and education sectors. The new National Curriculum in Music, requiring all pupils between the ages of 5-14 to engage with music through performance, composition and leadership, meant there was a fairly immediate demand for music practitioners who could facilitate music-making environments for young people, and their teachers, from a wide variety of backgrounds and experiences. Many orchestras, opera companies, concert halls and arts centres were also setting up their own outreach and education programmes, which required professional artists to communicate and engage with society beyond their traditional platforms. It was the perfect opportunity to synthesize the key elements and forces I had been pursuing since school - artistically, culturally, politically and socially.

During the 1990s, as a workshop leader, composer, performer and projects manager, this rather holistic, 'portfolio-based' passion for collaboration, creativity and connectivity developed into a thirst for not only coming up with ideas, projects and outcomes, but also for making sure that their impact was as connected to and sustainable for as many people from as wide a variety of backgrounds and contexts as possible. Whilst nearly always personally rewarding, it no longer felt enough for me to lead endless one-off projects and events that resonated at the time with whoever was in the room but had no lasting effect on those people or the communities and organisations around them. This was the driving force that led me into accepting a full-time role at Guildhall, learning from and supporting Peter Renshaw in establishing a lasting legacy for the work of the Performance and Communication Skills department and its Arts and Community Development project in East London.

The sense of personal liberation and *permission* – artistically, professionally and emotionally – I experienced through the last decade of the twentieth century was both exhilarating and extremely rewarding. But was it sustainable? As I 'rollercoastered' from one 'high' to another, mainly in the role of composer/leader/collaborator/performer in a diverse set of contexts (locally, nationally and internationally) with people from a whole range of backgrounds, ages and experiences, I became increasingly aware of the fragility of this evolving field of practice. These so called 'education' or 'outreach' projects that I, and many other practitioners were now facilitating and leading on behalf of arts and education organisations were like butterflies, blooming into beautiful processes, performances, events etc, lasting a few days, and then disappearing.

Having experienced such an exciting and meaningful synthesis of my own passions and beliefs, much of it through a combination of good fortune and an enabling environment of family support and key informal mentors, had ensured I was now engaged with something that was far more than a 'job'. It was something that had the genuine capacity to not only make a difference at one particular moment, but to have lasting impact for people, their lives and society. It no longer felt valid to parachute projects in, however uplifting and valuable they were at that particular moment, without being clear what the overall intention and strategy was. Otherwise there was a danger that it became more about the organisations involved ticking boxes in order to raise more funds and leaders such as myself fuelling our own artistic egos.

This work had emerged at the height of a Thatcher government that had blithely announced that there was no longer such a thing as community. Despite all the policies being implemented that were about gain for the individual at the expense of others, a movement had nonetheless managed to establish itself that focused on music-making with creativity at its heart, thereby demonstrating that more could be achieved when working together rather that separately. Organisations such as *Music in Prisons* and *Music for Life* (and there were plenty of others) were already showing what could be achieved through sustained, intelligent planning and delivery. My 'constant' was working with PCS at Guildhall and therefore it seemed a natural next step for me to go full-time at the School in order to ensure our developing field of practice became firmly embedded in the undergraduate and postgraduate curriculum, as well as in our neighbouring East London Community.

New Labour had already made it clear that access, creativity and inclusivity was to be at the heart of its agenda, so the time felt right by 1999 to consolidate our 15 years of work within the conservatoire. Following my experience of setting up, running and playing in a large-scale creative ensemble with professional colleagues called *iO*, built very much on the ethos and values of collaborative workshops, Guildhall Connect was set up in order to establish more sustained relationships with young people, their families and schools. The long-term intention was (and still is) to ensure *everyone* had the opportunity to take their musical and creative experiences as far as they wanted to, informally and/or formally into higher education and the profession. This became the basis for us building up partnerships locally, nationally and internationally, as well as building up our team and developing our curricula within the Guildhall School.

My priority for Connect over recent years has been for the creation of an efficient, workable and sustainable model that embraces both the formal and non-formal education sectors. An ongoing and obvious challenge along the way has been that the music generated by Connect participants is often embedded in a contemporary, vernacular culture that does not necessarily resonate with the core business of a conservatoire. In order to assist the evolution of its profile and position, the gradual consolidation of a broader administrative infrastructure took place to support the activity and to enable its ongoing development. As well as continuing to run access and inclusion workshops/projects, satellite Connect Ensembles (local, national and international), apprenticeship schemes and continuing professional development for teachers and leaders, a more ambitious progression route – a type of 'golden thread' – has begun to emerge through the programme:

A new 'non-formal' curriculum for young participants that offers genuine opportunities for sustained and personalised musical learning alongside a robust mentoring circle of co-participants, students, teachers, parents and Connect tutors.

A new Connect undergraduate programme set up for 'creative portfolio practitioners' who break down the boundaries between musical genres, arts disciplines, 'specialists' and 'non-specialists'.

A postgraduate programme/research forum (particularly through an MMus in Leadership and a proposed Collaborative Masters in New

Audiences and Innovative Practice) for the training and development of contemporary practitioners who collaborate, create and perform as artistic leaders, cultural producers and curators in a variety of contexts.

A continuing professional development programme offering lifelong learning to performing artists, teachers, project managers and creative producers.

Work also continues with the BMus and MMus Performance programmes through Performance Matters, Collaborative Practice, Workshop Skills, Professional Studies and postgraduate electives, as well as with relevant research initiatives such as exploring approaches to instrumental teaching and learning and improvisation. Crucial to Connect is its role as a laboratory, particularly in relation to the developmental work around creative and collaborative practice, leadership and the role of the musician as a 'portfolio practitioner' in society.

I have continued to dedicate time to my own continuing learning, research and professional development. A substantial part of this has come through an MPhil I undertook at the Royal College of Art from 1999-2004 – *Workshop practice in collaborative contexts: an evaluation of language, meaning and creative processes*. This postgraduate research enabled me:

to strengthen my own comprehension (as a composer) of how a variety of musical languages can work together in a collective music-making environment

to deepen my understanding (as a creative workshop leader) of how this participatory experience can have a positive effect on local community.

This research has had considerable impact on the approaches and practices implemented through the Guildhall Connect and Professional Development programmes. I have since been exploring how these creative and participatory learning experiences can be applied to inter-cultural and cross-disciplinary contexts. Examples include:

Joint Leadership (with Dan Fern, Head of Communications at the Royal College of Art) of *MAP/Making; Creating new landscapes in Music, Art and Performance*, a collaborative research programme (funded by The Leverhulme Trust) involving postgraduate students and staff from the Guildhall School and the Royal College of Art.

Joint Leadership (with Christian Burgess, Head of Acting at the Guildhall School) of *Open Call*, a laboratory workshop environment for

Guildhall actors and musicians exploring approaches to performance and communication through creative collaboration and improvisation.

Project-based field research into the role and function of the performing arts in society, particularly in Africa and South America. This has included an exploration of the African concept *ngoma*, where music, dance, theatre and storytelling are seen as a holistic 'one', rather than separate art forms.

A five-month sabbatical granted by Guildhall in 2006 has also enabled me to visit South America and explore the synthesis of sound and movement in contemporary 'Latin American' music (particularly Brazil and Argentina) across a variety of arts, community and educational settings. As well as drawing on *the heritage* of European, African, North and South American influences it embraces *the now*, from the natural environment to technology, and 'high art' to 'street level' culture.

My most recent role (2007-2009) as Head of Centre for Creative and Professional Practice at the Guildhall School has carried responsibility for the School's pioneering work within the fields of composition, creative collaboration & performance, electronic music, improvisation, jazz, leadership, music therapy and arts & community development. It has also continued to entail developing, advocating and facilitating programmes, projects and activities that involve students and staff integrating with the wider community, particularly in our neighbouring East London Community. As well as ensuring the continued growth and success of each Principal Study pathway, particular focuses of activity for the Centre of Creative and Professional Practice include creative and cultural learning, widening participation, inter-cultural and cross-discipline practice, music-making in formal/non-formal contexts, music technology with live performance and continuing professional development.

One of my most exciting and increasing aspects of my work over the past few years has been to help facilitate projects and activities across the School cross-departmentally, with this remit extending more recently to liaising with the Barbican Centre, and London Symphony Orchestra. During this time it became increasingly clear that an unparalleled potential existed as a Campus/Cultural Quarter through its range of arts and education programmes, validated degree courses, depth of expertise and state of art facilities. The range of styles and influences on offer to the public through the Barbican's programme in particular, from classical to contemporary, from 'street culture' to 'high art' continues to excite and impress me, as does the belief and passion of all those involved in the planning and delivery. Much of what I see and hear through the Barbican Centre complements and resonates with what I have being developing through my own free-lance work as a practitioner and as a leader of creative and collaborative programmes at the Guildhall School.

My recent appointment as Director of Creative Learning for the Barbican-Guildhall in September 2009 therefore presents an exciting opportunity for me to harness these two organisation's distinctive, progressive culture, along with my own passion and vision for artistic and cultural education in society. The potential for drawing together the learning and participation programmes of our two organisations and connecting them meaningfully with the artistic direction of the Campus at a local, national and international level is immense and something I had hoped to see happen for a number of years.

Of primary importance will be the co-steering of a 'joined up' Creative Learning model, along with the key mutual partnerships of the LSO, City of London Festival, the Museum of London and Serious Productions. This would help to shape the Campus's artistic process and outcomes in the future. What has already become clear from discussions between our organisations is that the broad concept of *education* should serve as the *driver* rather than the *label* to our thinking and development.

There is real potential for the Barbican-Guildhall to develop an international reputation for producing innovative and exciting work of the highest quality – work that not only resonates with the 'high art' world, but contemporary society as a whole. The Royal College of Art end-of-year shows attract over half a million visitors – including royalty, politicians, arts leaders, designers, curators, the cultural industries, tourists and the London community. Could a 21st century Creative Learning programme, closely tied to an internationally renowned arts centre and conservatoire, develop a similar reputation for producing excellent work and performing artists in the 'new' and 'contemporary' as well as the 'classical' and 'traditional' sectors?

As planning for our future campus gets underway it feels as good a time as any to consider the possibility of a laboratory, of new ensembles and companies (even a professional agency) committed to the creation of new landscapes in music, art and performance. This laboratory, particularly for young people at school, and in further and higher education level, will offer the widest possible access to participation in the arts without compromising reputations and aspirations for excellence. It will be an opportunity for the Barbican Centre, Guildhall School and London Symphony Orchestra to take all the performing and visual arts (music, drama, dance, film, gallery exhibitions) as points of departure for the creation of new work and the nurturing of collaborative multi-practitioners. Acting as a cultural catalyst at local, national and international levels, the Creative Learning programmes will provide collaborative environments for an emerging generation of young artists coming from a wide range of backgrounds, disciplines and experiences who are interested in extending artistic boundaries and deepening creative processes.

As Director of Creative Learning at the Barbican Centre and Guildhall School, I will be seeking to:

1. Provide inspirational leadership and management across the Barbican Centre and Guildhall School's broad spectrum of programmes. This will be achieved primarily through my affinity and passion for creating and shaping approaches to engaging in the arts for people of all ages across a comprehensive range of styles and genres.

2. Promote and extend the Campus's reputation both regionally and nationally. My vision will be bold, and one that sets out to be owned by all Barbican and Guildhall staff. This vision will seek to continue to build on Barbican Education and Guildhall Connect successes and have an empathy and passion for all art forms, as well as for the creative process. I remain particularly interested in demonstrating how inclusive, participatory arts-based opportunities can lead to genuine and robust progression pathways, which empathise and respond to the individual needs of young people, as well as promote excellence in higher impact group based activities.

3. Foster and maintain a long-term strategy for future growth, contributing as a member of the Senior Management Team to securing sustainable funding streams. A priority is going to be to consolidate current and, where appropriate, establish new sustainable programmes of creative and developmental arts education fit for formal and non-formal sectors. This will need to be realised through a range of intelligent and strategic partnerships, thereby maximizing the confidence, commitment and passion of the Barbican Centre, Guildhall School and London Symphony Orchestra stakeholders and audiences.

What is so exciting is that this new role is enabling me to enter into a period of renewed focus and prioritisation, both on a personal and a professional level. It is a natural evolution of leadership responsibilities for me, whilst also allowing me to continue to shape, curate, facilitate and engage with the human condition. As indicated in this testimony, my primary sources of inspiration lie in people and their communities, creativity and its effective implementation, and love, both as emotional energy and at a transcendent, spiritual level.

Many of the personal changes that have taken place for me over the past five years – meeting and marrying Rachel, the passing away of my parents and the birth of our first child Poppy – have heightened my awareness of just how extraordinary the potential of what we have to offer as human beings is. It therefore feels imperative that we do not waste this gift, this 'window of opportunity' we have been given over the past 25 years to demonstrate the extraordinary and transformative qualities of the arts across all walks of life, for all types of people, in a vast array of cultural settings. The sense of empowerment – beyond 'liberation' for its own sake – that this provides can, and surely will, take people and society to a new and as yet unrealised level.

6.2 D   Anna-Karin Gullberg

Co-leader and Founder, BoomTown Music Education, Borlänge, Sweden

BoomTown Music Education is a radical project at the centre of the regeneration area of Borlänge in Sweden. It offers an alternative form of higher music education for rock and pop bands, with an emphasis on informal approaches to learning, supported by experimental projects, business, networking and education.

I was born in Piteå from two quite non-ordinary parents (I realised ad hoc) – musicians and 'immigrants' from Stockholm who moved up to this very little town, Piteå, which started a folk high school in music in 1958. My mother got work as piano teacher there. They were supposed to stay for a couple of years but together with my birth, time went by and suddenly Stockholm, and the wild jazz climate my father came from, seemed very far away. My mother, who is still alive, was a classically trained piano teacher, whereas my father played mostly by ear (always in jazz but on the clarinet and piano he could actually read the notes). I think this is important for my view of music, knowledge, creativity, humanity etc. My mother was very ambitious, schooled, organised and worked within the classical field whilst my father learned by doing and always had a playful, spontaneous attitude to all things in life up to his death!

When the School of Music in Piteå (university college/conservatoire) started, both my parents worked there: my mother as teacher and later as Head of the School, and my father (very against his will to be honest) as a teacher in playing by ear. There was a saying about my father that his pedagogy looked like this: Arno (his name) came into the room, looked at the students and said (snapping his fingers) – one, two, one, two, three, four ...

When I was about 10 years old, hanging around in his 'classroom', I suddenly saw that the students had music stands in front of them, with regular classical notation on them, but they were playing (i.e., improvising), jazz music, as usual. I asked my father why and he answered: "you know they get so scared when they don't have anything in front of them, so I just put some classical notes up on the stands and then we start jamming!"

Of course, impressions like these have shaped my view of music education and if we now jump forward to my own 'career', I started off as a living mixture of these two roads – the formal schooled road and the informal, natural road. I was singing in church choirs and rock bands at the same time and didn't have any problem with that. When I was older I went to the ballet academy and focused on dancing instead of music. At the same time I studied psychology and science of history and ideas, and realised after several years that the entertaining business was not my cup of tea – it was superficial and I wanted to pursue the BIG questions. I started a research road in psychology of engineering and focused on brain and design questions. But I was always seen as a bit of an outsider (by myself and others, but friendly!) – as an artist – not square or domestic enough to stay in that research field. My professor in technical psychology said: "A-K, you are living the way you learn – do you understand how strange that is?" I didn't! At the same time I was a single mother to my gorgeous son!

When the School of Music in Piteå had the opportunity to start a research department, I joined the one and only professor and became a PhD in Music Education in 2002 with a thesis titled: *The School Way or the Garage Way – Studies of Socialisation in Music.* I was totally convinced not to do any ordinary thesis, printed in an ordinary format. I also stayed with my conviction that you should be able to stay living and passionate during those doctoral years – not only almost alive! Even after the dissertation and the post-doc stress syndrome, I continued to do what I think is important. Of course, we all have to pay a price for this attitude and personality, but for me to be anything else than autonomous and bold in my thinking, and to do what I think is crucial for humanity, seems to be impossible when it comes to issues I care about.

At this point I probably have to say that I am a nice person – not a 'climber' at all – but my positive upbringing gave me the opportunity to develop a healthy self-esteem and 'high moral standards' – together with a lot of energy, I have never really been prepared to conform. Of course I have had my share of the Academies gender issues, envy or frank suspicion of my 'higher motives', but I have also had very supporting managers that have honestly believed in my 'world-changing projects'.

Since my thesis I have lectured, done research and managed projects, but most important (with the exception of my two latest baby girls, no doubt!), is the BoomTown-baby! Together with Kaj Podgorski (a soul mate) in Borlänge, I have started an alternative higher music education for rock and pop bands. As perhaps you can see, I created the third way – the synthesis – not the school way *or* the garage way – I put an *and* instead. The students in BoomTown Music Education apply as a band. They use their informal learning processes to learn other subjects and they identify their own learning goals and decide the way to realise them. They almost examine themselves and from next year (if my will becomes the law and the Board of Faculty have the guts!), the students will be granted the money for themselves and will be able to choose which teachers and supervisors they need and want.

Needless to say, the whole pedagogical philosophy is very popular amongst teachers when they listen to it, but when it comes to realising this adventitious view of learning situations, they get scared and upset. I try to support all the personnel and encourage them to build up values, attitudes and mindsets they do not want, with the aim of constructing a learning organisation – but instead they get even more scared!

So, I think I could say that my driving force is at least two-headed: my conviction that as persons we are much more interesting and happy, and our relations more giving and fruitful if we are honest, real, authentic, alive, engaged, enthusiastic, bold and beautiful! To achieve this you have to be guided to look into yourself – into the content of who you are – and not only to the outside, to the form. This is a provoking thought for the academy, of course, but that is why I try to do it my way together with others who also want to stay a little bit more than just alive! I am not a dreamer but I am a romantic. I am structured and organised and try to design educational settings and situations where students have to develop their self-independence, esteem and awareness – not the ego. Of course, I don't always succeed (definitely not amongst my closest relatives – talk about lifelong learning!), but at least I try!

My other driving force is the fact that from birth I have had a feeling that I am here on earth to make a difference. I have always had a spiritual (not a religious!) perspective on life, on meaningfulness and a kind of seriousness when it comes to fighting for equality, growing in consciousness and reforming institutions to support spiritual evolvement. Sometimes I am a Don Quixote – but at least a happy one!

6.2 E   Joost Heinsius

Manager Knowledge & Innovation, Kunstenaars&CO, Amsterdam

Kunstenaars&CO is a Dutch organisation with the mission to support and guide professional artists in gaining economic independence. It explores and develops new working areas for artists from all disciplines (e.g. actors, musicians, graphic designers, photographers, fashion creators) in close cooperation with partners and organisations from other sectors, such as welfare, local projects, education or the business community.

Most of my life I worked outside the arts sector, as a writer, as a consultant: mostly within the field of volunteer management and relations between professionals and volunteers in all kinds of organizations from community level to national advocacy. In my free time I was active as an amateur modern dancer and thus knew many young, aspiring and struggling artists.

I am a curious person and like to work in a non-profit environment (although a fan of social entrepreneurship). I am good at translating social and professional developments into new services and products. Most recently I became experienced in raising the level of professionalism within the organization I work in.

All these qualities came in handy when I started working within the cultural sector 8 years ago. I had never seen such an amateurish organized sector, working in very traditional ways on a level that has to be called proto-professional. I was quite shocked. Also the organization I started to work in was full of people with lots of idealism and enthusiasm but with little knowledge of for example, project management, working together productively, etc.

In short, everything I knew had to be harnessed to help this organization develop into the professional organization Kunstenaars&CO which it is now. (Of course, we never finish developing ourselves further). Meanwhile we are also developing new principles in our work: it is better if artists learn to earn their own money rather than us giving them money. The art sector is too small to offer all artists enough income, so let us develop new markets which offer them new experiences, new ways of producing work that can be appreciated by other people. Many artists have found new meaning and a new purpose for example, in working with youngsters or handicapped people. And, yes, they still make good art. We are now developing means in which we can show that art has more possibilities, more meaning to more people than just art for arts sake.

Why do I care? First of all, it fulfills my professional curiosity and drive to ameliorate, to discover new possibilities for existing services, to link abstract policies into profit for real people. Secondly, I meet many people for whom content is their first concern and money is a means, not an end. (I have a weak spot for this kind of idealism). And thirdly, I once studied political science out of desire to change the world. I do not feel the urge anymore to change the whole world, but in helping to change the world I work in just a tiny little bit. Somehow that still feeds into this desire.

6.2 F   Renee Jonker

Director, société Gavigniès
Teacher for Creative Music Making Programme, The Royal
Conservatoire, The Hague

*As Director of société Gavigniès, a private fund for sponsoring music,
Renee Jonker has been in a strong position to guide and develop its specific
profile in   music education – especially in the area of creative and
collaborative forms of music-making. His dotComp programme continues to
train musicians in Dutch orchestras, opera companies and conservatoires to
engage in creative work within schools and the wider community. He is a
member of the Research Group in Lifelong Learning in Music & the Arts.*

"You can start playing when everybody is listening..."

Together with "please do as I do" this is my favourite instruction in a
workshop situation: participants have just worked on a small piece of music,
created by themselves in a short break-out session and are now about to
perform it in front of the whole group. This is the crucial moment where they
are no longer just pupils in a workshop: they are about to become
performing musicians that can only communicate what they've just been
creating if their audience will give them attention. "You can start playing
when everybody is listening..."

It always works! Always and in every circumstance participants in a
workshop will be silent and listen concentrating on what their fellow
participants have created. Sometimes nervous, knowing they will be the next
group to perform, sometimes critical but always involved and open to new
impressions.

In a nutshell this is what I have experienced as the most rewarding aspect of
a certain kind of musical formation that I have been promoting now for over
a period of nine years. A formation that can be defined by three aspects:
creation, collaboration and self-expression. Oddly enough, this should not
be seen in contrast with any other form of musical formation, yet many times
it is. Most of our music education is build on reproduction. It hardly
encompasses the creative aspect of making music. And of course, playing
together in an ensemble or orchestra forces you to work together with other
musicians, but how distant is that process from playing in a band and
creating your own music, your own style, the identity of your own group?
And how difficult it is to bring out the element of self-expression once
notions of the 'wrong notes' or wrong fingering start to dominate our music
making!

As a child I was exposed to music. Both my parents loved opera, there was
a piano in the house and my father had, as a school master, this rare quality
of being able to accompany any song sung by a child in any key. Yet he

couldn't read music. My early interest in playing the piano was immediately encouraged and I was allowed to have weekly lessons with a certain Ms Plaisir (Ms Pleasure), whose name contrasted strongly with how I experienced her teaching. My secondary school was a long way from home so that gave me the right excuse to give up my lessons.

After a few years, the local brass band asked me to help them out, playing the timpani in a piece that was mandatory in a brassband competition. They asked me simply because I was the only young person in the village able to read music. Playing the timpani must have reawakened my interest in music. I started playing the piano again, now reading through a vast pile of piano music that somehow was given to my parents, just for my own pleasure. The percussion playing was then suddenly very stimulated when my parents offered me the chance to attend the Rotterdam Music School. The sheer fact that this would allow me as a fifteen year old to leave the island where we were living to visit the city of Rotterdam every week contributed highly to my enthusiasm for this idea. For three years I attended this music school where my teacher turned out to be an advocate of contemporary music. In contrast to my class mates, I started to listen to broadcastings of concerts with music by Stockhausen (*Gesang der Jünglinge* made a big impression) and Kagel. Also I started to organise cultural events and concerts in my secondary school to fight the boredom I was experiencing, much to the confusion of the other kids.

I often ask fellow musicians 'when they were born in music?'. An expression I have taken from the Canadian composer and one of my musical 'heroes' Claude Vivier. Vivier grew up as an orphan and never got to know his biological parents, whereas his adoptive parents couldn't save him from child abuse by an uncle. After being placed in an orphanage, whilst singing in the boys choir he experienced what he has since described as his 'birth into music', followed later by a second birth while attending a performance of Stockhausen's *Hymnen* in Montreal.

Most people can answer the question when they were born in music. My personal moment of 'birth' must have been on a Thursday evening and not 'in' music but 'through' music. On Thursdays my parents would leave for Rotterdam to sing in an opera choir. They would return only late at night and as the noise of our car was easily recognised from a distance, this gave me plenty of time to switch off the television. In those days Thursday evening was the time of the VPRO broadcasting, devoted to avant-garde cinema and theatre. This was my window on a world that was strange, confusing, seductive, mysterious and magical at the same time, but in any case a lot larger than the world I had been living in. The movies of Fellini, Pasolini, Fassbinder, Herzog, Wenders, Truffaut, Visconti, Godard, the absurd theatre of Wim T. Schippers, the unique documentaries of Cherry Duyns and Hans Verhagen – they all had a great impact on developing my taste for art.

After seeing these kinds of films on television, it was only natural that I should enjoy the music of Cage and Ligeti, which of course made me a complete outsider with the other kids in school.

After attending the Royal Conservatoire in Den Haag (in those days and even now the place to be for contemporary music) it was just a matter of months before I ended up in playing in a percussion group that has given me both a formation and the most precious of experiences over a period of 15 years. I also quickly joined both the Asko Ensemble and Schönberg Ensemble in Amsterdam and later (on a temporary basis) the Ensemble Modern in Frankfurt. As a rather entrepreneural percussionist, these activities gave me the opportunity to collaborate with some of my early day heroes who without exception, became great teachers.

The pathway I had chosen wasn't the most natural one for me: I see myself as a person with more than one talent, but none of them developed to be especially outstanding. I managed to be a successful percussionist but had to work extremely hard to meet the demands of my profession. Many colleagues were faster and better. I turned out to be the manager and producer of most groups I played in and my duties as a leader increasingly stood in the way of my playing. It was only logical to stop playing after 25 years when I was given the chance to become Director of the société Gavigniès, a private fund for sponsoring music.

Ever since I became aware of my love for art and music, I decided not to become a teacher, especially since both my parents were practising this profession. Somewhere down the line, I must have become less alert about this hang-up. To my surprise, in helping to develop the education programme for the société Gavigniès I found out that I can be a good teacher. Even worse, I love teaching!

Nowadays a large part of my activities has to do with teaching: leading workshops, teaching classes, developing new curricula, mentoring. They are all about music, although I cannot and will not teach how to play percussion.

What I can teach people is what is reflected in those two instructions that I tend to use quite a lot: 'do as I do!' Not meant in a narcissistic manner, but only using the simplest of all instructions to invite people to enter a new world that is rich, challenging, enchanting and in which I can be their guide on an equal level. And inviting them to become performing musicians able to express themselves whenever there are people paying attention with that most precious gift: the true listening of an audience.

6.2 G Ninja Kors

Project Co-ordinator, World Music & Dance Centre, Rotterdam

Ninja Kors is a member of the Research Group in Lifelong Learning in Music & the Arts. The World Music & Dance Centre (WMDC) in Rotterdam is a unique meeting point for music and dance from all parts of the world. It serves as a performance venue and a centre for developing talent and research, but it also has a special interest in promoting neighbourhood-oriented activities that are aligned with the cultural diversity of its local environment.

We are not alone

As people in this world we need to constantly find a balance between the big and the small. The local and the global. The 'me' and 'us'. It is a fascinating balance because it signifies how we need to be aware of both a sense of self, of who we are and where we belong, and of the notion that we are part of a bigger whole that gives us room to grow and challenges us to improve ourselves.

> *Hurray for the internet! Hurray for travel! Hurray for cultural encounters! And now let's go home and listen to our treasures in the comfort of our own ipod.*

A bit of personal background, for context.

At the University of Amsterdam, where ethnomusicology is part of the package, I encountered a world of music from Asia, Arab music, African, Latin American, and European folk music. Presented to me by professors from a bygone age, the age of tape recorders and late-colonial times. They were from the sixties generation where 'encountering the strange' was considered a tool to better the world. The old image of the *noble savage* was still alive, in a strange way. Our professors had taken it upon themselves to preserve the innocent musics, in their purest form. They were the ones who had taken their recorders out into the field, from wax rolls recorded by Jaap Kunst to DAT recorders that got stuck when dirty. I remember the collection of recordings at the institution – scores of tapes with music made by dead people. There was some live music at the university as well, one of them the gamelan orchestra. I played gamelan for several years.

> *To fall into place in this massive but subtle wall of sound. To hear the notes coming to you through the throng of brass keys. To hear ornamentations do their somersaults and skipping jumps, only to land on their feet again at the end of the gong phrase. The gong phrase! Not landing on the count of one, like in most western music which leaves the rest of the bar to its own devices. No, the gong phrase ends on the count of eight, the final beat. The whole phrase works towards that beat, and every note comes together on that final note. The gong phrase carries within itself a sense of one-ness. It is strongly connected with the*

culture that developed it: the religious notions, how the universe fits together, how a community is formed. And most of all, it is a musical principle that gives identity to the music itself.

Halfway through my studies I took a course at another university, just for variation. It centred on the anthropological aspects of musicology and 'encountering the other'. Part of the course was to play Sundanese music, the music of western Java. It is different from Central-Javanese gamelan but the basic philosophy of the gong phrase is the same as in gamelan. The professor explained the gong phrase to his students and stressed the 'otherness' of ending music on the last count instead of the first. Yet then he took up the *suling* (flute) and presented us with a self-devised notation system in which the final beat, the gong, fell on the first count of the bar. We were astounded. Was the music not supposed to flow *within* the gong phrases? Was the first beat not one of the weakest – and certainly no place for the defining emphasis of the gong? Yes, our professor explained, but he had adjusted the teaching method so that his western students may understand it better.

For me, that left nothing to understand. I never finished the course. (I also never gave the flute back, I still have it somewhere.)

Teaching across cultures

"Adjusting the musical culture itself for the purpose of educating those who do not understand". I don't see the point. This concept holds within itself a presupposition that one must simplify in order to teach, to transfer. More often than not, this is not necessary, and the culture as a whole is actually easier to understand than trying to fit bits and pieces into another culture.

Having said that, it is inevitable and therefore understandable that something, some aspects of a music are lost as it travels from one context to another. It is up to the teacher, together with the culture bearers, to determine what should definitely stay in. What to leave in, what to take out – I believe that in order to make that choice, it is important to know what exactly we want the other to understand. Because that aspect should not be compromised – that would defeat the object of teaching. Determining what that aspect should be, that is central in all examples of good world music teaching. It is a large part of what constitutes quality: integrity. The designer of the education (the teacher, the master, the coach) has a strong understanding of what he or she means to convey, and makes sure that it leaves the musical culture intact.

Another aspect that determines quality is aim, purpose. If you want to set up a project to improve purely musical quality, let it be about purely musical excellence. If you want to improve living standards in a certain area or group, let it be about that. Activities can have more than one aim but it is difficult to combine several aims in one when choices need to be made. There is a real danger of compromising *everything*.

Music is a social activity

The tricky thing here is that music, as I said before, is a social activity. It takes place within a context of society, culture, community. In short: music is people. In order to work on one aim, one needs to take into account the context in which music thrives.

For example, many of the projects of the WMDC in Rotterdam deal with cultural groups and social development. Because music is a social activity, and because WMDC is in the middle of a large multicultural (and multi-generational, and multi-social, and...) urban community, WMDC concerns itself with music projects that carry within them a strong social component. This is true on many levels of music making.

For the community projects with Caribbean brass bands, where the social dynamics are as important for the learning environment as are the musical instruments. For the talent development summer schools where music-making as a group is central to the learning process. For the joint production and marketing of top afro-caribbean bands where young musicians are actively recruited to take part in the rehearsals and performances to provide them with valuable experience and musician networks. For the gospel choirs where our project leaders need to engage with religious communities to reach the best singers and find the social 'glue' to keep the group together.

All this does not make WMDC a social institution. Our aim is not to keep young people out of trouble, or to relieve the elderly immigrants of loneliness, or to provide a platform for political debate, or even to provide young people with career opportunities. Our aim is to facilitate the development of music (and to some degree dance and other arts) and to make that development visible. In order to reach that aim, we need to care for the other things as well.

So how does that work re: distribution of energy and quality?

Engaging in different kinds of musical (and therefore social) development, on different levels of musical mastery, opens the door to a more inclusive concept of quality. A concept that is sometimes called 'flexible' because it adjusts to different contexts. I find that to call it flexible is actually not very respectful. It is not about 'adjusting standards', lowering or increasing them as the situation sees fit. The quality should always be of the highest rank; I think that in every situation it should be the aim to reach the utmost. To reach for the stars, as one of our project leaders Mimoun Himmit puts it. It is that everyone involved works *to the best of their ability*. This makes the concept of quality not so much flexible, but relative. This is not the same.

Whatever the project is, the aim is the same every time: to facilitate the development of music (and to some degree dance and other arts) and to make that development visible. To the best of our ability, meaning that we cannot leave the social environment out.

Space

The WMDC is lucky. In its development phase it was decided to keep the core of the building, the performance space, central. An open space was created that has good acoustic qualities, many uses (although not enough) and more importantly a good feel to it. Many groups feel at home in the WMDC, and the space facilitates easy mixture of groups and people. It is a professional performance place where people are also at home during the daytime when they are eating lunch, practising etudes or waiting for other people. It is relatively easy for musicians, all kinds, to claim the space as their own, something that happens frequently and almost always with success.

The building facilitates how we work on our aims of developing and promoting the edges of the musical genres, just like our social engagement with the city around us. It is important to understand that this does not compromise our commitment to the social aims in any way. We're not just in it for the money, or to milk the Caribbean brass bands for their current popularity. Exactly *because* it is important to the central aim, the engagement is real. This is also why we invest time in developing the restaurant facilities of the building, for example.

Apple

So how does this resonate with the target groups, the ultimate quality assessors? So far it resonates well. Sometimes WMDC struggles with its identity that lies between developer, educator and performance venue. The public needs pigeon holes. We provide them with it and present ourselves in Rotterdam as the latest in world music and cross-over performance. We're a stage. And just like in real life, behind the scenes is where the new generation is happening – without the pigeon holes. Like a tree that waves in the wind, but it's the roots that soak up the ground water and the trunk that carries it upwards. Let us be the roots that tap into unseen streams, and let us be the trunk that pumps the juices around. That way we will grow leaves that in turn give shelter and, ultimately, nourishment. You need a whole tree to get apples.

6.2 H Sara Lee

Artistic Director, Music in Prisons

Set up in memory of Lady Taylor, the wife of the late Lord Chief Justice, the Irene Taylor Trust 'Music in Prisons' has been working at the forefront of arts and rehabilitation since 1995 under the leadership of Sara Lee. The individuals that Music in Prisons works with are some of the most socially disadvantaged and excluded. Many have faced a range of challenges including abuse, violence, addiction, mental health issues, exclusion from school and homelessness.

My first adventure into Her Majesty's Prisons was slightly unusual but something was right about it. I was wondering what to do when I left college and a chance place on a new course and a fortuitous list led me to HMP Wormwood Scrubs and the start of my life working inside.

The first gig was a memorable one and stands out as one of the most powerful and important musical and personal moments in my life to date. A man who had served many years inside came to the performance with a piece of music he had written but never heard, hoping that we might be able to play it for him. We performed it and to this day I can remember my feeling as we were playing it and his response to that. Instantly this man had genuine respect and kudos amongst his peers - something I know to be important in life but what I quickly realised to be vital to anyone's survival in prison. He had been elevated and looked proud and was very pleased to take the praise.

We were told that the performance had had a big impact and the group was asked if anyone might like to come and teach music for 2 hours a week on a regular basis. I said yes. I had been intrigued by the building and the people in it and wanted to understand more about the feeling I, the man and the audience had experienced that evening. 25 years on and although quite different, my passion is still there. Increased knowledge has only brought more of a desire to make what the man and the audience felt available to more people, as I believe music and the process of creating it makes a massive difference to people's lives. The content of my work may have changed but the same things about it still make me happy, make me angry and drive my motivation to continue.

Over the years it has been amazing to be in a position to offer people who need and deserve it, a voice, the chance to be heard and a new opportunity. For me, the work throws up more than just the challenge of guiding disparate groups of people through a music project. I love music and am fascinated by people and what makes them tick, so it is a privilege to be able to use these two things in combination in my working life. It is remarkable that you can go into such a dark and austere place yet be able to create something beautiful within it. The combination of containment and musical freedom is a paradox but there is something really exciting if a little bizarre about giving people in prison this metaphorical freedom.

Much of the work is about taking musical risks with people and with yourself. With music there is no way you are going to know everything about everything; the possible musical areas groups can delve in to are incredibly wide and part of the joy of my work is that I can learn new things all the time. Young people especially are privy to genres of music arriving and passing really quickly and almost every time I work I am faced with a new type of music - which in reality is only probably the placement of a cymbal crash away from something I was told a month previously but nevertheless is different enough and important enough to the young person for me to make sure I listen.

To see everyone I work with immerse themselves fully in what is at times a difficult and challenging process for them and to see them responding to me, to each other and to the music they have written affirms why I am so fortunate to work in this way. The inclusive nature of something where everyone's opinion and skills are accepted, valued and combined does wonders for a person's confidence. To see musical skills develop is brilliant but to see self esteem and confidence grow is just amazing.

What matters is that we come out at the end having created something beautiful, something of quality and something of which we can all be proud. The journey can be difficult as well as fascinating as each week I meet different people, some with musical skills but most without them. Some find them along the way but everyone finds something, ranging from feeling safe, feeling challenged, feeling a sense of achievement, having got to the end of something or getting to the end and having people appreciate what you have done.

One of the most exciting aspects of the work is never knowing who you are going to meet, therefore not knowing any of the challenges you are going to face. To this day I still get excited to see what might happen in any given situation and to have to puzzle my way through things with participants and colleagues. I like the fluidity of it as well as the fact it is risky and I love watching people's personal and musical development throughout the week. It is incredibly satisfying to work in a team that pulls in the same direction despite none of us really knowing the direction we are going at the outset. One of the best parts of my work is that my colleagues are people who have the same work ethic and commitment as I do. They are people I totally respect as musicians and people and there is always something to learn from them. I love stretching/developing/ finding my musical skills and they help me do this. I am genuinely challenged sometimes and people I work with see this; they can help me, they can come up with ideas and they can show me things. This boosts people and gives them deserved pride - someone has asked for their help and taken what has been offered. Getting to the end of a project and seeing and hearing about the positive changes people have seen in themselves continues to make me smile.

It matters to me that some people in prison come out with no more than they went in with. One of the recurring things I see isn't so much people *not* having skills, just not having the basic human reserves with which to begin to find them. In life you need to start with a firm foundation and for many, that means simply helping them onto the rung where they see they can do something and where they won't be cussed for f***ing it up. The fear of failure for some is often all consuming; some are brave enough to confront it and others are not. Music is the vehicle I use and so much of the confidence and self esteem needed in life can be gained through taking part in a music project. They are not a soft option and not for the faint hearted; certainly not an easy ride. They can be a huge challenge, often throwing up unlikely scenarios where other things are uncovered during the process. Music and the process of creating it touches the deepest of emotions in all of us and somehow the fact we are all going through it together makes it all the more meaningful. We know that when we hear certain pieces of music we either have written or just love to listen to, it gets to us. People in prison are just the same. We all have emotions; it's just that sometimes theirs are more raw and undiscovered.

Many of the people I work with unanimously agree that their Music in Prisons experience is one of the most exciting and challenging projects they have ever undertaken. Some freely admit that the whole process was difficult; simply having to work together as a group and listen and respect other people's ideas is often a new concept but when they make it to the final performance it's great to hear everyone's appreciation and honest acknowledgement of their personal achievements – in many cases they had not realised they had anywhere near the potential to see something through to its conclusion. It is always rewarding to see how people grasp the essence of a project and take the opportunity on offer to them.

It matters to me to strive to always give my best to people and in the vast majority of cases people respond with the same measures. I say to them that I have the same kinds of feelings as they do when I am playing and writing music; I worry that I don't know something well enough or whether I am going to remember something or play it in the right place. I get a good deal of pleasure from working out how on earth to make things work and how to engage people. The process starts on an even playing field which is initially difficult for some to comprehend, bearing in mind that their previous school experiences and dealings with adults have not always led to such equal and positive relationships. People are more likely to take risks if they feel supported so I have to cultivate and provide a safe and supportive environment for people to experiment.

Maintaining quality has always been at the root of my work and it is my desire to retain that quality that keeps me questioning things. However, my driving force is the same as it has always been – I get an enormous sense of satisfaction creating great music with people and seeing them achieve things they thought were impossible. I love the fact I would not have met and seen the creativity of the people I have worked with and what it has done for me as a musician had I not walked in to prison for the first time. It simply reaffirms the far-reaching and sometimes totally unexpected benefits creative music making has on all of us.

6.2 I   Debora Patty

Education, Yo! Opera Festival and Laboratory, Utrecht

Since the 2005 Festival, Yo! Opera has increasingly seen itself as a laboratory exploring different forms of creative collaboration and performance practice. This has ranged from direct work in the community to pursuing new avenues in training, research and development. For the Festivals of 2005 and 2007 Debora Patty was responsible for organising the Operaflat in the Utrecht district of Overvecht.

Peter asked me to write a personal testimony about myself, my beliefs, values, goals, motives – basically, about what matters to me and how these things relate to what I do. For example, in my work at Yo! Opera Festival but also in my personal life, in my part-time study for possibly becoming a primary school teacher, and the things that I enjoy, in general.

For me it all starts where I was brought up – my family. I was born and raised in a Christian family. Faith still has a big role in my life. It tells me I have been made for a reason, that I have been given a set of principles and talents to enjoy life to the fullest and to help others do the same. That is my responsibility. That is about the quality of life. That is why I am here.

I love the theory of multiple intelligences (Howard Gardner) where the basic assumption is that everybody has been given a unique combination of those intelligences and qualities. Everybody has a favorite way of living and learning and that is something that we have to keep in mind when we communicate to others.

Opera contains more art disciplines than just singing. In relation to the intelligences, this makes my work very interesting. I like the fact that we can offer kids different ways of expressing, of being creative. You can sing, write, act, compose, be a musician, or be more in the background by for example, making the scenery and props.

This is also my drive as a (future) primary school teacher. Not to force kids to learn in just written language, but to make things visual and tangible. Not just to learn on your own, but also together with your class mates – by listening, by doing or by telling. This approach sometimes clashes with time management, with traditional structure, or with government policy which says that language and maths should be the main focus of your education programme. In a (practical) way this is very understandable. We need 'quality' in terms of results and quantifiable statistics. But when it comes to a rich learning environment that inspires, tickles, that really fascinates and is meaningful, that facilitates relationships and social skills – when it comes to that, then you want 'quality' that is permanent. Again it's about the contribution to your journey in life, and the beautiful views you don't want to miss because you were looking at your fuel gauge.

One of the main reasons why I chose to study to become a primary school teacher is the contact with the children. When Yo! Opera started its education projects in schools, my career as education manager began. This was in 2006 with the project 'Water'. Together with about 75 kids we made an opera on the terrain of a water treatment plant in Utrecht. This was just the beginning of a long-term relationship with the school, 'De Rietendakschool', where we still now work.

I noticed that I really enjoyed being in contact with the children – in talking with them, but also in talking with the teachers who work with them, not only for one hour but for a whole week. I wanted that too! Not just to work with them in an artistic context, but to help them to discover how to find the height of their school building, to enable them to find words for making a poem, or to talk with them about the meaning of democracy or about volcanoes. This shared journey contains all the aspects of life – in which, I think, art and creativity have a very important role, because they touch your inside, your identity, your emotions, and the way you look at things.

At the centre of it all is 'relationship'. Your relationship with yourself, your relationship with others and the way you connect these two. I believe that honesty, openness and integrity are key words. This also counts for the way you work with people as an organization.

Yo! Opera works with a lot of different people: (student) singers, (student) composers, teachers, pupils, communities. Most of the time mixed in one project working in collaboration. The challenge at first is to take a look at your motives for engaging in such a shared venture. Why do you want to work with young composers? Why with children? Why with these children? Why with this school? Or with this art organization? If you cannot give a clear answer, there is a danger that you are just 'using' the other in order to achieve your (artistic) goals. The benefits should be for both parties. As the initiator of a project, you should be aware of this, as this is your responsibility when you establish and nurture a relationship. It is the responsibility of Yo! Opera to create conditions in which conservatoire students, high school pupils or professional opera singers are at their best.

When I talked about the main reason for studying to become a primary school teacher, I mentioned the long-term contact you have with kids. When I think of reasons for not yet having made the step into the classroom, I think of the fact that I love working in the creative industries – where people have crazy ideas, where emotions, voices, colours, movements and daily reality are being challenged or are being transformed into something that enables you to see things differently. I love the fact that we as human beings have the capacity to create and to stun each other with ideas and beauty. For example, I'm a big fan of street artists like 'Banksy'[1] ,'Os Gemeos'[2] or the photographer 'JR'[3] who use the street as a stage to make creative statements – about life, what should be different, about beauty, communicating, playing and about lightness. I love the freedom that art brings. It allows you to cross (unwritten) boundaries or barriers that are blocking your view or keeping you from playing. I see this in Yo! Opera projects like 'Water', 'Opera uit het Hart' or 'De Operaflat' where the gap between your imagination and normal life disappears and everybody becomes part of the game again. Because secretly, I think that we still all want to play...

1 http://www.youtube.com/watch?v=lyGZIwKL-0c&feature=related, www.bansky.co.uk/
2 http://www.youtube.com/watch?v=VuTi4nZv_cl, http://www.lost.art.br/osgemeos_01.htm
3 http://news.bbc.co.uk/hi/in_depth/8091890.stm, http://jr-art.net/

6.2 J   Linda Rose

Project Consultant and Founder (1993), Music for Life Wigmore Hall and *for dementia*, London

In 1993 Linda Rose founded Music for Life with the support of Jewish Care. As a pioneering project it developed interactive, creative music workshop programmes for people living with dementia. Work takes place in residential homes, hospitals and day care centres. The project aims both to enhance the quality of life of its participants and to demonstrate to staff the emotional, social and physical potential of people in their care. In 2009 Music for Life transferred to the Wigmore Hall which recently formed a new partnership with the charity for dementia. *Linda is now participating in the research project Healthy Ageing through Music and the Arts, as part of the Research Group in Lifelong learning in Music & the Arts.*

REASONS

"Why do you keep chipping away at that huge piece of rock?" the little boy asked Michelangelo. "Because I know there's an angel inside trying to get out."

"Why do I keep gazing at, stroking, whispering to
this body in a bed?" I ask myself. "Because I know
there's a person inside trying to get out."

John Killick (2008, p.19)

I think I am nosey. If there is a hole in a tree, if there is a dark doorway, if there is a person with a puzzled expression, I need to peer in and explore further. I am told, generously, by a friend as we explore this idea that I am someone with an insatiable curiosity.

In trying to build a picture of why and how Music for Life came about, I have had all sorts of conversations, both with myself and with others. I am told that yes I am curious, that I like to be connected and that I am secretly subversive. I like creating unexpected and what initially seem to be impossible relationships between individuals and groups of people. I love watching people find themselves and know, from my own experience, this happens slowly. I like the challenge of changing systems but know this happens slowly too, and am patient.

Once the sporty, active participant I have changed into the observer, looking on and processing. I like to watch people, anywhere and everywhere, at railway stations, in traffic jams, in restaurants, or engaged on our projects. I am interested in the places, the contexts in which people live their lives and how they respond to them, or are shaped by them. I believe that all people are creative until the very end of their lives and that empowering people to find themselves is the most meaningful thing I can do in my life. All of this I suppose underpins the growth of Music for Life.

Setting out at 18, I had no grand design or lifelong ambition – simply a fear of the years ahead and a need to fill them with something more meaningful than the school years I had left behind. Not blessed with a memory for facts, I came to believe that questions were more important and more exciting and life changing than answers. I loved the kind of quizzical 'What if....' questions, the kind that involved leaps of imagination to land in a place that seemed impossible to reach. Children are particularly good at this and as a teacher I was excited by the child who questioned. As an adviser, I was most interested in the teacher who questioned, and now, the musician who questions the purpose of his music-making, the care staff who allow themselves to observe, to question their assumptions and to wonder at the amazing potential remaining in those very vulnerable individuals in their care. I am always learning from those I work with, and journeying with them has been the most privileged and exciting place for me to be.

At times, I am plagued with ideas and possibilities, which I have to bat away at night so as not to be overwhelmed. Music for Life began as one of these possibilities. It came into my mind to build a relationship between some voluntary work I was involved in with older people and some community work with music students in order to change the lives of older people in care. It evolved organically into something different and new, away from its beginnings, through the connections made over the 15 years of its development. Paul Klee's 'taking a line for a walk', comes to mind here – starting with a line and allowing it to go where it suggests. Unlike my previous work as music adviser in an education department of a large city council, there were no constraints on Music for Life. It had not been done before and I was in control. There were no politicians imposing frameworks, and I was now totally free of local government. I was left alone and was at last able to work in complete freedom.

Tracing back along the line that has been the evolution of Music for Life, I find many and various influences. I have been inspired by wonderful people. There are the pioneers who became my mentors and who often mysteriously knew each other or knew of each other, despite their different disciplines. They encouraged me to think in new ways through their own quests. They believed in my potential, when I have been so uncertain. They served as models, as I too grew to see the capacity in others to bring about change. I have been inspired by the musicians who have come into this work. bravely searching the depths of their being, risking the vulnerability that ultimately takes them to a new and meaningful place in their lives, They have opened themselves to each other and to the people with dementia they have worked with, in the most honest and moving of ways and have revealed some of the deepest motivations from their own disciplines and their own beings. Throughout the time that the project was developing, I have watched our young adopted daughter in her on-going struggle to find who she is and have been inspired by her strength despite numerous set-backs. I have learned how a young person with a disrupted early life may experience difficulty in both forming and in trusting relationships, but I have also seen the richness that is possible in meeting the struggle to relate. There are points in my own upbringing that resonate with this and have guided the direction my life has taken.

I know that I am driven by a deep-rooted need to connect, which I have been lucky to be able address in my work. I am intrigued by the paradox of what has been developed, the complexity of the project and yet the sheer simplicity of the message it embodies. Maybe the project brings me the kind of peace I yearn for. Often we are engulfed in a kind of silence that is more powerful than words and that exists also as an integral part of the musical experience. I see it so brilliantly and so simply described by John Killick (1997, p.10) in his poem 'You are Words', where he gives voice to a person with advanced dementia:

> But will you permit me to say
> that you have the stillness of silence
> that listens and lasts.

There seems to be such an urgent need today to identify outcomes of work and to 'go public', before we even know what we're about, before we have had the time to develop our ideas and practice. By contrast, Music for Life has remained low key, growing slowly over many years. True to my early training as a student teacher, the work has been subject to constant reflection, refinement and the search for precise words often for imprecise feelings. But all this is combined with a belief in my instinct for what may be the way forward. I can still hear the questions ringing as I write this – what is instinct, is it informed judgement, is it a kind of collective knowledge, is it a kind of internal truth and so on...I am led back to the first book I was introduced to by Peter Renshaw, in the first week of my college course a lifetime ago. RS Peters (1964), Professor of Philosophy of Education, writes:

> I am reverting once more to my feeling of muddle that first awakened my interest in the philosophy of education... We used to spend hours in conferences discussing what our aims were. I have felt muddled ever since (p.8).

In surviving the strain and confusion of the project's early days I too have emerged knowing that this is it. Uncertainty will always be central and is in effect the very stuff of the project. Music for Life is not a methodology but rather a journey to embark upon with the possibility of emerging from the confusion to find something of oneself along the way. Its values and beliefs are transmitted from one to another, just as some sense of what is important was transmitted to me. This has been and still is subject to constant testing and integral to my own personal and professional development.

The project has taken with it so many people from so many different walks of life and encouraged them to support and participate – and fund. This is a constant source of amazement and delight for me for they are recognising and sharing this set of values, a belief in what is essentially human and important in life – a need to relate and respect. In writing this, I have looked back again to those who have influenced my work over the past 40 years and notice that the literature that they have introduced to me also carries this theme, despite working in different fields. RS Peters, talked of 'respect for persons', Carl Rogers, Professor of Psychology and Psychiatry 'On becoming a person', Professor Tom Kitwood, a pioneer in the field of dementia care, 'Dementia Reconsidered; *the person comes first'*.

Now the work is growing beyond my remit and I will watch others take it forward. It is not so hard now. The baby has grown up and the beliefs of others will need to guide it now. I only hope that it continues to be a source of learning and inspiration, but also, as it has always been, a struggle for a kind of truth from which everyone who is part of it can derive the greatest rewards.

> To a large extent, a person is what he does in life. If his occupation seems to him an important one, which he holds in respect and through which he can enrich both

himself and his society, he cannot help but feel that a large part of his life is important and respectable and enriching (p.4).

Bennett Reimer (1970)

References

Killick, J. (1997). You are Words in *You are Words*. Also in *Journal of Dementia Care*. London: Hawker Publications Ltd.

Killick, J. (2008). Reasons. In *Dementia Diary – Journal of Dementia Care*. London: Hawker Publications Ltd.

Peters, R.S. (1964). *Education as Initiation*. London: University of London Institute of Education and George G. Harrap & Co.

Reimer, B. (1970). *A Philosophy of Music Education*. Englewood Cliffs, New Jersey: Prentice Hall, Inc.

6.2 K   John Stephens

Music Education Consultant, UK

For over 50 years John Stephens has been a pillar of music education in UK – former teacher, County Music Adviser, HM Inspector, Staff Inspector for Music with the Inner London Education Authority, founder of the Music Education Department at Trinity College of Music and adviser to numerous major organisations such as Youth Music, the Britten-Pears School in Aldeburgh, The Sage Gateshead, the Royal Opera House and all of the London Orchestras. He has been especially keen to bring the professions of music and education closer together.

Reflections

A few weeks ago I attended the 'Trooping of the Colour': over 200 men and women of the Royal Marines parading their marching and musical skills on Horse Guards parade ground. It was a colourful and exciting occasion that brought back memories of some seventy years ago when, every Sunday morning, on the cross-bar of my dad's bicycle I was taken to nearby Eastney Barracks to watch, and listen to the Royal Marine band on parade. I eagerly anticipated each Sunday for the spectacle, the ritual, the music and what today would be called 'bonding' with my dad: during this period our family was pained by the frequent hospitalisation of my mother and in some way the music was a comfort when she died before I reached my teens. I took the band tunes home with me in my head and sang *A Life on the Ocean Wave* and other marches throughout the week often parading an imaginary band across the lawn. Sousa, Alford and the rest might have wondered what this six year old was doing to their creations and doubtless Lieutenant Colonel Vivian Dunn, who was then in charge of the Royal Marine band, might have commented on the lack of drill.

Remembrance of early musical experiences include the hearty non-conformist church singing, and radio, or as then the 'wireless' programmes, are also tucked away in the corners of memory: *Music while you Work* (a regular lunch-time spot on the airwaves) alongside *Cwm Ronda* and other hymns, psalms and anthems in church. Musical opportunities did not come directly through school until I reached what was then known as the sixth form (aged 16).

By the year of my eighth birthday, the marines from Eastney barracks had all gone off to be cockleshell heroes in the Second World war whilst I, an evacuee, began to learn, first the piano and then the violin. Nightly visits to the air raid shelter in the garden were set alongside an increasing interest in music. I later realised that the 'Home Front', as the civilian population was called, found great comfort and support from musical activity and I too absorbed the cultural environment of the time: listening, between news bulletins, to music programmes.

I keenly mastered Bach's *Jesu, joy of Man's Desiring* because Dame Myra Hess, a notable pianist of the day, had made her mark with a piano arrangement for her regular war-time recitals at London's National Gallery. As I now realise, this was an age in which music was valued for the emotional and spiritual support it provided in a stressful time: Vera Lynne's *There'll be Blue Birds over the White Cliffs of Dover* and other popular songs had significance to all of the families whose fathers were away fighting for King and country whilst their wives valiantly coped with trying to maintain as normal life as possible.

Church life at this time extended beyond the two Sunday services and afternoon Sunday school: there were meetings and clubs on week nights. Music of one kind or another was required for these occasions and as pianistic talent was in short supply, I invariably found myself asked to accompany singing or provide interludes, background music: the thin war-time paper of Piano Folios containing arrangements of orchestral works and simplified version of more complex piano music was a staple diet. There was an expectation that I would play whatever was put in front of me, and if necessary transpose to suit the a particular voice. Needless to say, sight reading and transposition skills advanced at the rate of knots.

Other teenagers in the church community began to develop an interest in music and, with the addition of a few school friends I started an 'orchestra' made up of whatever instruments we could muster. Arrangements of the music had to be made and I quickly found myself handwriting parts, sometimes ambitiously beyond the competence of the players. I even tried my untutored hand at composition, writing amongst other pieces a three-movement violin concerto that I remember to be based largely on arpeggios and the kind of chord sequences to be found in hymn tunes. The orchestra had to be fully equipped so, with the assistance of my grandfather, who had been a shipwright in Portsmouth dockyard, I made them wooden music stands: sturdy but inflexible. Many rehearsals and much encouraging of the slow learners, I eventually arranged for the orchestra to give a concert in the church.

Applause at this and subsequent concerts was doubtless more directed to our efforts and enthusiasm than the musical worth, but encouragement was there in plenty. Likewise, at school where there was then no musician on the staff, the organ-playing chemistry master, recognising my keen involvement in music, offered to give me regular organ lessons. The Novello Organ Primer carefully led me through the complexity of three manuals and a concave pedal board into the world of Karg Elert, Mendelssohn, Bach and the like. In my final school year a music mistress arrived to rush me through A level that was then known as Higher School Certificate.

By this time an enthusiasm for music - making and listening - had focussed and I strongly wished to share with others the feelings and excitement I had in this involvement: it was akin to a missionary zeal. I found in music a deeply rewarding emotional involvement, satisfaction and fulfilment that I realised I had the capacity to pass to others. Thus when my dad asked what I wanted to do with my life the answer, as I clearly recall, came directly – 'to teach music'. The training and career that followed always seemed to reference back to this decision made at the end of schooling, aged eighteen.

When the day to start teaching finally arrived, I found myself in front of a class at Southsea Secondary Modern School for Boys. Morning assemblies included lusty hymn singing from the boys accompanied by a Broadwood grand piano the wooden frame of which pulled the tension of the strings in and out of tune according to the weather. With the help of many of the thirteen masters on the staff, I mounted concerts and musical productions that were mostly rehearsed before and after school as well as during lunch breaks. The boys were loyal and committed, many arriving for an 08.30 rehearsal having already completed a paper round and taken younger brothers and sisters to school. Here I learnt through direct experience, the significance of the social value of music-making and its importance for a school community.

The local Music Adviser, John Grayson, had a considerable influence on my development: he became my 'hero' figure, providing wise counsel and advice, mentoring and, in today's lingo, CPD. He also gave me many musical opportunities, including assisting him in Methodist services played on the three manual Willis organ of Wesley Central Hall. His carefully methodical approach to teaching is now years out of fashion, but he had a keen understanding of pedagogy (how to teach) that has sustained me throughout my career.

Arriving at a large newly opened comprehensive school in London-overspill Harlow I quickly found myself in the midst of musical activity which included directing the local operatic society, playing the church organ and leading its choir, alongside organising many musical activities in the school itself. A neighbouring comprehensive school had already established its musical reputation with a Saturday morning music school offering individual instrumental lessons and I felt that this should be replicated in my school. I recall that, in discussion with my Headmaster, I said that if it was not possible to open such a centre I was teaching in the wrong school. He quickly found a way through the county hall bureaucracy to enable me to launch the school's own music centre.

Sir Robert Mayer and his wife, music benefactors of the time, took an interest and supported the musical developments in the town, notably by helping in the appointment of the young Alberni Quartet to the town. Performing and teaching commitments demonstrated how improvements in the quality were achieved through the perspective of this professional ensemble. The importance to music learning of the professional ear wove its way into my psyche.

The role played by John Grayson earlier in my career was strongly embedded in my ambition and I applied for, and was appointed, County Music Adviser for Shropshire after a four year stint at the comprehensive school. It was a considerable wrench from the daily contact with young, developing talent and, whilst establishing and conducting the Shropshire County Schools Orchestra was, in part, compensation, the early days in Shropshire showed how much I missed teaching: since when I have always admired the skilled and dedicated music teachers who sustain their effort by staying in the classroom throughout their career.

Earlier experiences, organising the Schools' Music Festival in Portsmouth, running the music centre in Harlow and gaining various music diplomas en route, provided a backdrop for the developments I promoted in Shropshire. Encouraging teachers to advance their professional skills, I engaged leading music educators and musicians of the day to bring to this somewhat remote county the latest thinking in the practice of music education. It was a great good fortune that the Education Officer and other advisor colleagues were at the time involved in the preparation of the Plowden Report on primary education and this had a considerable influence on my thinking and understanding of how children learn.

Shropshire schools were receptive to the composers whom I invited to work and write for them. Amongst the many whose music was performed in the county was Gordon Crosse who had made his name writing works for BBC Schools' programmes. With him, I learnt of the importance for the composer to visit and work alongside the prospective performers: viewing the site as an architect might. The process of composition was as important as the finished product. My commission of Gordon Crosse's *The Demon of Adachigahara* found its way into the repertoire of the day, introducing many pupils to contemporary idiom.

At this time I had very little notion of the working of HM Inspectorate, although I knew the local District inspector as an enthusiastic supporter of choral activity and the specialist music inspector as a valued friend. It was therefore something of a surprise that I should be taken to one side and asked if I had ever thought of applying for HM Inspectorate. I had not but, as asked, gave thought to the suggestion and subsequently made an application.

The team of some dozen music specialist HMI was a great stimulus to thinking about music education and the opportunities offered to the role of HMI gave me experiences that I would unlikely to have met in any other post. I visited schools and colleges, including independent schools, throughout the south of England and become engaged in numerous courses and conferences for teachers and lecturers. These were often of ten days duration which gave time for some real development. Quite a number of the courses involved HMI from other subject disciplines and working with such colleagues gave me practical experience of relating music- making to drama, movement and other arts disciplines.

This was an era when the role of HMI was to inspect and have knowledge of the delivery of the curriculum with the purpose of informing the Secretary of State and to improve schools themselves. To this end HMI published numerous documents, leaflets and booklets, reporting on good practice and feeding back to the profession an assessment of the strengths in subject disciplines. I became involved in many such exercises, including the writing of the music statements for full inspection reports. These were always discussed and not infrequently challenged by other HMI: a learning process in precision in the use of written language. Whilst music was still at the core of my work these wider opportunities broadened my perspective and began to open a political scenario that I later found important.

Following a second advertisement for a Staff Inspector for Music with the Inner London Education Authority (ILEA), it was suggested to me that I should make an application. I was subsequently appointed to lead a large team of teachers, advisers and professional musicians for the largest education authority in the country. The size of this education service, sheer critical mass, provided opportunities not available to other, smaller units. An educational television unit, learning resources centre, specialist careers service that included advice on music careers and many other initiatives worked alongside those specific to music making. A Music Teachers' Centre, Saturday Centre for Young Musicians, Holiday Music Courses, including the London Schools Symphony Orchestra, Concerts by professional musicians, visits to English National Opera and other London music venues were all part of the fabric of a comprehensive provision for music.

The service linked work with pupils and students to that for adults, through distinguished departments like those at Morley College and City Lit. It attracted attention from those working in music education overseas and offered opportunities for such visitors to London to hear and learn about the integrated structures and policy for music education. The development of the education service to make provision for a rapidly changing social and multi-cultural society was, for musical activity, within my sphere of influence.

I had to understand the developing ILEA policy and interpret it within music activities: a keen political awareness was essential. Numerous schemes, backed by the local politicians, sought to raise the profile and the quality of the provision for music and with such a wealth of professional musicians (of all genre) living on the capital, I was determined to do everything possible to bring together the worlds of education and music. The motivation and drive of my early career was now challenged to interpret ideals into action. It is for others to judge how far this was successful. Suffice to say that, when the government of the day abolished the ILEA, support for the continuation of the music service came from distinguished musicians, Michael Tippet, Simon Rattle and the like, as well as leading educationalists of the day who recognised the worth of the ILEA music service.

I found other outlets for my energies and experience; firstly establishing a Music Education Department at Trinity College of Music and then advising on the setting up of the Lottery Funded, Youth Music. Advisory and consultancy visits to numerous organisations including the Britten-Pears School, The Sage Centre in Gateshead, the Royal Opera House and all of the London orchestras, took forward, along with numerous school advisory visits, my zeal for bringing the professions of music and education closer together.

So, what forces have sustained and nurtured this belief in the value of music and the importance of the educational process? Why am I still excited by the performances of students and young people? What depths of curiosity compel me to continually ask 'why?' in almost every musical encounter? How does the political imperative drive me to the 'What would happen if....?' question. Like pebbles on a beach, picking up one to examine only reveals another. I'm a beachcomber and, fortunately the landscape is rich with opportunities for reflections.

6.2 L   Judith Webster

Director, Nuance Music Ltd
Course Leader, PGDip Creative Leadership, Royal College of
Music, London

*For Judith Webster her early career in music therapy brought together two
important aspects of her life in a creative context – her love of music and
her interest in working in challenging social contexts. When she was
appointed in 1993 to run the new Community and Education Department for
the Royal Philharmonic Orchestra, she found that her experience in music
therapy affected the way she approached the training of professional
musicians, the way she set up community projects, the nature of her own
musical involvement and the way she shaped programmes for different
organisations. Subsequently all her work has been influenced by these
connected strands of experience.*

No one was more surprised than me when I had a career change and moved
from music therapy to running a new Community and Education Department
for the Royal Philharmonic Orchestra (RPO). Six months previously I had
not known that such departments existed. However, it turned out that my
training and experience as a music therapist was totally relevant to the work
I subsequently led, and it hugely informed my approach to everything I set
up from that point.

On arrival at the RPO, the first key decision I made was to provide
professional development to the orchestral musicians who chose to be
involved in community and education work for the first time. Rather than
teach them how to be a teacher or workshop leader, and provide them with
lots of tricks and clapping games which they could use in workshops, I
decided to focus on their own musical skills – giving them opportunities to
learn to improvise, to work without notation, creatively, flexibly and freely
with other musicians from different traditions. Remembering my own fear of
improvisation when first training as a music therapist, I considered it vital to
support them through this process by doing it with them. I was more familiar
with improvisation than they were, albeit a less skilled player. I felt
instinctively that I needed to make a relationship with each of them in music
as they would relate to me differently than if our relationship was one of
'management and player'. This was one of the most important decisions I
made, and enabled me to gain their respect, and to challenge entrenched
views about management and what to expect from me. It also allowed them
to realise that I understood the implications of what I was asking of them,
understood their fears and demons. As a result, they respected me and we
began our journey of discovery together. As an orchestral musician myself, I
gave a great deal of thought to the roles they play within the orchestra, how
the psychology of, for example, a rank and file violinist might differ from that
of a principal trombonist and how these might affect their responses to an

improvisation workshop with colleagues. An important influence on my approach to setting up this new work was therefore my own awareness of personal identity, how it was expressed in music and how to work with this creatively.

The other key decision I made was that I should understand the core identity of the orchestra itself – its DNA, its essence, what made it tick and how that showed in its playing, how it collectively expressed itself. In my judgement, it was this that would determine the kind of work we should initiate in a community setting. It would guide me in setting up projects – who with, what we would do well, how we would approach the work. Once again, this proved to be a crucial decision which affected the type of challenges I offered the musicians through their evolving community engagement and context. I used my music therapist's insight to steer their individual and collective professional/personal development. Through continually reassessing this, I was able to unlock high levels of motivation and watch them grow into new creative roles, with a sense of achievement and pride in their work. They re-connected with the reasons they took up music in the first place, sought out musical and social challenges and faced new situations with relish and commitment. This was the opposite of what I had been told to expect from them.

Another unflinching belief was that if I focused on the development of the musicians themselves, ensuring that they never had a bad experience in what was a new and daunting type of work for them, and that they were fulfilled and challenged as musicians and people, then this would inevitably result in a high quality of work, and that their engagement with external partners would have integrity and depth. This absolutely proved to be the case and I watched as hardened professional musicians from what was regarded at the time as the 'cinderella orchestra' in London, opened their eyes and ears to new experiences, researched unfamiliar musics and communities in preparation for new projects, and volunteered for more opportunities which would extend their horizons further. I am absolutely convinced that my belief in them, and the possibility for change, was a key factor in that change becoming a reality. I empathised with them – as an orchestral musician myself – and did not take on the negative expectations which were handed to me. Just like in a music therapy session, I took them as they were, accepted them and allowed them to find new ways of existing and coping with their professional lives.

Once I had tuned into the DNA of the orchestra, I then needed to create appropriate and developmental opportunities for the players to work in. In my assessment, the orchestra was earthy, uncompromising, gutsy, passionate, and possessing huge warmth and compassion. So I sought out challenging social contexts where our work could question the status quo and make a difference. The orchestra proved to work best when working with offenders, young homeless people, children with special needs and their families, and in tough youth club settings. They were fantastic at working with underdogs – and could relate to the psychology of their situation in their own way.

In this testimony, I have only really considered the work as it relates to the development of the musicians. However, it should be said that my music therapy background also informed my approach to setting up external partnerships. It was imperative that the community partners, just like the orchestral musicians, had a clear and honest understanding of what we were trying to achieve together, what we could not achieve and how we might expect to reach our shared goals. Key to this was ensuring that the musicians and partners all understood their different roles, and respected their own skills as well as those of the partners.

The other key area influenced by my music therapy background was the content of the artistic and musical experience itself, in a community based context. This has come into focus even more strongly for me now that I am involved in the training of workshop leaders in my current role at the Royal College of Music. My music therapy training taught me to explore a wide range of musical tools and devices in order to connect with a client. These took the form of diverse musical idioms, different tonalities and harmonic progressions, the conscious use of different intervals for different effects, different timbres, styles and rhythmic patterns, the use of different types of instruments for different reasons rather than random selection and so on. I was very conscious of the need to provide differentiated musical challenges for individual members of a workshop group, whilst maintaining the engagement of the larger group. Although the music therapy setting differs from that of a group workshop, and it is inappropriate to work to the same intensity, I have always felt that it is important to enable any creative team to take collective responsibility for the needs of a group and to find ways of challenging them appropriately, without undermining the overall focus and leadership. I therefore tried to draw musicians' attention to this responsibility and to lead by example through my own engagement with the creative process and participants' needs as a part of that team. This heightened awareness by the musicians results in greater impact, stronger support for the artistic leader, and more effective learning experiences for participants.

There is so much more I could say regarding my views on what constitutes quality within the context of community engagement. However, space does not permit further exploration. Although I have now been working in community contexts with professional musicians for far longer than I worked as a music therapist, it is still my music therapy training which is the strongest influence on my continuing work, and it is my continued emphasis on my own personal development that enables me to call myself a reflective practitioner, constantly challenging other musicians to challenge themselves.

6.2 M   Robert Wells

Programme Leader, Professional Pathways, Guildhall School of Music & Drama, London

Robert Wells is a creative music leader whose experience is rooted in different musical and cultural contexts. Whilst teaching at NewVIc sixth form college in East London, he first collaborated with Guildhall Connect and subsequently moved to the Guildhall School where he is especially interested in developing pathways and progression routes that will allow students from a range of musical and social backgrounds to enter the School. His joint Case Study with Heloisa Feichas describes introducing the principles of Guildhall Connect to the Music School at the Federal University of Minas Gerais in Brazil.

Context

I feel that the contexts in which we are raised have a huge effect upon who we become as adults, our values and our beliefs. As a child, I experienced cultural displacement from two very different vantage points. I was initially brought up in an affluent area of Hampshire but didn't have the same background as many of the children in my school. My parents had both been forced to leave school at 14 and did not have 'professional jobs' like many of my friend's parents. My range of experiences was limited in comparison to many other children: for instance, we didn't take regular holidays abroad; on the last day of term I didn't have flash toys to bring to school; the types of people I came into contact with via my parents were quite different from those other children met; and my parent's expectations of the type of life I may lead as an adult were far more limited than the aspirations of many of my peer's parents.

At the age of 11 all of this was turned on its head, when my family returned to where my mum had been brought up. The area we moved to had high unemployment due to a local dockyard that had previously been the main source of employment, being shut down. The area also had the 11+ system and I was 'selected for non-selective education'. Within my new school environment I was again a cultural vagrant but now for completely the reverse reasons. This experience profoundly changed my understanding of identity, belonging and the world in general.

A few years later, at the age of 23, having recently completed a masters degree in music, I was again made to think about how powerful the context of your upbringing is, in deciding your path in life. Searching for work I stumbled upon a job teaching music in a prison. I didn't particularly want to teach at this point, however with few other options I accepted the job. With virtually no teaching experience and little sense of what to expect or what I should do, I began teaching prisoners. What I discovered shocked and changed me. I began with a de-humanized view of the inmates, based upon films and the press. I expected to discover 'evil' people but this could not have been further from the truth. I quickly began to realize how like me my students were. It dawned upon me that if I had been brought up by different parents in a different location I could well have been on the other side of the desk. I was also struck by just how much wasted talent there was in the prison, how much our society suffers from not using this talent and how simple and yet complex this situation is to change.

Expectation

Other's expectations affect our achievements. I believe that we create our own personal reality; however, we also exist within the realities of others. Although there is a conflict, the impressions they have of us profoundly affect the opportunities that we are offered. There was a study done in the 1960s during which researchers fooled teachers into believing that a few, seemingly unremarkable students, had very high IQs. Within a small space of time, the highlighted children began to out-perform their peers. The only explanation for this is that the teacher's expectation of the young people had suddenly shifted.

I think I witnessed this first hand, in both positive and negative ways, during my schooling. The school I moved to, aged 11, was failing in virtually every imaginable way. The teachers had very low expectations of the students and were consequently failing them. This was doubly unfair given that many of the students could ill afford to be let down at school given the additional social baggage they carried. When I was in Year 10 the school was 're-launched'; we were given a new building and an almost complete change of staff. This change led directly to me becoming a musician.

From quite a young age I had always had a keyboard in my room. I enjoyed playing on it and although I didn't have lessons, I had taught myself to read music, play by ear and compose music. I loved the time I spent playing; it was a retreat from the world and a safe space, often meditative in nature. Music was the thing I enjoyed doing most. Despite this, I had never considered music as a profession. It was way outside my parent's experience and music lessons, like most lessons at my school, were far from informative.

When the school was re-opened we got a new music teacher. Unlike my previous teachers he was inspirational. Realizing that we were all likely to fail the music course we were doing, he started after school clubs and even opened the school on several Sundays for us to have additional lessons. Interestingly, given the lack of interest most of us had for school, the majority of the class turned up to these additional sessions. After about a term he pulled me to one side and asked if I would be interested in studying A Level music at the school, a course he was looking to introduce the following year. His belief that we could meet his high expectations, that we could be successful, was exceptionally powerful and transformed my life.

The belief that others can achieve great things if placed in a supportive environment has informed and affected my own teaching. This was probably most evident whilst I worked at NewVIc, a sixth form college in East London. At the prison I had become frustrated by the penal system. I had seen one inmate pass through the entire system three times in less than a year, which made me realize that prison more normally habituated than reformed inmates. I felt that I needed to work with young people at risk of entering the prison system before they got to that point.

NewVIc was a revelation....an oasis. The college, only a few years old, was in the heart of London's East End, which is deprived and diverse in equal measure. The attitude of the tutors was that the students could achieve any goal they set themselves. As staff we were encouraged to try new ideas, challenging ourselves, the students and a number of orthodoxies surrounding how best to teach the performing arts. This environment proved to be hugely beneficial both to the students and the staff.

Transformative power of the arts

I am not a natural scholar. At school I was prone to daydreaming, mostly favouring my imagination over the classroom. As a child I loved inventing things and was very happy playing with lego, sketching, writing poetry and composing music. I was less happy sat at a desk and largely opted out of the thing called 'work'. I didn't particularly enjoy primary school either socially or academically; this was much the same at secondary school. It was not until I was 16 that anyone spotted quite how creative I was but since then the change within me has been closer to revolution than evolution.

Although I had experienced first hand how powerful art can be, I didn't realize that it could have the same affect upon others until I began working in prison. One of the courses I led for young offenders involved 'making a band' in a month. Whilst learning to play an instrument or sing was an important part of the process, I was fascinated to see the change in the student's behaviour from the first session to the last. Session one always involved a lot of disagreements and swearing, without focusing on group skills. All these issues naturally disappeared as students became engaged in collective music making. Experience of this environment clearly benefited students, but it also profoundly changed my perception of music.

I explored this idea even further whilst at NewVIc. Within the Performing Arts Department all of the staff had creative backgrounds and were practicing artists. Our approach to teaching was therefore to deliver courses as if the young people we were working with were an arts company. The curriculum was filled with large-scale public performances, often in high profile venues, frequently involving partnerships with outside artists and arts organizations. We expected students to perform as professional artists, in a curriculum based upon shared exploration and risk. As a teacher/artist I was massively fulfilled; I had the opportunity to create amazing projects with freedom and funding rarely seen amongst arts professionals. More importantly, I was aware of the visible and massive effect this had on the students. The changes were not subtle; students who had arrived at the college with a few E and G grades at GCSE left three years later as highly motivated, high achieving young people. A large number of these young people now work in the arts and have successful careers in their own right.

The importance of providing access to high quality arts opportunities is now central to my work. I think it is important that these opportunities are as inclusive as possible; however, all too often we limit the scope of this type of work to young people. Frequently in our society there is a focus on 'our future', without realizing that without opening these opportunities to everyone the 'future' will remain within the 0-16 age group. NewVIc was inclusive and I saw the impact of having a diverse range of people working together in a supportive and co-operative manner. I was also lucky enough to work on some projects that involved a mix of people from a variety of backgrounds and ages. In response to our divisionary media, which bases its income upon highlighting the differences between varying groups, publicizing the rare occasions these divisions lead to violent acts, we need to bring people from different backgrounds, ages and races together. I honestly feel that this is the thing that the arts do better than any other media. I would even go as far as suggesting that this is the purpose of the arts, so far as they have any purpose.

How is it that we damage others with art?

Having had amazing experiences through my A level and undergraduate music courses, the experience of my masters degree was shocking and damaging, nearly making me give up music all together. My masters was the first time I was really confronted with strict cultural elitism. I was so happy to be doing music when I started my A level, that I had not really questioned why my study was dominated with music largely outside of my day-to-day cultural experience. During my BA I went to a relatively forward thinking college and was allowed a large degree of freedom to explore ideas and styles that interested me. When I was asked to try new things out it was done under the umbrella of broadening my musical palette, and I was able to understand how doing so would benefit me. This freedom was lacking during my masters, during which time I was expected to conform to a mono cultural ivory tower imbued music style. There was little or no attention to 'my voice' as a composer, to my artistic interests or my imagination. I was taught techniques and expected to accept and use them within my music. There was clear prejudice against anything not describable as dissonant art music. It was off limits to admit considering the audience's response to your music, or for that matter, the performers. Within this environment I began to struggle. Having started the course focused on being a composer, the year ended with me simply wishing to pass the qualification. I did not understand how such a disconnection between 'university music' and 'real music' had come about. It appeared that the purpose and context of music was never considered. Coming from this experience, my time teaching in prison which followed this course was yet more profound and answered many questions I had been contemplating.

Over the last few years I have found myself meeting increasing numbers of people who think like me, and more importantly, have begun to gain the influence to change things. When I was asked to join the music staff at the Guildhall School of Music & Drama, a little over 3 years ago, I knew that I would be culturally displaced. In my opinion Conservatoires suffer from a number of ills. Despite the huge changes in music and the music 'industry' during the 20th century, subject areas and pedagogical strategies have remained virtually unchanged over the last 100 years. Students are hot-housed in a way that separates them from mainstream culture. There is a macho attitude surrounding the music making, with certain issues being 'off limits'; physical and psychological pain are to be expected. Things are approached in a quantitative manner; students discuss how many hours they practice rather than the quality of the practice in which they are engaging. Technique is a focus and personal engagement with the music through more creative means is somehow lost. Rather than considering the 'value added' to students attending the School, there is a culture of sink or swim, of judgement rather than learning. Students are de-humanized and treated as 'musical automaton'. Successful and unsuccessful alike incur damage to their psyche. I feel that this is a perverse use of music and something that our culture should feel ashamed of having produced.

This culture is changing at the Guildhall and the School is seen as a pathfinder institution for many other conservatoires world wide. We are running some highly innovative programmes that deal with the issues above. The School is heavily involved with the wider community, working with a range of partners to blur the sense of separation between the School and the rest of the society. Pathways and progression routes are being developed that will allow students from a range of musical and social backgrounds to enter the School and excel. World wide there is interest in the techniques we are developing. Our approaches are beginning to be trialled in a number of schools and will have a lasting affect on music education and more importantly on the role of music in our society.

6.2 N   Marga Wobma-Helmich

Director of Education, Participation and Programming, National
Ballet and Nederlandse Opera, Amsterdam

*Marga Wobma-Helmich led and developed the education programme of the
Concertgebouw in Amsterdam. Her department of more than 10 people
reached out to some 30,000 children every season and consisted of four
areas: programmes for schoolchildren: primary and secondary schools;
training programmes for primary school teachers; participation programmes;
courses for adults. On 1 October 2009 she started as Director of Education,
Participation and Programming at the National Ballet and Nederlandse
Opera, Amsterdam.*

During the last few months I've cursed Peter Renshaw quite often. When
Peter asks you a question there is no way you can or want to say no. He's
much too charismatic and wise to be able to refuse any request. The
question was to write a personal testimony. 'It may be partly biographical –
your story – illustrating what drives/motivates you – those significant
moments that have helped to shape who you are and what you believe in. In
other words, those things which underpin and give a direction to your work
(Peter Renshaw, 31 May 2009)'.

I was feeling a lot of resistance to writing a personal testimony and I needed
to sort out why this feeling was so strong before starting the actual writing.
Finding the answer to this question gave me a clearer view on my motivation
in my work, as well as the philosophy behind it. My main objection to writing
a personal testimony is that I'm a strong believer that as an arts manager it
should never be about you as a person. I love to speak about my work but I
don't feel comfortable speaking about myself when a larger audience is
listening, or in this case, reading. As an arts manager – and for me in life
generally – your ego shouldn't get in the way. This is partly a natural
awareness and partly developed during my life in which I've been active
exploring eastern philosophy and spirituality. But I realise that most things
happening in life are the result of human action, and that who you are and
what drives you have an important impact on how you relate to other people
and how you manage to do your work. It can be interesting for other people
to know about these aspects from people who are working in a field you're
interested in yourself. That's why I do end up writing this personal
testimony!

The driving force in my life and work doesn't feel like 'a force'. What I do is a
natural way of existing. For me, music is the language that is most related to
all different kinds of aspects of being a human being than any other
language. It started in an active way with singing in a youth choir and
playing the harp and as a listener to all different kinds of music. The house
where I grew up was filled with music with my parents playing the piano and

singing, and my sisters playing the piano and violin. The question whether I wanted to play an instrument was never asked; the only question was which instrument I wanted to play. Asking the first question would have felt the same as asking if I wanted to grow up. It's a useless question because growing up is a given fact of life. Just like making music. The only question is how you want to grow up or how you want to become musically active.

In the same way that music was a natural part of my life, so was organising. I was on the board of the choir and a youth organisation during my secondary school period and continued being involved in organising projects when I was a student at conservatory. I loved being involved and making things happening. After a few years it became clear that my talent at organising was of much more use than my talent at playing the harp. This resulted in a position at the conservatory, organising concerts, gigs, projects and festivals. During my years at the conservatory I started to become more and more involved with the primary and secondary school for ballet and music which were part of the institute. This brought me back to my previous goal: if I had not been selected for the conservatory, I would have studied to become a school teacher.

An invitation to replace the artistic assistant of the general director of the Concertgebouw during her maternity leave gave a temporary new direction to my career. This was followed with the question to set up the education department at the Concertgebouw: and I was back 'home'. Whilst working there I learned so much about the field of music education and music in general. I had the chance to see so many examples of what music can mean in a person's life and to exchange ideas with people working in this field. It helped me to give direction to the education work at the Concertgebouw which over the years has become much more about involving people in an active way, trying to make it possible for people to experience the joy of making music as a starting point for exploring music as a listener. To do this within an institute where music is performed to such a high artistic level brings two worlds together, which is important for both worlds. Communicating through music, as with communication in general, should always be two-way communication.

What keeps me motivated to do my work is that my energy comes from a natural resource. I love what I do and I have the opportunity to keep on developing in many different ways – as a creator, as a facilitator and as a leader. Quality is always an issue in all areas – for the performances and projects, for the preparation, in how you communicate your ideals, in how you try to motivate people to join you on this journey. It's not that I believe music is the only or strongest language in making the world a place worth living in. It's because music is the language which enables me to communicate and make a contribution to our society.

6.3   Case studies

6.3 A   Eugene van Erven
Researcher, Community Art Lab, Utrecht
Associate Professor, Theatre Department, Utrecht University

*Eugene van Erven lectures in the Theatre Department of Utrecht University;
he directs a triennial International Festival of Community Arts in Rotterdam
and is a researcher in the Community Art Lab Utrecht. He is a board
member and artistic consultant of Stut Theatre, Utrecht and the Rotterdam
Neighbourhood Theatre. His Case Study of the Story Kitchen, Haarlem
presents an authentic example of community art.*

My name is Eugene van Erven. I am 54. Professionally I am a theatre
scholar, drama teacher, community art organizer. Privately, I am a musician
in a latin band, a sportsman, father to an almost 17-year-old son and
husband to his mother, a nurse who migrated from the Caribbean to Holland
37 years ago. Between 2004 and 2006 we lived and worked for two years in
Aruba, her native island. Her mother had migrated there from a small town
in Surinam in December 1943 to work as a live-in maid for the family of an
educated Surinamese man who had been recruited to work in the Lago oil
refinery. My own parents, the son and daughter of a gardener and
electrician respectively, also migrated, albeit less spectacularly. In 1964
they moved with my brother, two sisters and myself – heavy dialects and all
- from a small rural village a stone-throw away from the Belgian border, to
what to our eyes was a bustling metropole: Holland's fourth largest city,
Utrecht. From walking to school on a sandy road through the wheat fields I
had to learn to quickly lose my odd accent to be accepted on the streets of
an urban working-class neighbourhood, where we had moved into an
upstairs two-storey residence with no garden or balcony. I quickly adapted
and learned to love the city. I believe that experience lay the foundation for
a life of intercultural communication and, together with the village theatre
that my uncles and aunts were involved in back in the rural south, for my
lifelong interest in community art. I believe in the power of art made in close
collaboration with the people who live in these places and for whom active
involvement in the arts is not self-evident. After many years of worldwide
travel, ever higher education, and moving up to middle-class status, I still
identify with them.

I do not have the space here to elaborate on the many potent examples I
have seen of community art under dictatorships, or indeed on the violent
deaths of some artists I knew, who were killed because they were too good
at their work. The contextual challenges of community art in the Netherlands
in 2009 are obviously far less dangerous but not less complex. And even

today it helps to exchange experiences with colleagues working in, for example, Peruvian slums. They marvel at Dutch urban regeneration projects (which, to their minds, demolish perfectly fine apartment complexes) or artists complaining about subsidies (which do not even exist in their country).

Today, I lecture in the Theatre Department of Utrecht University, direct a triennial International Festival of Community Arts in Rotterdam (ICAF), and conduct research through a city-funded outfit we call the Community Art Lab (CAL). Through CAL we gather basic information on as many Dutch community arts projects as we possibly can and store it in a data base (www.communityartdatabase.nl). From that general collection we (that is me and my part-time assistant Margreet) select a number of projects that we try to monitor with greater precision. Since mid-2006 we have documented approximately ten such enterprises. Some texts and video clips from this research can be found on the English-language pages of www.community-art.nl.

When it comes to determining quality in community art my main point of reference is community-based theatre, the workings and effects of which I have witnessed first-hand through my association as a board member and artistic consultant with Stut Theatre (Utrecht, established in 1977) and the Rotterdam Neighbourhood Theatre (est. 1992). Both these professional theatre organizations create original plays with working-class and immigrant residents of urban areas that are culturally and artistically underserviced. The mutual care and trust generated in their work and the power of the resulting shows is impressive. Audience surveys focusing on identification reveal that their plays truly communicate with their intended audiences. For the participants whose lives form the inspiration for the scripts in which they themselves perform, our video documentation, in-depth interviews and long-term monitoring indicate an even greater impact. So we know that this kind of theatre works in community settings, as long as the professionals involved (who direct, write, and produce) are very flexible indeed, are unambitious when it comes to mainstream status, can quickly establish trust and confidence through a gregarious and genuinely caring attitude, and can muster deep-felt concern for the often complicated lives of the people they work with. They must also be high calibre artists who possess the ability to shape the material that comes from the participants into exciting and meaningful products that those actively involved can be proud of and that contain local cultural parameters so that they communicate with a public for which they are primarily intended.

Over the years, I have come across many projects that label themselves as 'community arts'. In the worst cases these are concept-driven, autonomously created site-specific works in which a working-class or immigrant location is used as exotic backdrop and some locals are fitted in as token participants. The cultural parameters that shape the style and form of such projects are alien to such places and to the people who live there. Audiences and critical acclaim are recruited downtown. In the best cases I know, however, an entire neighbourhood is permanently infected with the arts activities, which are sustained well after the professional artists, who have propelled it in the first place, have left.

I want to introduce you now to what I consider one such good case, which is quite different from the community-devised theatre I referred to earlier. I will also attempt to explain why I believe it to be so good. It is called The Story Kitchen. It is situated in the so-called 'slaughterhouse' district, a one-hundred-year-old working-class neighbourhood in the east of Haarlem, an area with approximately 3,000 houses that, since the 1980s, has become multicultural. The Story Kitchen is the brainchild of visual artist/theatre maker Titia Bouwmeester and musician Ted van Leeuwen, who both worked for many years with the internationally renowned site-specific performance group Dogtroep. This company specialized in spectacular, technically sophisticated colourful outdoor shows in industrial or otherwise colourless sites, but rarely created these short-term interventions with local participation.

Since they left Dogtroep in 2003 and organized their own company, called Vijfde Kwartier ('5th Quarter'), Bouwmeester and van Leeuwen have been collaborating increasingly intensively with local people and their stories. For several years they did this work wherever subsidy happened to be available, but they became increasingly frustrated with the lack of interest on the part of project sponsors and municipalities to continue the work after they had left. Working in a working-class neighbourhood in Delft in 2007 served as a catalyst:

> Delft was one of the first times we worked in an actual neighbourhood. Before that, we worked in more enclosed environments, like a hospital, a prison (both with Dogtroup), a centre for asylum seekers, a psychiatric ward, a home for the elderly. In those places people already share a situation in common. Not in a neighbourhood, which is diffuse and where everyone wants something else. In Delft I discovered that you need to do more than turn people into documentary makers of their own lives. You also need to give people direct influence on their own existence. And because the people who live there are so diffuse, you also need much longer than the three months we had, to truly get to know the people, to generate reliable local support for the work, to find out what they and what you want and what is possible, in short, before you can begin to make something together. (Personal interview with Titia Bouwmeester, 28 October 2008)

A crucial success factor in this kind of work, Bouwmeester discovered, was to be frequently and very visibly present in the location. This is why they jumped at the opportunity when they were invited to do a new project in Haarlem's slaughterhouse district, a place they could ride their bikes to from their home elsewhere in the same city. This time, Bouwmeester also wanted to train key people who were already involved in social initiatives embedded in the area. Two women, Geja Muffels and Rozine Salah, were driving forces in a new community centre for migrant women when, in December 2007, they ran into Bouwmeester, who was exploring the neighbourhood on her bicycle. Muffels and Salah have been key figures in The Story Kitchen since then. A third gem was Ruud Barnhorn, a young and energetic primary school headmaster who had been appointed Project Director of a new so-called Broad School. A Broad School is a mixture of a community centre and a primary school, but the one he had in mind would also include a workshop for artists and a community kitchen. On the recommendation of Muffels he decided to ask Bouwmeester to help design the facility. Through their constructive, creative, and reliable participation in the planning meetings, the artists organically met and gained the trust of other stakeholders, such as the local representative of the public housing corporation 'PreWonen', politicians, social workers, the chairman of the informal neighbourhood council, and the editor of a digital neighbourhood newspaper. As a result, The Story Kitchen literally grew along with the Broad School and generated broad support from official organizations and regular residents. For 15 months now, the project has been a constant process of fine-tuning, adjusting the planning, and trial and error, explained Bouwmeester: "this work is continually searching for where the energy is and then to build on that and to place your personal ambitions as an artist on the backburner" (ibid).

Constantly fostering an ever stronger relationship with stakeholders and seducing neighbourhood residents to become actively involved, The Story Kitchen started in April 2008 with a series of pilot storytelling encounters in an empty school building a few blocks away from where the new Broad School would be located. During several afternoons, civil servants, social workers, housing corporation representatives and women from Geja and Rozine's 'Mother Centre' drank tea, sampled home-made Middle Eastern snacks and shared stories connected to recipes. They were seated at long tables surrounded by recycled kitchen cabinets ('Story Cabinets') filled with ten television monitors connected to DVD players on which short documentaries made by children about their mothers were looped. In essence, this was an artistically shaped dialogue which explored social, cultural and difference of status and power. The pilot effectively convinced stakeholders to continue with The Story Kitchen and to invite 5th Quarter a role in designing the Broad School. The tangible result of this partnership was the inclusion of two workshop spaces for art, a large kitchen operated by the Mother Centre, and a spacious central area with tables and chairs that could easily be converted into a performance space.

Broad School 'De Hamelink' was officially opened on 11 October 2008 in a spectacular event orchestrated by 5th Quarter. The playing ground was filled with 600 flags made by women from the neighbourhood under guidance of several visual artists. The schoolyard orchestra, run by former friends of 5th Quarter from the Dogtroep days, had created percussion instruments from recycled materials with the primary school children. They performed along with five professional musicians including a sas-player from the nearby mosque. A choir of elderly folk from the area sang a specially composed song. The kitchen was in full swing with cooks from many different cultural backgrounds turning out a variety of snacks. Many hundreds of people showed up, thanks to 5th Quarter's own publicity campaign, the mobilizing efforts of the housing corporation, welfare agencies, and neighbourhood volunteers, and that other unpredictable success factor – good weather.

Between October and December, visual artists then went into the classrooms to work with children on six-week project cycles, not as teachers but as artists with a great deal of freedom to experiment. Another visual artist was put in charge of a workshop to artistically shape tablecloths of recycled fabric and family album photographs printed on textile. Bouwmeester and van Leeuwen started to film portraits of women preparing (and talking about) their favourite dish. Sometimes by zooming in on hands only, this allowed them also to include Muslim women who otherwise might not have participated. From 10 through 13 December all of these activities culminated in eight public neighbourhood meals (lunch and dinner), which were all sold out.

Seated in De Hamelink's central meeting area at tables covered with the most fantastic table cloths (some of which even included pieces of original wedding dresses), visitors were treated to a screening of the elaborate preparation of a Moroccan appetizer accompanied by two musicians playing live music. Towards the end of the 5-minute documentary the actual smells of the dish being prepared on the screen began to emerge from the kitchen. When the film ended, the kitchen doors opened and the dish in question was brought out in sufficient quantities to serve everyone. The main course (Kurdish) and desert (traditional Dutch) were offered in a similar combination of film, music, smell and taste. Simple, effective, and very meticulously produced with substantial local involvement, it provided once again artistically-shaped dialogic space that mobilized all the senses, generating conversations that would not have happened otherwise.

By this time, many people in the neighbourhood knew who Titia and Ted and 5th Quarter were. They had been visibly present in the Hamelink a few days a week, uninterruptedly since the summer. They were there when parents dropped their children off to school, when middle aged people dropped off their parents to attend the day-care for people with Alzheimer's, and when migrant women from the Mother Centre showed up to cook in the kitchen or simply chat over coffee or tea. Inspired by The Story Kitchen neighbourhood meal in December, some of these women took the initiative to start cooking lunches. These have now become a very popular Wednesday afternoon event. There is even talk of setting up a small cooperative catering business.

Meanwhile, with the support of the provincial archive, the Slaughterhouse neighbourhood association, and the district's digital newspaper, which started in February 2009, 5th Quarter continued its quest for local stories through a photo project. Clustered in thematic groups, former employees of the slaughterhouse and of the nearby railway repair shop, former shop owners and others were invited to bring old photos to the Hamelink on Wednesdays. Incredibly, people came in droves. Word of mouth, countless telephone calls, announcements in the digital newspaper, and the sheer desire to meet with people one had not seen for years, explained this unanticipated success. Tangibly, this phase of the project yielded a beautifully shaped book with photographs and stories that was presented to Haarlem's deputy mayor on May 9th. An exposition of these photos and stories was opened in De Hamelink on the same day, again accompanied by live music and with some of the stories being read out loud live by their owners. In the middle of the exposition was a tree created by primary school children under guidance of visual artist Ulrike Bartels. It had tiny speakers suspended from the branches from which audio recordings of some of the original stories could be heard.

On Saturday, June 13th, I witnessed a concert in the park. The programme included children's songs from many cultures, which had been recorded along with the photo stories between February and April. Professionally re-arranged and supported by a live eight-piece band, fifteen of these songs were performed by primary school children, a Turkish teenager and Dutch, Iraqi and Afghan adult women.

After the summer 5th Quarter will work towards a large-scale apotheosis of The Story Kitchen in the form of a roaming site-specific performance of some of the most powerful stories it has collected so far, set in actual living rooms throughout the neighbourhood. Knowing Bouwmeester and van Leeuwen by now, it will be visually stunning, (probably including still and moving images), musical, literally tasty, meticulously produced, and emotionally moving, through the respectful representation of local stories that matter. The event will very likely generate great pride among residents, who will, I suspect, regard it as at least partly owned by them. And when, after November, Bouwmeester and van Leeuwen move on to other projects, artistic activities will continue in the Slaughterhouse district, if Geja Muffels, Rozine Salah and school director Ruud Barnhorn have anything to with it.

Surely, a crucial success factor in this project is the sheer luck of having three energetic and visionary people like Muffels, Salah and Barnhorn in the neighbourhood, along with an open-minded editor of a digital newspaper servicing the area, an active residents' association, and a cooperative public housing authority. Another success factor is the decision by Bouwmeester and van Leeuwen to visibly embed themselves in the neighbourhood and their ability to convince key stakeholders to include them in the design of the Broad School, which gave them a strategically central basis to operate from. Their genuine interest in people, the unwavering energy and artistic professionalism they put into designing and producing activities and events, and their flexibility to change concepts and plans when the circumstances required it, did the rest. Building sustainable alliances with individuals and key organizations in the neighbourhood over a two-year-period, and accumulating trust and expanding local support with each new activity, are keys to making the site specific performance next October (2009) not only the conclusion of a successful creative partnership between professional artists and a variety of local entities, but also the beginning of sustained creativity in the slaughterhouse district for many years to come. "The neighbourhood should be able to design and produce its own cultural climaxes from that point on. Only then The Story Kitchen will have really mattered," claims Barnhorn (personal interview, 28 October 2008).

I intend to test Barnhorn's challenge, for sustainability is indeed one of the most powerful indicators of community art. The quality of these projects cannot be judged by assessing a single performance alone with criteria borrowed from a mainstream arts discourse. Of course one can judge the quality of the song arrangements and the technical ability of the professional musicians involved in the concert on Saturday 13 June, but one should also look at their sensitivity towards the neighbourhood singers, and how the songs communicated with this particular audience. Furthermore, one should consider how the concert fitted into the sub-projects that preceded it and how it will feed into others that are still to follow (like concerts in all of Haarlem's primary schools). The outsider's artistic assessment of these kinds of projects, in short, should be balanced by an assessment of the social and ethical quality of the work viewed in its totality. Such an overall view is not complete unless it is informed by the perspectives of participants, intended local audiences and other stakeholders. Community arts require a new kind of critic – and new kinds of artists.

6.3 B Heloisa Feichas

Professor Adjunto, School of Music, Federal University of Minas Gerais, Brazil

Robert Wells

Programme Leader, Professional Pathways, Guildhall School of Music & Drama, London

PROJECT CONNECT IN BRAZIL

Introduction

This case study explores the experience of 24 undergraduate students from the Music School at the Federal University of Minas Gerais (EMUFMG), Brazil, enrolled in the optional course 'Music Education and Social Projects'. Designed around principles developed by the Guildhall School's Connect team, the course had three related aims:

1. To encourage students to consider the variety of roles musicians can have in society;
2. To train undergraduate music students as creative music facilitators able to work in a diverse range of social contexts;
3. To create sustainable links between the University and social projects;

The course was delivered by Robert Wells from the Guildhall School of Music & Drama and Heloisa Feichas, lecturer at EMUFMG.

The idea of bringing this project to a Brazilian reality came from our questioning of the gaps in undergraduate music students' learning. The music school at EMUFMG is based on the European Conservatoire model, a system which is both chronologically and culturally displaced within modern Brazil. The 'master/apprentice' hierarchy, which can encourage reliant behaviour in students, is pervasive. The study of performance, composition and conducting is decontextualized; rooted in the European classical tradition, students explore only a fraction of the diverse musical life of Brazil. There are scarce opportunities for students, including those studying Music Education, to engage practically with the wider society. Collectively these issues frequently prevent students from developing into conscious, self-aware, creative musicians who can positively add to the society of which they are a part. We felt it essential to develop new opportunities for students so that they could explore the connections between their musical interests and the social and cultural landscape of contemporary Brazil.

The introduction of Connect's practices was one way of doing this. Guildhall Connect's work focuses upon collaboration. Participants engage in group composition tasks, collectively creating the music that they perform. These sessions expand a range of intelligences, for instance their interpersonal and musical intelligences.

As students gain a practical and theoretical understanding of Connect's processes there is a natural development of their leadership skills. These skills are transferable to a number of musical, educational and social contexts. This is particularly relevant in Brazil where there has been a steady increase in the number of Brazilian NGOs supporting social projects involving music. These projects frequently engage communities through musical activities, however in many cases the pedagogical approaches are based on old models, frequently involving the reproduction of existing music. We hoped that engaging students in this project would make them re-consider the role of a leader/teacher within both the formal and non-formal educational environment.

Connect in action: the course in UFMG

The group consisted of 24 undergraduate students in their early 20s. There were 10 male and 14 female. 14 students were registered in the Music Education course whereas eight were doing Bachelor degrees in Performance; one was doing Composition, one was enrolled in Conducting and one was on a vocal studies programme. Officially those registered on the Bachelor in Performance play the following: Percussion (1); Flute (3); Harp (1); Piano (2); Cello (1). However, most of the students are multi-instrumentalists, the range of instruments being diverse and including different types of percussion, recorders, escaletta, accordion, cavaquinho, bandolim, viola caipira (10 strings) and glockenspiel.

The course was divided into three parts:

1. Introduction to philosophies underpinning the programme - led by Heloisa Feichas;
2. Intensive month of sessions (8 hours per week) culminating in the delivery of a short project with young people from a social project at the University - led by Robert Wells;
3. Continuation of practical work with increasing reflection, leading to delivery of a second short project, this time as part of a visit to a social project - led by Heloisa Feichas.

The structure of the programme was in part determined by Robert's availability to travel to Brazil. In an ideal world the theoretical and practical aspects would have been more interconnected and the pacing of sessions slightly different. We were concerned about having too much theory at the start of the course and by the timing of the first project.

Students' expectations and identities

In the first session students sat in a circle and were asked to talk about their expectations of the course and question their musical identities. What they expected to develop during the course in terms of knowledge and skills, who they are as musicians, and their future career goals were all explored. They were given time to think about the questions and everyone had his/her turn to speak out. Their responses were recorded. Students were also asked to keep a diary during the course in order to be aware of their learning process and observe their changes.

The students had been told about the aims of the course prior to its commencement, so had a general idea about it's aims. According to their personal musical experiences and backgrounds their expectations and musical interests varied. However, some categories appeared similar for many students. From their responses it was clear that most of them were motivated to develop aural skills. They seemed aware of the need to improve their listening skills including picking music up by ear. All students, even those enrolled in the classical course, expressed high motivation for playing and listening to popular music expanding their knowledge of popular styles. Those students with a particular interest in popular music also tended to stress the importance of performing in groups and made clear that they saw the course as an opportunity to acquire and develop ensembles skills. Actually thirteen members of the group were already engaged in ensembles of different types and stated the benefits of playing together.

Education and social transformation were frequently discussed. Six students were already engaged in different social projects; eight students talked about their interest in music education believing music to be a powerful tool for changing societies. Interestingly, some students who had begun on performance courses had already been considering developing as teachers having engaged in optional music education courses.

Seven students discussed the need to improve their composition/creative skills. Few of the students had experience as individual composers. The idea of composing collectively was quite new for the majority, as was the concept of leading an ensemble engaged in this practice. Improvisation was mentioned as a skill for musicians to develop.

When asked about 'who are you as a musician', most of the students talked about their musical tastes. Out of twenty four students only one affirmed being a 'classical' musician and stated a wish to play in classical orchestras. All of them are passionate about popular music, especially Brazilian popular music. Many students also had mentioned their 'passion' for music. Some of them had started another course in the university but the 'passion' for music was stronger and led them to change courses. 'Passion' was often related to playing an instrument and listening to music. They were asked to keep thinking about their musical identities throughout the course in order to be conscious about who they are, what they would like to change, which skills and knowledge they would like to acquire and how they were changing.

The challenges

Students faced a number of challenges during the course. The programme was demanding in terms of the diversity of skills needed and the group's lack of experience in this area of work. Based upon the experience of delivering similar courses at the Guildhall School and in other similar institutions, certain issues were expected to arise, others were rather more unexpected. Throughout the course situations challenging students most were considered, by the tutors, as areas for learning. These became topics for and helped to shape the practical content of the course.

The ability to make decisions and find consensus was a cornerstone of the course. For many students the level of freedom being encouraged was challenging. Students frequently looked to the tutors for 'the answers' rather than finding their own solutions at the start of the course. They struggled to make independent decisions, and failed to recognize the impact of their decision-making approach on others. There was often an overemphasis on verbal communication leading to unnecessary debate. Rather than trying an idea, the group preference was to debate it over a protracted period, slowing the pace of a session and reducing the overall creativity of the group. Even non-musical tasks, such as separating into small groups, took large amounts of time early on. As these issues arose and students reflected upon them they became increasingly aware of the effect interpersonal skills had on the work they could produce and consequently on their own role within the group.

Structuring ideas and developing musical material also proved challenging. Whilst most students were comfortable composing in the moment, improvising, and 'jamming' together, they did not have the skills needed to create fixed musical ideas. In the first few composition sessions students produced lots of sketches and musical ideas, unfortunately few of these were in any sense 'finished'. Students also found it difficult to conceptualize how different musical ideas could relate to each other or be shaped to create larger musical structures.

Conflicts also arose between students based upon their differing approaches to music. Classically trained students were happiest using questions such as 'which scale should we use?' as the starting point for collaborative composition tasks. In contrast, students with a popular music background preferred to play, allowing the musical direction to be led by the sound of the music being created. As students with different backgrounds were mixed together, this frequently led to students complaining about the approach used by others. These issues diminished as students took a more practical approach towards decision-making: the classically trained students spending less time discussing theoretical issues, and all students being more accepting and aware of their differences.

A big challenge, and area of much debate, was gaining a clear understanding of the role of the leader. At first they associated the concept of leadership to authority; the leader was the person who made decisions. This concept transferred into the classroom, many students considering the role of a teacher to be the person with the answers. In this course emphasis was placed upon students' ideas; their challenges set the agenda for further exploration, and the tutors more frequently asked questions than gave solutions. Because of this many of the students came to challenge their preconceptions of leadership and the role of the teacher in an educational context.

Working with social projects

First experience: at the Music School [1]

We had planned to work with two different social projects to deliver a one-day workshop at the University. During the day students would work with young people from the social projects *Projeto Cariúnas* and *Projeto Corpo Cidadão,* leading an entire day of activities culminating in an early evening concert at the school's concert hall. Due to problems of schedules, *Projeto Corpo Cidadão* could not take part and *Projeto Cariúnas* could only attend during the afternoon. This was a significant constraint which added significant pressure on the undergraduate students to produce something in only a very limited amount of time.

After a collective warm-up the group divided in two. The young people from the social project were quieter than expected, making it difficult to centre the creative process on the young people's ideas; this was particularly apparent in one group where the students struggled to create a melody. Time was a significant factor here; it was difficult for the students to build the relationships necessary to solicit ideas from the young people and consequently there was a tendency from the students to put forward their own ideas. This tested the student's burgeoning interpersonal skills as they attempted to make the young people feel more comfortable.

This was the first time the students had led a creative workshop, and despite a number of challenges, the session was a success. By the end of the creative session strong musical material had been created. The additional time constraints had focussed students thinking on their own interpersonal skills, reinforcing the work done in preceding lessons. The ability to share leadership and trust each other had been critical to the success of the workshop. The following day there was a session to reflect upon the workshop and it was clear that although it had been quite stressful, the students had learnt a lot from the experience.

1 Footage of the session is available at: http://www.youtube.com/user/CulturalAdventurer

Second experience: at 'Projeto Cariúnas'

The first experience with the Social Project *Cariúnas* marked the end of the course with Robert. The students however continued their collaborative composition work, further developing their skills in preparation for a second project, this time visiting *Cariúnas*.

During the second experience all of the students noticed that their skill levels had improved. The sense of collaboration was stronger, they were able to enjoy the process far more and were more satisfied with the musical results. Despite this they still had questions about shared leadership. Even where clear roles had been decided prior to the workshops, those involved felt challenged by the situation. The lack of a central figure was hotly debated. Many students felt that there needed to be a single person leading the process, whilst others thought that taking collective responsibility strengthens the sense of the group.

Outcomes from the evaluation: students' responses

There were two formal moments of evaluation. The first one was after the initial project with *Cariúnas*. Students were asked to divide into three groups and create mind maps focusing on what they felt they had learnt during the course. The main categories that came up from the analysis of the mind map are in the following table in a hierarchical order:

Group 1	Group 2	Group 3
Composition	Composition	Composition (collective)
Leadership	Leadership	General learning
Group working	Music	Group working
Concentration	Teaching	Leadership
Informal learning	Group feeling	Teaching

Within the *Composition* category there were sub-categories such as creativity, originality, connection of ideas, innovation, adapting musically (acceptance of unusual/unexpected material), sense of collective, detaching from your own ideas, language adaptation, contextualization. Improvisation was also mentioned as an important area that had been developed.

When discussing *leadership* students pointed out the importance of learning about humility, patience, sharing, making mistakes, knowing when to be passive and active, being ready to act, developing commitment, listening to others, knowing the limits of leading and being led.

When talking about *group working* students considered all the stages of the process including warming-up, collaborative composition and performance. They learned about the importance of humility, of getting on well with each other, having a good atmosphere, compromising, having responsibility towards the group, coping with adversity, trusting and respecting each other, being comprehensive, tolerant and sensitive to the group, having the ability to listen, knowing the limits of ones action, having positive attitudes and a sense of unity, putting yourself in somebody else's place, having a sense of commitment, developing a sense of the group (group feeling), and having an understanding of musical and technical issues. Students also mentioned the pleasure and satisfaction of working in a group.

Other issues mentioned as important in their learning included concentration, teaching strategies, an awareness of their learning processes, body consciousness and music. They also pointed out some characteristics from informal learning practices such as playing by ear, improvisation, sense of liberty and spontaneity.

The second moment for course evaluation and student self-assessment was in the last session. In a circle again, as in the very first session, each student talked about the impact of having taken part in the course. They were required to reflect upon the process and speak about what they considered most important. The process of collaborative composition was mentioned as the most important thing learnt by most of the group. They stressed many related skills that had been acquired such as being spontaneous, having the freedom to create, improving their listening and compositional skills and respecting others ideas. Almost all the students who already teach have been trying to apply the *Connect* principles and described their experiences as positive though challenging. Leadership concepts are still not clear for the majority of students and in most of the discussions they showed doubts about the leader's role. Despite this most students were highly motivated to keep using the ideas explored during the course.

Conclusions and future plans

The course was initially intended as a single semester programme. Long before the course had finished students asked if it could be extended for a second semester. Students were keen to develop the ensemble that had been created in class wishing to compose and perform together more regularly. A number of the students had become very interested in working in social contexts and had begun volunteering to lead music sessions on social projects. A second semester course has now been written and 22 of the initial 24 students have elected to take the programme.

Connections between the university and several social projects have also been developed. During the second semester programme it is hoped that students will engage in longer placements increasing their skills and creating further links between the young people in the projects and the university. There are also increasing opportunities for leaders from social projects to meet and share their practices due to this work, creating a more interconnected community of music leaders across Belo Horizonte.

6.3 C Anna-Karin Gullberg

Co-leader and Founder, BoomTown Music Education, Borlänge, Sweden

Response to three questions

1   *How do you and others see your 'institution' – a 'family', a 'way of life', a 'learning organisation', a music education programme, a 'conservatoire'?*

This particular question is of course, very, very interesting and I must say that we have had several meetings about exactly this issue! I think that I and my close colleague, Kaj Podgorski, see BoomTown as a family and a way of life: I suppose this is a mixture of the idealistic side of us and the entrepreneurship attitude in us. It is definitely **not** a conservatoire but of course, when I am in my workplace – the School of Music – it is a kind of course package within the field of Music Education. I am also a PhD in Music Education, so my formal legitimacy is within that field. But both Kaj and I in our shared world of 'innovative adventure' do not really care about such formalities. We see things in terms of the big picture, and different forms of legitimacy are just useful ways of giving us the credibility and empowering us to reach our goals.

The 'family' is also quite obvious at the moment since the physical place, BoomTown, is under construction – both in terms of people and buildings. When it has been running for, let's say five more years, what will it be then? Well, I don't know – a semi-institution, maybe? Our hope is that our pedagogical philosophy that supports a learning organisation, self-independence and the students own learning goal and musical taste, can lead to an organisation of learning that does not institutionalise people. But who knows? I think that the BoomTown project and the inventors or creators (Kaj and myself) will also go our separate ways some where during the journey – it probably has to be that way. This is a very personal point of view but I think this is unavoidable when you are the creator of a project.

When it comes to 'others' I think that the students and the community see BoomTown as an exciting music place, with separate activities within the popular music field – networking, business and education. The community politicians also see it as a way of transforming a traditional 'Manchester' working city into a modern city responding to the needs of the 'information society'. It is a brave management in Borlänge that has put a quarter of a billion Skr (approximately £21,000,000) into the music project BoomTown. I can talk mostly from the BoomTown Music Education perspective even though Kaj Podgorski and I are the mental and spiritual leaders of the whole of BoomTown. The other two 'legs', networking and business, have a lot of community work on their agenda, but I am not all that informed about how they really interact with other community actors. In the School of Music the impressions and opinions are at least three-fold. The most interesting aspect of our educational activities is the progressive, new thinking. This is supported by experimental projects like BoomTown Music Education (BTME) which can never be long-term. The third response is plain un-interest, as developments are seen as too threatening and foreign compared with the conservatoire tradition. I don't think what we do will become a programme either – it is a couple of years in the students lives and careers, a few years in their musical journey and not a vocational programme.

When I talk about BoomTown in research conferences and music networks I get a lot of interest and questions about the pedagogical design. Some teachers also ask what I will do when 'Högskoleverket' (the institution that investigates and judge higher education quality) comes to see what we do. I say that I will greet them and will be very satisfied to be able to present a higher education that really lives the standards of higher education! I think I can say that the reception of BTME has been very positive in every presentation – both because of its uniqueness and also because as a researcher in music I managed to put the results of my thesis into practice and created a new possibility for other people. BTME could probably be a more well known 'brand' these days, but the problem for me is to get time for writing, publishing and presenting!

According to Kaj, the triple helix – community, business and education under the same umbrella – also generates positive reactions and curiosity amongst people from the music business. Probably there are also people who see BoomTown as a crazy project that steals community funding from health care and other welfare institutions for supporting lazy youngsters to do such unimportant stuff like playing music for fun. They are always there – and that is good –but we have to sharpen our arguments!

2 *How do you define the 'quality' of what goes on in your music education projects?*

This is a tricky question that is under constant discussion, as it should be! First I think that we are working along the whole continuum from artistic integrity to musical entrepreneurship. So quality at the first pole is a student that has grown in consciousness, an artist that can make his or her own artistic and personal choices (and re-choices) and can handle the consequences of a chosen direction. The other pole is an artist that people want to listen to and pay money for! The quality within a bigger perspective is the opportunity these students are given. To be able to strengthen your musical skills (in a broad sense) together with your friends in the band and with new music-making partners, in a way that you prefer to learn things and in a context that includes people from the music business, top quality rehearsal rooms and recording studios. With teachers that are 'forbidden' to judge your musical taste, only tease it, together with supervisors that you have chosen to extend your musical repertoire. With 'crazy' challenging teachers that question your self-image (in a supporting way!) and together with you, develop new personalised strategies for your self-realisation and support your creative ambitions. That to me seems like 'quality'.

We are also concerned with pedagogical research into the structure and design of education, the organisation of learning contexts and how this supports, or not, students' motivation and progression of learning. I think BTME is an interesting pedagogical experiment in music knowledge building.

3 *How would 'quality' be determined?*

This is an area where we have paid with a lot of blood, sweat and tears (and money!) – both in terms of competence development work for the teachers and in conversations with the students. We are working with pedagogical documentation and in combination with the students' (and the bands') own learning goals (that we set together), we are trying to set and develop common criteria for quality. One could say that the first 'pole' (as in question 2) is measured by following the students' learning processes by observation, interviews, self-assessment, log-books etc. and later on in dialogue with the students about how well they have reached their learning goals and in what way that can demonstrate this.

The other 'pole' is more about products. For this we use external examinations (we are developing a process that could use a reference group for assessment purposes), together with recordings, live gigs, written music critiques, fans' comments etc. for assessing how well they are succeeding in established music areas.

The first 'pole' is the difficult one in several obvious aspects, but also because higher music education (in my opinion) has never had these aspects of quality expressed as explicit criteria, but rather more like an implicit wish. Teachers had hoped for students to have developed these qualities and they nurtured a common belief that if a student can play a specific repertoire, he or she has in fact also developed other qualities. So, this is still quite untravelled land for many teachers and they, as well as the students, need a lot of training in seeing and documenting process criteria.

This is also a growing (but still small) discussion at a national level, as how to assess artistic processes in higher education within the fine arts. For example, what is creativity, musical groove, timing, excellence etc? I suppose this field is only just in its infancy!

6.3 D   Joost Heinsius

Manager Knowledge & Innovation, Kunstenaars&CO, Amsterdam

Kunstenaars&CO is a national organization which employs about 75 people. In The Netherlands there is a law on work and income for artists that offers artists a temporary sub-minimum income for a maximum of 48 months. We have the legal task to advise on who to admit to this provision. We also receive a budget to supply artists who participate in this provision with training, counselling and work experience. In recent years more and more artists use our services who are not part of this provision. The rest of our income comes from (EU) projects, working for city governments, etc.

Kunstenaars&CO (Artists, Culture & Entrepreneurship) has the mission to stimulate economic independence for artists. In the firm belief that independence is a necessary condition for a professional working life, we see the artist as a professional who is able to put his/her competencies into the work he/she is committed to. Those competencies are not only about being artistic or being creative, but also comprise general competencies such as being able to influence others, to lead a process, to negotiate, to network, to be able to translate his/her unique contribution meaningfully into contexts other than only the art sector. Last but not least, since the majority of artists are small entrepreneurs (whether by choice or by necessity), they also have to be capable of finding work opportunities, of managing themselves well and of managing the different sources from which they draw their income.

This is not a small task and it is easy to see why many artists do not succeed in all of these aspects. Most of art education concentrates only on the artistic side and does not prepare artists for the working life that is ahead of them. Nor are there many opportunities after finishing their education to systematically reflect on these challenges together with fellow artists. Lifelong education for artists is very necessary, but certainly is not offered within the world of most artists (and this is an understatement).

We are also convinced that there is much to be gained from working outside the art sector as an artist. Responding to different contexts requires artists to redefine their own skills, testing them with professionals from other fields and developing new kinds of art. Working in communities, in business, within health care, within other public sector organizations helps artists to redefine their art, to develop new forms of art which are just as valid on these new 'stages' as traditional art is on its own particular stage.

Changing the context has three other healthy effects: it generates new sources of income for the artists, it brings recognition from new audiences and it shows that art can be of more social value than just art for arts sake.

Kunstenaars&CO has developed a wide range of services to foster this professional development. We offer more than 40 different workshops and courses, on networking and project management, on how to organize your business and on how to present yourself better. We also offer longer continuing education for artists who like to work with children in classrooms and for experienced artists to learn how to set up projects within business and public organizations. There is also a shorter programme on community work. In total more than1200 artists participate in this whole programme. As a form of support we offer a mentoring programme where young artists can team up with well known professionals in their field to learn the tricks of the trade. In addition there is career counselling and coaching. Career counselling concentrates on making career choices and on learning to focus, whereas coaching is more directed at getting clear as to what the mental barriers are in developing each individual's career and in taking steps to overcome them. Each year there are some 300 artists involved in these programmes. Within these services self-reflection, self-management and an active outgoing attitude are the key words. Learning by doing and reflecting on their practice afterwards are essential professional competencies for artists when they go out and engage in the world.

Next we offer work experience opportunities through different projects in a variety of contexts outside the art sector. These opportunities range from designing the decorations for the annual Writers Ball to designing art for 12 roundabouts within a city, and from co-creating an innovation room for a world-wide operating chemical company to workshops with children in deprived neighbourhoods. We organise more than 60 of these kinds of opportunities which involve some 400 artists from all disciplines. One of our principles is to mix artists from all disciplines, not only to create better results but also to let artists experience the advantages of working together with people from different backgrounds. This is seen as a necessary experience and skill for each professional.

We recognise that artists now have to take into account the changing society in which we live. In major cities more than 50% of young people come from different ethnic backgrounds – a reality that many from the traditional arts world do not want to deal with. Artists from different ethnic backgrounds can also have trouble fitting in: on one hand because they are not familiar with the traditions and codes of behaviour within the arts sector, and on the other hand because the art they produce is either not ethnic enough or too ethnic and thus fails to subscribe to the standards of 'high' art. We run a programme to coach these artists to find out their own way of dealing with these mixed messages. Not surprisingly, we see the same discussions coming to the surface in our own organization.

Of course, all these developments present higher arts education with a huge challenge. The working practice of the future artist is much more varied and context sensitive than it was in the past. How can artistic quality be maintained whilst at the same time training students to be prepared for a working life that has never been experienced by their present teachers and directors? How can we find new didactic models that respond to the situations of real life after school? How can we transfer a new image of the artist of the future when the present image is still dominant within many parts of the arts sector itself?

For some years now we have been offering workshops on the business elements of a working artist's life, but most of these take place on the fringe of the curriculum and have no connection to the core of the education. Three years ago we started a project, supported by the Ministry of Culture, to engage higher arts education in developing new models of training, new ways of looking at their context and also strengthening the sparse nuclei of good practice within the art schools. The burden, in our opinion, lies not only on arts education. The art sector itself has also to take responsibility in providing opportunities for further learning and reflection.

The last tier of our work is devoted to research. We really do want to know what the results are of our work, but also how the working life of artists evolves and what are the decisive steps in their careers. This kind of research is still in its initial phase. We disseminated research into the effects of some of our community projects where it showed it can have positive effects on the competencies of the people involved (for example, illiterate migrant women who worked with theatre makers to learn the Dutch language better). And we started research into the numbers and economic conditions of artists in The Netherlands.

Kunstenaars&CO sees itself as a builder of bridges, both within the arts sector as a promoter of continuing education, but also connecting the arts with the world out there where there is a lot to gain, not only as new sources of income but also strengthening the position of art within society as a whole, to show that art can really contribute, can be of real value to real people.

6.3 E Lucy Hunt

Former Projects Manager, Professional Development Department, Guildhall School of Music & Drama, London

*As its first Administrator in 2002, Lucy Hunt became the backbone of
Guildhall Connect, organising workshops, performances and festivals for
young people in East London. Her role further extended into Projects
Manager of the Guildhall School's Professional Development Department,
which includes an MMus and Postgraduate Diploma in Leadership.*

**Initial workshop experience of the Leadership Programme October 2006 –
A Case Study relating to Quality**

In September 2006 the first ever mixed cohort of MMus Leadership students
began the programme. In previous years (2004 and 2005) students were
made up of Guildhall graduates and in one case a friend of a Guildhall
graduate. In 2006 the students came from a range of backgrounds, music
colleges and countries. They were a mixed group instrumentally.

As part of the induction to the programme a residential project was held at
the Britten Pears School, Snape Maltings in Aldeburgh for the cohort of 10
students. The group was accompanied by 2 tutors: Paul Griffiths and Sigrun
Saevarsdottir, their 2 year old child and a project manager. The group
stayed in three rented properties in Aldeburgh.

The aims of the residency were:

- To bond the students as a group/ensemble

- To allow the tutors and project manager to get to know the students

- To start to introduce the ethos of Connect such as working as a team,
  mutual respect, listening to each other, promoting creativity etc.

- To introduce the group to workshop-leading techniques and begin to
  develop these skills

- To run workshops in local schools

- To raise awareness of the Leadership programme and of the
  educational projects run by Aldeburgh Music

- To recruit young musicians to an Aldeburgh Connect project taking
  place the week after the residency

During the first 3 days the students were led through a series of introductory
games and activities and began to learn and develop the skills required in
creative workshop leading. They were given tasks, divided into groups and
began to devise material for schools' sessions. The schools' sessions were
to give the students, some of whom had never been to a workshop, an initial
introduction to leading. Workshop teams were given tutorials and the chance
to test their ideas on each other.

On the Thursday the students delivered 3 creative music workshops:

- a sixth form A level/yr11 GCSE music group of about 20 for advanced instrumental work at Thomas Mills School

- a yr 7 class for vocal/body percussion work at Thomas Mills School

- a mixed group containing 20 year 11 GCSE Music pupils and 8 Post-GCSE/Music Tech pupils at Leiston High

These were led by the previously arranged workshop teams and observed by a tutor.

On the Friday there was a final session at Farlingaye High School, with two groups of 25 students from Years 10 & 11, who were all basic instrumentalists, and were joined by some teaching staff. This session was led jointly by the two tutors who were supported by the 10 students.

During the workshops several things became apparent:

- Some of the skills involved in being a workshop leader such as communication skills, clarity of instructions, the reading of a group, presence, and charisma are intrinsic and not necessarily related to musical ability

- Despite being well planned, workshops can go wrong if the leader cannot show flexibility towards his/her ideas

- Communication skills are paramount both between leaders and between leader and participant

- Musical ownership of the young people affects interest and engagement levels

- Shared leadership particularly for new leaders is hard to manage as some of the skills involved need to be learnt and successful sharing relies mainly on trust which does not exist between strangers

- Confidence in giving instructions is paramount

Personal realisations

Until this series of workshops I had never seen a bad workshop leader and an unsuccessful workshop, therefore I had not really considered in depth the layers of thought that have to be active within the leader's mind at all times and the range of aspects that can in fact go terribly wrong.

I realized that some of our very experienced tutors were unaware of some of the actions they used when sharing ideas and co-leading a group and that I could, through observing and pointing certain things out to participants be helpful to their learning.

As I watched students who were of a very high musical standard struggling with very basic workshop skills I felt very proud of the calibre of people I work with, and felt slightly daunted at the task of training people in this field.

As the Leadership programme has developed:

    teaching staff have vastly improved the way they explain how to approach group creative music making and what is expected of students

    several trained students have become very strong leaders themselves

    the separate elements of the programme have become more robust

    it is clear that certain traits of a good workshop leader can be spotted at the time of audition. This has been given various names including 'the X factor' and 'magic dust' and is a gut feeling from the panel based on raw potential, enthusiasm, openness of mind as well as good rhythmic skills and musical ability

    it is clear that those who are committed to the work and feel that it develops them as a musician become far stronger leaders

    tutors and graduates have been encouraged to commit to a programme of continuing learning and development

6.3 F Renee Jonker

Director, société Gavigniès
Teacher for Creative Music Making Programme, The Royal Conservatoire, The Hague

The dotComp programme of the société Gavigniès

The société Gavigniès is a private fund established in 1998 by the late Madeleine Margot. Herself a pianist and lifelong teacher and lover of chamber music, this Swiss-born musician decided to leave her fortune to a private foundation that was called after the small-sized cello she once had bought: an instrument made by the French *luthier* Gavigniès. A highly symbolic name, the instrument was a gift to her by the great love of her life, a Dutch cellist and member of a well-known string quartet.

After Madeleine Margot had passed away the first Board of this Foundation (with amongst its members conductor Riccardo Chailly and the director of The Netherlands Opera Pierre Audi) decided to appoint me as Director of this fund. I was asked to investigate how this new fund could develop its own profile in a field in which many funds were already active in promoting and sponsoring music in The Netherlands. After a year of research, it was decided that stimulating new forms of music education would become the core of the Fund's activities. This enabled the société Gavigniès to develop its own profile. Apart from supporting activities and projects in the field of music on request (as most funds do), this Fund was also able to initiate its own programme.

This new approach started just before the internet revolution took place and with no other connotation than the Dutch expression for the typographical sign ; (=punt comma / dot comma) and the word to compose, the programme was given the name puntComp (=dotComp). From the beginning composition, the creative aspect of making music, was central to the programme, which was inspired by the education and community music programme of the London Sinfonietta.

Formerly I had been active as a percussionist mainly in the field of contemporary music, working with such groups as the Amsterdam-based Asko Ensemble and Schönberg Ensemble, Ensemble Modern in Frankfurt and often in close collaboration with composers such as Karlheinz Stockhausen, Györgi Ligeti, Györgi Kurtág, Mauricio Kagel, Wolfgang Rihm, Heiner Goebbels and Helmut Lachenmann. I also became very interested in the outreach programme of the internationally known new music ensemble, the London Sinfonietta. As I saw the number of people attending contemporary music concerts decrease, whilst the average age of the audience was increasing, I had already experimented with developing programmes to reach out to young people in schools in Amsterdam. These attempts were based on no training and little experience in education.

The first thing the dotComp programme had to do was to invest in training professional musicians, offering them a chance to develop and enhance their skills in leading workshops and setting up outreach activities. Over a period of three years, musicians connected to the London Sinfoniette Educational programme came to The Netherlands and trained various groups of musicians: Peter Wiegold, Fraser Trainer and Matthew Barley came over regularly to lead three days of workshops.

In the beginning participants were recruited from the ranks of the Dutch new music ensembles (my 'old' colleagues, since I had given up my position in these groups to devote my time to setting up the société Gavigniès and its dotComp programme). Soon other musicians signed up, some of them with a strong focus on music therapy. A crucial step was to bring this training programme to the Royal Conservatoire in The Hague as a warm-up event for its Music Teachers programme. In The Netherlands musicians who want to become music teachers in schools attend a course offered by conservatoires.

The first series of workshops led by Trainer and Barley caused a sort of a revolution in the Music Teachers Department of the Royal Conservatoire. Students demanded that a lot more of this kind of training should become part of their curriculum. Two of the most outspoken advocates of this 'movement' also turned out to be very gifted with their leading skills and later became the first 'home-grown' workshop leaders of the dotComp programme: Niels Vermeulen, who is connected to Yo! Opera in Utrecht and Jurgen van Harskamp, who is working for the Concertgebouw Education Department in Amsterdam.

After having participated in some 20 different workshops led by English workshop leaders, it felt natural for me to start my own practice in leading workshops and training colleagues. I was appointed as a teacher for the new curriculum 'Community Music Making' (CMM), later changed to 'Creative Music Making' in the Music Teachers Department of the Royal Conservatoire. This was followed by an assignment to develop an introductory programme for all First Year students (classical, jazz, composition, early music, conducting, sonology) that would include workshops on group composition and improvisation according to the principles of the dotComp programme.

This forced me to work out a structure for the training sessions as well as a description of the 'method' involved. This also confronted me with the lack of literature or a clear description of the leading and guiding as it was introduced in The Netherlands by the English workshop leaders. Even more strongly, when asked for such a description, time and again the English workshop leaders made clear this was the kind of work that would not fit into a methodological description and could only be learned 'by doing'.

Backed up by resources from the société Gavigniès, I started to look for partners in this professional practice. One of my first partners was the newly appointed 'coordinator for education' in the Amsterdam Concertgebouw, Marga Helmich. This highly prolific concert hall has developed an educational programme that is outstanding and has gone through a rocket-like development since Helmich (now Marga Wobma-Helmich) started out as their first employee. She is now leading a department with more than 10 people which reaches out to some 30.000 children every season. Together with Marga Wobma-Helmich, we designed a programme where groups of schoolchildren would be introduced to contemporary music concerts in the Concertgebouw by means of workshops in which they would create their own pieces, based on musical material derived from one of the pieces performed in the regular programming of this concert hall. The musicians performing would visit the schools, but the workshops were led by trainees from the dotComp programme. The société Gavigniès had invested in a large set of instruments (basically percussion) for these activities.

Reflecting on the results, it was felt by both Marga Wobma-Helmich and myself that the level of workshop leading and the number of Dutch musicians able to do this, needed to increase. So new trainings were organised led by Hannah Conway (a former LSO apprentice animateur) and Tim Steiner, a teacher from the Guildhall School of Music & Drama. The Concertgebouw has continued to develop this part of their educational programme but the need for high-level workshop leaders has only increased and needs attention.

My attempt to find new partners was given a boost in 1993 when all of the 13 Dutch government-supported symphony orchestras decided to include educational activities in their annual week of nationwide promotion of classical music. With the help of Marga Wobma, the administration of these orchestras (some of them at that moment without staff members for education) were led to the dotComp programme of the société Gavigniès. All of a sudden I was confronted with the request to roll out a training programme for 12 symphony orchestras (the world famous Concertgebouw Orchestra preferred to organise its own training through the educational department of the Concertgebouw (i.e., the building – both are different entities, but they work together in education). The project was given the title 'componeren in de klas' (composition in the classroom) and led to many initial attempts to start educational activities by these orchestras that would go a bit further than playing Britten's *Young Persons Guide* or Prokoviev's *Peter and the Wolf* in front of a concert hall full of noisy children.

It would be interesting to analyse why this project was a success with one orchestra and a failure with another, when the programme was set up in the same way: orchestral musicians were invited to follow a training in their contract time (concentrating on how to assist workshop leaders as a representative of an orchestra and on how to engage themselves as professional musicians in communicating with groups of young people who have no background in listening to classical music). The orchestral players would than assist in several workshops led by former students of mine at the Royal Conservatoire or former dotComp trainees. With at least six orchestras this was the beginning of setting up educational activities which have continued to include a form of 'componeren in de klas'. The three orchestras of the Dutch Public Broadcasting now run their own educational programme and have been organising their own training programme (with Fraser Trainer and Mary King). With all these activities it can be said that they have been received with great enthusiasm both from the musicians in the orchestras and from their partners in local schools. But there also seems to be a glass ceiling in terms of the quality that is achieved in these kind of activities – quality in terms of musical level, the impact on the community and the sustainability of these activities.

Apart from these partnerships with Dutch symphony orchestras, the Amsterdam Concertgebouw and incidentally The Netherlands Opera, the société Gavigniès has initiated partnerships with Yo! Opera in Utrecht and Dario Fo in Poeldijk. The latter being a local initiative called after the well-known Italian writer and director that established an organisation for community opera in a rural part of The Netherlands with a remarkable history of activities. For all these partnership one could say that a certain status quo has been reached that is more of a stand still than a promise for future development.

It is felt that analysing the current situation of outreach programmes and community music activities by these organisations, including the dotComp programme of the société Gavigniès itself, is very necessary. Questions should be asked like:

- what has defined the limits of the programme so far?
- what explanation can be given for failures in the programme?
- how can 'quality' be defined for these kind of activities?
- what is this 'glass ceiling' that all parties involved experience, especially when they have put their full energy and enthusiasm into these activities?
- what is missing in the formation of people leading and organising these programmes?
- what is missing in the formation and training of the musicians leading workshop programmes?
- how can one define the outlines for a partnership that is successful?
- what are the specific conditions that make a successful partnership between an educational initiative (like the dotComp programme) or an educational institution (like the Royal Conservatoire)?

This need for evaluation has increased since new partnerships are to be developed by the société Gavigniès in the near future. These partnerships will expand the activities of the société Gavigniès abroad: the Melodi Music project in Pimville and Soweto (South-Africa), the exchange programme of the Royal Conservatoire in The Hague with the University of Legon in Accra (Ghana) and with the Sarasvati School for Young Talent in Djakarta (Indonesia). All have applied for support from the société Gavigniès for developing outreach programmes. The challenges to invest in partnerships in a very different cultural context are enormous and it increases the demands on the quality of the dotComp programme substantially.

Almost nine years after launching dotComp the société Gavigniès is still the only partner for professional organisations in The Netherlands able to invest in training and development for what is widely seen as 'the Guildhall method' of leading and guiding workshops – i.e., workshops that concentrate on the creative and collaborative aspects of musical formation.

There are now more institutions in The Netherlands engaging in educational activities that include composition (the Dutch Wind Ensemble, Ensemble De Ereprijs, Asko and Schönberg Ensembles), but these projects all lead to new pieces written by individual (young) composers and arranged by the professional musicians of the ensembles. For a couple of years Jos Schilling, of the Utrecht Conservatoire, has been leading a programme that is called 'the Guildhall method' (which has resulted in a publication by the Gehrels Institute) but this programme seems to have had little effect on establishing educational activities by the larger cultural institutes in this country. The Royal Conservatoire in Den Haag and the Prince Claus Conservatoire in Groningen have started a Joint Masters programme in which the principles of this 'method' form the core of one of the four compulsory modules.

It should be stated that the dotComp programme has not been evaluated over the years and that systematic records about its various activities have not been made. Also the documentation of various activities has been poor (evaluation reports, participant satisfaction questionnaires, logs, filmed footage or recordings in sound). Yet there is a list of most of the people who have been involved and it is most likely that many of them would be willing to reflect on the various activities and hand in reflective statements.

6.3 G Ninja Kors

Project Co-ordinator, World Music & Dance Centre, Rotterdam

The Brassband School in the South of Rotterdam has been going for three years, since it was founded in 2006. The central idea is for brass bands to develop themselves beyond the point where many of them have been for several years. To this end the Brassband School (BBS) provides rehearsal space, band coaching, and professional development for the band leaders, directors, and brass musicians.

Brass bands

Brass bands are an integral part of Dutch 20th century musical history. They were an important part of village and church culture throughout the 20th century and were brought to the Dutch colonies. Brass orchestras and ultimately bands sprung up in Indonesia, Surinam and the Netherlands Antilles (Aruba, Bonaire, Curacao) in the Caribbean. The repertoire in those communities was at first tightly connected with the churches but soon the trumpets and trombones found their way out of the churches, away from the control of the Dutch *paters,* and into the local music circuit. With the changing context the musical idiom followed suit, and new musics were born. Nothing makes a party like a trumpet. (This process is wonderfully described and illustrated by Rob Boonzajer Flaes in his publication *Brass*

Unbound: Secret Children of the Colonial Brass Band. Amsterdam, Royal Tropical Institute, 2001.)

Surinam became independent in 1975; the Antilles are still part of the kingdom. Many young people come to the Netherlands to study because the Antilles do not have a university to speak of. With them, as is so common, comes their music. In Surinam and the Antilles the brass music became an integral part of the carnival, leading the street parades. In the Netherlands there is no real Caribbean carnival, except for a large summer festival in Rotterdam. The brass bands that sprung up among the Antillean migrants and Surinam immigrants were founded mainly for cultural purposes: to keep a bit of home going in this strange cold land. It was soon found, however, that there is also a lucrative economic side to the bands: while on the islands the bands play *only* during the carnival, in the Netherlands they are a welcome addition to any festival, opening, party or other occasion.

Brassband School

The term brass band is a misleading one. The bands consist mainly of drums. Trumpets and trombones (no other brass instruments) are added to bring in the melody. Usually two or three players are added to the regular band of drummers. There are comparatively few brass players available and they play with many bands, upon request. As such, because they are few, they often ask high fees. The lack of competition also means that there is little need for further development. Once you're good enough, you're good enough. This was holding back the bands as a whole. The Brassband School (BBS) was founded to tackle this issue, and to develop the Caribbean brass tradition in the Netherlands.

A partnership was made with the Battle of the Drums, a large event that is held each year prior to the Summer Carnival. During the Battle of the Drums the Caribbean brass bands battle each other in a fierce competition. The jury looks for musical quality from both the drums and brass section, using such criteria as originality, musicality of performance, composition and arrangement, ensemble playing and stage presentation and choreography. From the start of the partnership with the Brassband School, all participating bands are also required to include brass instruments. The Battle of the Drums is an important incentive for brass bands to improve themselves.

The Antillean community is strongly social in the sense that social structures are defining in all areas, business and pleasure. The same goes for the Surinamese. In order to really reach the brass bands, one needs to be aware of how the social infrastructure fits together and how communication works within the community. The project leader of the Brassband School does not have an Antillean or Surinamese background but he is a community musician with an extensive network in many cultural groups. He has worked for several years in the communities of Rotterdam, of which the Antillean and Surinamese are a substantial part. He set up the BBS in Rotterdam South, a 'challenged' area where many Antillean people live. He did this by engaging brass bands in the development, and offering them rehearsal space in a building of the Rotterdam Music School (SKVR). The music school does not offer courses on Saturday and the first year made the building available for the brass bands. Since rehearsal space for 25 drummers and brass players is not easy to find in a densely inhabited area, it is quite a draw.

An added benefit is that the brass bands can get band coaching from external professionals, if they want. Teachers are available as well, to teach the musicians (brass in particular!) as well as the band leaders. The teaching body is mixed and consists of both self-taught leaders from the Antillean community and professionally trained teachers from Rotterdam Conservatoire (Codarts) and the Music School (SKVR). The exchange is easy to see: while the self-trained musicians receive background knowledge and skills training in didactics and theory from the trained professionals, the conservatoire diploma holders become acquainted with the musical idiom and social codes of the brassbands. After all, while the Dutch brass traditions are slowly disappearing with the demise of the traditional village communities, the Caribbean brassbands are growing everywhere like mushrooms. A typical case of shifts in the work field.

Thin lines

So far the Brassband School has been a success. This is largely due, as is often the case, to having the right people in the right places at the right time. An intern who turned out to be extremely efficient in working with the bands, is now one of the central people in the everyday running of the School. The project leader is exactly the right person for the job, holding a steady balance between trouble shooting, ambition and continuity. The teachers involved in the project are dedicated and, most importantly, ready to learn. The brass bands are eager to learn and improve, and musicians dedicated to spending time on learning their instruments. Of course, not everyone comes every week. Some musicians occasionally drop in, others are very ambitious and travel from other parts of the country to follow lessons at the Brassband School. The teachers need to accommodate this if they want to reach the ones who are indeed serious about their development.

The main challenge lies with the social and economic infrastructures of the bands and individual musicians. This is a potential mine field since many people depend on the brass bands for a substantial addition to their income. It is therefore important for the Brassband School not to be a threat to the economic situation of the bands and musicians involved. However, seeing how the BBS is training brass players who will inevitably work in the market that was once the domain of only a few trumpeters and trombone players, some interference is unavoidable. This is why some of the key people from the brass field were involved with the Brassband School from the beginning. Their income, once mostly coming from playing with the bands, has the potential to shift to teaching. They become the new 'cadre' for this fast-growing sector in the Netherlands.

This mechanism is not a natural one within the brass band community. Development of the bands and the music has never been top priority; brass bands have always been there for cultural and economic reasons. Ergo: good enough is good enough. This means that working on the improvement of the bands and the music, making that extra step, requires a mind-shift in many of the participants including the teachers and band leaders. Winning the prestigious Battle of the Drums is an important incentive since it cannot be won without serious investment in the quality of the band. Winning means popularity.

Social work?

Another balance that needs to be found and maintained is the balance between social and artistic aims. The WMDC and its partners may be primarily concerned with musical development but most brass bands in the Netherlands that currently come into existence, start because of social aims. Antillean youth are regarded as a risk group in Dutch society and many initiatives by social workers and youth organisations include starting up a brass band to 'keep the youth off the street'. (It is effective, mostly, but when the money is gone after a few years, sometimes so is the brass band. Which leaves the interesting question: what happens to the instruments? This could mean history repeating itself!) Some of the political interest in the Brassband School comes from the same corner; and not without reason. The brass band leaders deal not only with musical and didactic matters but also need to concern themselves with other social issues of the band members such as social and economic deprivation and for example, teenage pregnancies.

The effects a brass band can have on young people on the edge of society are undeniable. The Brassband School has developed into a hub of this activity and has the potential to be an important access point to many issues that face this group. But we need to be careful with this. The first priority is the bands! New music is composed and arranged, new musical concepts to the participants (such as polyphony) are introduced into the performances, brass players and teachers are trained to a higher level. The first target, after all, is the music. In order to target the music, we need to be aware of and take care of the social environment. And in turn, the development of the music feeds into the social climate as the bands improve and the music is picked up and taken seriously by a wider audience – including other musicians.

6.3 H Sara Lee

Artistic Director, Music in Prisons, England and Wales

One of the main reasons Music in Prisons (MiP) projects have a high success rate is due to the continued emphasis on quality rather than quantity. In a time where getting value for money often means getting as many people as possible in a room in one go, we are fortunate that people realise and accept that the impact of a project on an individual is far more meaningful and long-lasting because of the quality of the experience.

Many factors are crucial in achieving and maintaining this quality and it is how these things combine that make the work so effective. MiPs project team is one of the most important factors in its success. First and foremost they are all amazing musicians but very importantly, each of them has the specific social skills needed to work with sometimes challenging prisoners and the patience to deal appropriately with the vagaries of the prison system. The core team has been working together regularly for many years and because of this, has been able to develop an enviable working relationship built on trust, support and a strong musical understanding. Having a team that is secure in its function means a positive and high quality experience will be delivered to the participant group every time. It is the sensitive and enthusiastic approach of the project team which leads to such dramatic and positive responses from participants and this firstly enables the creation of music of the highest quality and secondly offers them an experience that will have a positive influence on their futures.

Participant-led working demands that as musicians, the team has to be exceptionally versatile on a variety of instruments and in a variety of styles. The projects are about people learning new skills on new instruments and writing new music so the team needs to possess these skills in order to share them. Having excellent musicians gives the participants something to aspire to and is a clear indication that they are being asked to engage and participate in something of exceptional quality. Seeing this assures people the project is worth investing in.

Leadership within the projects is fluid and roles within the team have to be interchangeable as with regularity one of the team is drawn away from the front to work with someone one to one. At this point, in order to keep the momentum going, another member of the team has to take the lead. There is an absolute need to be able to communicate appropriately and with clarity in these situations; with the participants, prison staff and the rest of the project team. The situations are often complex and involve all sorts of other 'outside influences' and to be able to make a quick yet calm and accurate judgment on how to proceed in any given situation is essential. On one hand the project team has to display confidence and authority whilst on the other hand it has to work in amongst the participants as a member of the band. To get the balance is sometimes tricky but achieving the balance makes for a great working partnership.

The project team works effectively because the musicians possess not only a deep understanding of the context but have a personal authenticity and an absolute integrity and respect for the work and the people participating in it. It is a skill to be able to assess individuals quickly and accurately and to gauge the right time for each of them to make the next big step both musically and personally. The team instinctively knows how far to push people, when to leave them alone and when to coax something out of them. It is about having an innate understanding of people and very importantly an innate understanding of oneself. Any form of musical or personal ego does not work in the prison environment as the work is solely about what the participants can achieve with the team's support.

In any situation, good management is one of the keys to success and organising projects in prisons is no different. It is often as difficult to get into a prison as to get out of it and there are many hurdles to overcome before any kind of intervention can happen within them. Personal relationships and a keen understanding of what you are walking into are crucial at this stage as you are often dealing with people who have little or no understanding of the work. At this stage you *have* to understand their position and work closely with them to enable them to understand yours. If good relationships are built you will be welcome and you will succeed; if anything is taken for granted then the project will be in jeopardy.

The project team always strives to get the best from the people we work with and the best from ourselves. Much of the delivery process is about assessing the work as it progresses and you need to have a team that is familiar and comfortable with each other to do this effectively. As a team we don't go in with a 'plan' but as a result of this must be confident enough in our own/team skills to be able to respond to a particular person/ group/ situation.

From the outset we show the people we work with that we are coming in on a high level. If they see us taking pride in our work then the likelihood is that they will also take pride. It is clear to all of them - and they have said it on many occasions - that we are people who know and care about what both we and they are doing. We bring in great instruments for them to play and great musicians for them to work with. This shows an immediate investment in them, something too few of them have experienced in their lives before. Many feel blown away by this and the effort that has gone in to it, but everyone responds. At the outset, some shy away from it, some feel immediately anxious about failing, others just dive in. All these feelings must be accepted and worked with; it can be a delicate balance between understanding someone's feelings and at the same time instilling in them the confidence they can do it.

If equipment is broken, we mend it. It shows the group that we take pride in our work and that they can be a part of that. Importantly, it lets people see we think they are worth something. The equipment is good, the team is good and when you invest in all these things great results are achieved.

There is a big focus on the performance at the end of a project as it is a great mark of achievement and allows individuals to get immediate praise and appreciation for what they have done. It takes a huge amount of confidence to take part in a project which has the potential to open you up in ways you may not have been before and it takes an even bigger effort to present your work in the final gig. Many people have never started *and* finished something in their lives so this is a massive step into often unchartered and frightening territory.

Time and effort is put into mixing and designing the project CDs as this is another very important aspect of the whole process. To have something tangible that you can be really proud of and to have the opportunity to let family and friends hear what you have achieved is a wonderful and positive link back to life outside.

Finally, in order to maintain the quality of the work over a long period of time, space for reflection on all aspects of the management and delivery is crucial. This allows the exchange of information, ideas and suggestions between prison staff, MiP management, the project team and participants. It gives each party a chance to discuss and process all that has happened and therefore move forward with knowledge and confidence that attention to detail and musical quality will never be compromised.

6.3 I   Debora Patty

Education, Yo! Opera Festival and Laboratory, Utrecht

THE OPERAFLAT

The Operaflat

The idea is simple. You have a flat in Utrecht: 8 floors high with 13 doors on each floor. Behind the doors are opera singers. Every door is marked with a red heart balloon. When you see one, you know you are allowed to ring the doorbell. And when you do, the door opens and an opera is being sung for you, as if you were part of the story. This was the second edition of The Operaflat in 2007.

Background: The Operaflat 2005

The first edition of the project, The Operaflat, took place during the Yo! Opera Festival in 2005. The theme of the Festival was Community Opera. For 5 days Utrecht was filled with opera: in buses, in a children's hospital, community centres, on the streets and in a flat in a district of Utrecht called Overvecht. The idea was to ask the residents to welcome one, two or three singers in their doorway. But there weren't enough opera singers available for this day – so in the end behind every door there was a different genre: opera, jazz, folk. It became a place where everybody who loved to sing, had a stage. The project was one of the most successful parts of the programme. It was accessible and fun. But it was also a very intimate experience for both singers and audience.

The Operaflat 2007

In 2007 we decided to repeat the project. The goals were:

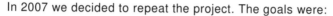 To research new forms and structures for making youth opera

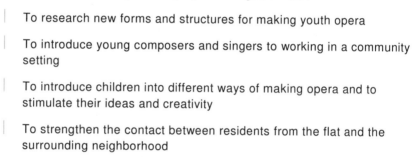 To introduce young composers and singers to working in a community setting

To introduce children into different ways of making opera and to stimulate their ideas and creativity

To strengthen the contact between residents from the flat and the surrounding neighborhood

This time we collaborated with 9 conservatoires in Holland: The Hague, Amsterdam, Rotterdam, Utrecht, Arnhem, Zwolle, Enschede, Tilburg and Groningen. From each conservatoire we invited singers and composers to make a one-minute opera. We also invited children from an elementary school from the same district as the flat to write the libretto.

The work started in January 2007 when the project leader and the artistic director spent evenings visiting the flat to ask the residents if they wanted to participate either again or for the first time. Some of the people who lived there in 2005, during the first edition, were happy to do it again. But in this flat there is also a lot of moving out and moving in. People sometimes call it a pigeon house. So there were the end, 25 households were involved in the project.

In March the workshops started in the elementary school. We asked a writer and a drama teacher to help the children write a libretto for a one-minute opera. The assignment was to write an opera about an encounter in a doorway. This working process took about 6 weeks, 1 hour a week. They made operas about hairdressers in love, fathers and mothers, bus drivers and sad teachers.

In May the teams met each other for the first time: writers, composers and singers. Each child officially handed over their libretto explaining how the composer should read the story. Musical rehearsals took place in September and were directed by a professional composer. For the drama rehearsals (the week before the big performance) the teams worked with professional theatre directors.

Day of the performance: November 3 2007

One of the first things that happened that morning was that two residents said they couldn't participate anymore. One was sick and one thought that the performance would take place a week later. So, as a solution, some doors had to facilitate two operas and one team decided to perform in one of the elevators.

Another thing that also was uncertain on the morning was how many of the young writers would show up. It was a Saturday, no school day, so it was all up to the motivation of the children and their parents. We gave a couple of children the task to make a video report that eventually would be part of the professional documentary that was made of the day. Luckily, more children showed up and were able to see what the result was of their libretto and their story. They were very proud.

The singers had a tough day. Some operas were performed more than 50 times but we heard no complaints. In fact we only saw very enthusiastic singers who were amazed by the effect their singing and performance had on the audience. One singer sent us an e-mail afterwards telling us how the project had an impact on the way she now saw herself as a singing student. She said her teacher also saw the difference. But I think it is fair to say that this kind of project is not attractive to all singers. There has to be a curiosity and a need to experiment, to grow and to explore.

The role of the residents was a small one. It was their job to be there. Some residents gave the key of their apartment to the singer so they could walk through the flat to see the other operas. Some residents made snacks for the audience. Just as in 2005, their reactions to the project were very positive. For some people it was more than enough just to be there on that day. Others were interested to be more involved.

What I learned

As the project leader of this project I was involved with all the different parties: singers, composers, children, teachers, residents – afternoons in classrooms, evenings ringing doorbells, days of artistic rehearsals. I think that this is also what makes The Operaflat such an interesting and exciting project. The combination of different people – artists, pupils, experienced and new opera makers, young, old, national and international. There was a lot to learn and we learnt a lot.

In general

Personally I learned what it means to think out of the box. I was quite shocked when Anthony (Artistic Director) showed me the size of the flat where he imagined the project would take place. But with each week I learned that the whole flat contains families, individuals, old people, young people – people that were enthusiastic, people that were grumpy. The mega flat became personal.

I am amazed by the chemistry you get when you put different people together and introduce them to something totally new and crazy, like an Operaflat. They had to connect with people they would not normally meet. They had to find their position, they learned from each other and they were surprised by what they were capable of doing and what it meant for others.

But, with all these different groups of people, you have to be very clear about what you want from them. What do you want them to learn? What can they contribute to the process and the project? What are their qualities? What space do you give them? I think that we are now more and more conscious of the implications of this kind of project for our organization – about our artistic goals, our social goals and our priorities.

Working with students

When you work with students in this kind of project, you need students who are 'up for adventure'. You will not receive an everyday libretto. You will not sing on a normal stage. You will not have people around you who immediately know what you mean if you 'talk art'. And you will have to like it or at least, be open to liking it. You will also need support and understanding from your singing teacher – someone who will help you in your journey, even though it may not be his or her journey.

Working with children

What adventure can we offer children? What contribution can opera make to their development – to having a good time? I remember a moment during one of the first rehearsals where one girl for the first time heard the musical translation of her libretto about 'hairdressers in love'. The look on her face was priceless. She was so proud. In the November 2009 edition of The Operaflat we gave the children more space in making the opera. Not only writing lyrics, but also influencing the composition and the performance.

This meant a change in the working process. The division of roles is now blurring. And that's when you really have to start communicating.

In addition, the role of the teacher is very important. In 2007 this was not easy because the work with the children was after school. We had almost no contact with the children's teachers. I think working together with teachers helps you to shape your ideas and translate them into a project that connects with the qualities and the interests of the children. It makes it more possible to integrate the project into the curriculum. And again, the learning goes both ways. Teachers learn what art can do for their youngsters, whilst we, as an arts organisation can learn how to connect our artistic ideas with the reality of young people. It has made us more realistic. We now see through more glasses, not just through the artistic one.

Working with the residents

After the first edition I received a lot of reactions from residents who were so surprised by what had just happened in their flat. Nobody ever comes to that building if they have no reason to and people live next to each other for years without really knowing them. But after the first Operaflat, this changed. Two ladies started drinking coffee together. Young couples started doing things together. This was wonderful to hear of course.

The question then arose whether their contribution was enough both for them and for us because they didn't really have the opportunity to say anything about the content of the opera. We just simply asked them to be at home that day. For some people this low key contribution was sufficient reason to join in. It didn't take a lot of time and in exchange they had a wonderful opera experience. But some people wanted to be more involved.

So in 2009 we decided to take it a step further by letting the young people interview the residents as a starting point for writing a new opera. It was an experiment – a way of exploring the space that is available for people to join in, to really matter, to have an influence on the content and to have a voice.

Personally, I think that this is crucial – not just to put people in your project because you need them (or their door or a nice libretto), but to really think about the possible exchange. The learning goes both ways – to open the opera doors, to let people in, to start conversations and to leave them with a handful of new skills, new relationships, new experiences and new dreams.

6.3 J Luciana Prass

Department of Music, Institute of Arts, Universidade Federal do Rio Grande do Sul, Porto Alegre, Brazil

This Case Study takes the form of a commentary by Benjamin Smith (graduate student in Ethnomusicology at University of Illinois) after several interviews with Luciana Prass, discussing her experience of the Samba School, 'Bamba da Orgia' in Porto Alegre

Luciana is the leader, the *mestre*, of our illustrious 'U of I Samba Ensemble'. She grew up in Porto Alegre, completed her undergraduate degree in classical guitar, and then went on to write a Masters thesis on the city's oldest samba school, Bamba's in 1998. While the south of Brazil is not known for samba – the associations are more with Rio de Janeiro for Carnival or with Bahia for *samba de roda* – it does boast a long tradition of samba schools. For the project Luciana participated in one complete annual cycle and part of another, in which she played *tamborim* (also named *caixeta*): a small membranophone, with a wood frame, plastic head approximately six-inches in diameter, struck with a stick of six or so bundled knitting needles. Several of these *tamborins* march at the front of the *bateria*, or percussion section. In the last few years they have been played most often by women, who also choreograph arm and body movements to add to the visual appeal of the performance.

Luciana's choice of *tamborim* is informative on several levels. Samba school members come almost exclusively from the lower class, thus the price of a *surdo* – the large bass drums – or a *caixa* – the snare drums – would be prohibitive. The schools themselves, called *quadras*, are usually located in poor urban areas. Each samba school has its own instruments, which the performers are allowed to use. *Tamborins* are the exception. Because they are so small and inexpensive – "ten dollars or so," Luciana said – performers buy their own instruments. By playing the *tamborim* she not only remained within the gender expectations, but also avoided taking an instrument away from another (presumably poorer) player. This was important, she said, because it was already clear to everyone that she was an outsider. "Especially because I am a woman, (...), and white skin, and with glasses, and with different clothes, maybe. Most of the people there are lower class, working class". The choice was therefore a strategic move to minimize the already great social distance between herself and the majority of the percussionists, or *ritmistas*.[1]

Her time at Bamba's was transformational for Luciana on many counts. In addition to *tamborim*, Luciana also 'unofficially' learnt to play the other instruments in the *bateria*. Thus, as the *mestre* of her own samba ensembles, she is able to show students how to play all the parts on all the

---

1 Luciana comments: "But not just this - other *ritmistas* played better than me because they had more experience... it would be impossible to put the *mestre de bateria* in a situation where he had to decide between me - a white woman from an academic setting - and another *ritmista* - black, probably lower class, but playing better than me, of course..."

instruments. In our ensemble she does this primarily via demonstration. For instance at our first two meetings, when we were learning new pieces, she would first begin with the *surdo* parts, playing the drum, giving some explanation and then having the players take over. Then she would do the same with the *caixas*. Having demonstrated those patterns, she would set the two going and then proceed around the room adding the voices of the *atabaques* (tall conical membranophones), *repiniques* (metal-framed, double-headed membranophones), *ganzás* (metal shakers), *agogôs* (double cowbells) and *tamborins* solely by showing. Only in cases where players failed to grasp the demonstrations quickly enough did she resort to writing rhythms on the blackboard; this happened very rarely. I had been paying close attention to how she taught the parts and was curious how it related to what went on in a 'real samba school, like Bamba's.

"And so, the way you lead the ensemble here, is that, is that how they would teach people at Bamba's? The new people, or...?"
"No. In Bamba's I don't teach."
"No, but is that *how* they teach?"
"Oh. Oh, no. I think that is different, because I explain things using words. And there all the time the people explain to me by doing."
"Yeah."
"I say, 'Oh, I don't understand. How can I do this *tamborim*?' And then, 'Oh, you need [to] do 'taca tchica taca'.' [demonstrating in the air]"
"But you do both. See, that's interesting. I've noticed that you do both. You...you'll often start..."
"Yes."
"...explaining, you get, like, the *surdos* and the *caixas* going..."
"Yes, yes."
"And then you just go around and show people what to do."
"Yes, yes."
"Without talking."
"Yes, I try to do this. I don't know, I think I want to [build] a bridge [between] these two forms of understanding. This is because when I start[ed] teaching in academic settings I perceived that people would start to read music and then start to put...ah..."
"'Turn off,' you mean?"
"Yes."
"Turn off their ears?"
(Mimicking a horn player in the orchestra, tapping his foot, reading from sheet music, not paying attention to the rest of the orchestra)
"Um, dois, três...du, du, du, du, du, du, du, du...quatro, cinco, seis, sete..."
"Right."

"And [they] don't hear that in the rest there are a lot of things happen[ing]. (laughs) And the orchestra [is next to] you. And I start to emphasize with my students the importance of aural learning".

Thus, at Bamba's and then in her own teaching Luciana became convinced that "everyone can learn this. Some people (just) need more time" and that by removing the medium of explanation or sheet music, players focused more intensely on the sounds themselves and on each other. These realisations were significant because they greatly impacted on the attitude she brought to the samba ensembles she led at the music and arts school in Porto Alegre where she taught for 8 years.

Similar to the place of popular musics in US university and conservatory settings a few decades ago, samba is not taught at the secondary level, because of its lower class associations. Practical musical instruction is in Western European classical music. Luciana even reported that the older, more culturally conservative members of the university faculty were suspicious of her starting a samba ensemble, for they considered it out of place and were worried that the students might have "too much fun". Of course, Luciana conceded that it is a lot of fun, but she also has substantial reasons to justify its value to the students, who included those from the music, theatre, dance and fine arts departments. The initial ones were musical: students who saw themselves as 'rhythmically challenged' (my phrase) but learnt to play with great facility. They also benefited from the demonstrative teaching style uncommon in the conservatory setting, and finally, they learnt the importance of listening to others, not just playing in tune and in time. In doing so Luciana took a set of pedagogical principles she had been exposed to at Bamba's, which she had found effective, and then transplanted them to the arts' university. And, while this alone would have been a significant revelation for a music pedagogue, in fact the importance of Luciana's experience at Bamba's lies beyond the musical realm and bears directly on deeper values she finds in teaching her ensembles.

Having read literature on microtiming and participatory discrepancies, especially in relation to African American musics, when we sat down to talk after our third rehearsal I was curious to know how Luciana heard the ensemble. My worry was that, even though she had avoided using Western notation, many of the musicians were 'translating' her demonstrations into strict note values which do not correspond to the correct 'feel' of the rhythms. And while her answer speaks tellingly to the question, the course of the conversation took us into broader territory.

"So my question is when you, when you hear people downstairs playing...it sounds terrible to you, or it sounds...?"
"No, no. Really terrible, no. We... In some moments I feel that we are

doing... Last Monday, we feel in some moments 'Wow! This is...,' when we are doing *breque* 2. It's too perfect. And then, sometimes, whoa, we lose our concentration...because it's very important that people hear the whole battery, and the first time, it happens with me too, we start just thinking [about] our instrument and, oh, in reality you don't hear the others".

"Yeah."

"The swing starts to happen when you adapt your instrument, your rhythm with the others and perceive, 'Well, when I did this, I hear the surdo.Oh, this batida connects with this from surdo and this from snare drums and... But this is very difficult and this is a group job. It's...ah... This is for me the most interesting in this set, because you start to... to... to play together, but play together is not just playing together. You need [to] connect with other people, you need to start [to] really feel these things, and your concentration... And this is very interesting, for me... This is the most interesting... Because of this I start to teach a samba class (laughs)."

"Because of that feeling? Or because of..."

"Yes, because of that feeling [that] you perceive, 'Oh, [I] need other people to do my job. I'm not alone.' [...] And this is a kind of metaphor that you can, ah, transport, translate to other settings. [...] You can think this way, think together, to construct some knowledge together."

Music in colonial and post-colonial Brazil has never just been music. The political implications of musical practices have always been palpable to her inhabitants from the hegemonic demonstrations of European operas to the guised rebellion of candomblé. Today many Afro-Brazilian musics are being utilized by the disenfranchised classes to solidify counter-hegemonic positions and, thereby, lay claim to rights, monies and properties. Luciana's comments, however, suggest a more abstract lesson that can be drawn from playing samba: that by playing, not together, but as one interdependent whole, we (re)gain a glimpse of our fundamental state of interdependence – one that can be "translate[d] to other settings". We are not alone; samba makes this self-evident.

6.3 K Linda Rose

Project Consultant and Founder (1993), Music for Life Wigmore Hall and *for dementia*, London

Brief Outline

Music for Life is a project working with people with dementia and those who care for them. It aims to re-build confidence and trust for people who have become isolated and disempowered through their condition. Central to the work are the music workshops in which 3 musicians encourage communication and connection through the music they improvise together. Both the musical and the interpersonal skills of the musicians are crucial in this work. With support from the senior management of the setting, the musicians work to develop a cohesive group where each participant, whether a person with dementia or a member of staff becomes responsive and open to the possibilities for relating to any other in the group on an equal basis. The workshop space becomes a place for all kinds of exploration, experiences ranging from the most joyful and celebratory to the gently amusing and teasing to the saddest sharing. Both the music and the quiet spaces between the music in the sessions are created and owned by individuals in the group, and responded to in different ways by everyone in the group.

Project structure

After many years of exploration and experimentation, a framework has developed for the project. Each project lasts for 8 sessions, one session a week for 8 weeks. Each workshop lasts an hour and sits between 1 hour of preparation and 1 hour of de-briefing with staff and musicians. Each project involves 8 people with dementia, 5 staff and 3 musicians. The work affects all participants and at times has different emphases. Some projects are geared towards musician development, raising awareness for those new to the area to understand more about the ways dementia can affect an individual and so influence the way they relate in a workshop. Some projects are focused more towards care staff development, helping to develop more reflective practice, and occasionally projects have no formal training agenda but are simply a place where the musicians can develop new ideas and extend their existing work.

In every project the 1-hour workshop for the people with dementia is a protected space. Training, development and reflection go on both within and around this - in the hour before or after the workshop, in the days between sessions and in the days before the project arrives at a setting and after the project leaves. However, the workshop itself is the most important space for learning and the experience of the workshop provides the material for both personal and professional reflection. Significant changes occur for many of the people with dementia who participate in the project, but its legacy lies also in the extent to which care staff are affected. Staff are increasingly able to notice their own responses and the responses of others in the group and are encouraged to talk about their observations. The outcomes can be better teamwork, raised confidence and self esteem, and greater willingness, even excitement about developing care practice. This leads to a happier more motivated workforce and therefore better care for people with dementia.

The impact of the work spreads when the senior management recognises these changes in both residents and staff and explores ways to sustain the learning. Often this involves finding the time for staff to meet and to continue to talk together in the more personal way that the project encourages. Put graphically, imagine the music workshop without the music, a film without sound. You will see communication and responsiveness through the warmth of body language, the sustained gentleness of eye contact, the carefully organised space, and in many other ways. It is not the role of the staff to model the musical skills of the musicians but they can learn from their ways of working and integrate their learning into everyday care, activities and relationships of their own. Learning here is not about how to run music workshops, but rather about ways of communicating. Person-centred care is currently a central concern for improving practice in dementia care and is modelled in this project.

Case Study of a Staff Development Project

Setting up the project

The location for a particular project is identified by the Music for Life project director or manager, together with the dementia care officer who has an overview of residents' needs in homes in the area. Prior to the start of the project, the manager and senior staff meet with project leaders to share information about the project and the care home. Here staff development needs are discussed as well as practical questions such as appropriate spaces to work in, staff rotas etc. The project makes significant organisational demands on a home or centre and so it is important to establish a trusting relationship early on where managers feel confident about the quality of the investment as well as leaving them excited about the potential of the project for improving the lives of residents.

Meeting the staff team

A second meeting is held to select the people with dementia who are to participate in the project. This meeting again involves senior managers together with any members of staff who might be interested and available to attend, and in particular the 5 staff identified to be on the project over the 8 weeks. Here they meet the musician who is workshop leader for the project and the dementia care trainer with responsibility for spending time with the staff to reflect on their experiences of the workshops week by week. The focus of this meeting is to help the staff to select the residents to take part in the project and to introduce them to some of the people they will be working with. Again this is also about confidence building as staff are often particularly shy in the company of the musicians, commenting that they lack musical skill and fearful of being exposed in the workshops.

So, it is even at this early stage that the staff development work begins. The project itself is not easy to describe and involves musical experiences that are generally unfamiliar. Staff learn about the project as the meeting progresses. The process of selecting residents together is part of the initiation into the ways and experiences of the project. The lively discussions that ensue as residents are discussed and prioritised for the 8 places in the workshops provide opportunities to talk about examples of work in other homes and centres, where similar behaviours have been encountered and outcomes of the workshops can be described. Staff are already getting to know each other and their residents in new ways, listening to the perspectives of colleagues who may work differently, and who may experience individual residents in different ways. Gradually, as they explore the needs and interests of those in their care, a group of eight emerges. A final check ensures there is a variety of personalities to provide a balance of energy in the group and a balance of needs, leaving the staff with the opportunity to fine tune the list amongst themselves and with other colleagues, ready for the project's arrival a couple of weeks later.

The musicians and the space

Shortly before the project begins, the workshop leader holds a rehearsal with the two supporting musicians. He has also talked with them about the home and the residents they are to work with. The main purpose of this rehearsal is to devise with them the 'opening theme' for the workshop series. This is the framework for the improvised piece, which will mark the cornerstone of each workshop, providing a secure and predictable start and end to each session, but also with the opportunity to be shaped in response to the mood of individuals or to the group as a whole.

On the morning of the workshop, the project room is set up, the circle of chairs carefully set out, the observers chairs carefully placed. The range of percussion instruments is laid out in the centre of the circle, taking account of sightlines, accessibility and interest in the shape of the layout, often with a 'centre piece' maybe a djembe to look inviting and aesthetically pleasing. The musicians then improvise together, exploring the possibilities of their opening theme and developing ideas freely. Here they re-establish their relationship with each other and sensitivity to each other, in preparation for the workshop with its need for both flexibility and focus.

At all times, the quality of their music-making is paramount. For their music to communicate they need to be at the height of their musical skill. Their playing must matter and mean every bit as much as any public performance on the concert platform. The musicians often comment that it matters more to them and has greater meaning, as the integrity and quality of their playing directly affects the extent to which they will connect with the person with dementia. The demands are great, as they also need to be aware of more than one response or initiative from the circle at any one time and be responsive to each other, sometimes relinquishing a long awaited opportunity to work with a resident as another interaction has already begun. Sometimes the skill involves moulding two pieces together whilst giving a sense of personal attention to each resident. This is a challenge, and is often the subject of discussion in the debriefing. The work requires '360° radar' according to one musician. The musicians need to keep everyone in the group safe enough to cope with unpredictability, risk, trying something new. They need to be prepared to be out of their own comfort zone whilst at the same time inspiring confidence in the group.

The workshops

From the moment that staff bring residents into the room, the workshop begins. Aware of the vulnerability of those in the group, every moment is important, from the warmth of the initial greeting and welcome to both staff and residents, to the care in inviting people to join the circle. Musicians respect the need for space to settle for some people and for others, the wish to engage in social interaction. For residents, this initial connection may involve conversation or hand-holding or for others, quietly 'being' beside someone as they absorb their new environment, the circle of people, the chairs, the instruments. The musicians' interest in them and their care staff, and responsiveness to them all impacts on the confidence any participant may have to even be in the room.

The workshop itself invites people into a musical relationship, in a variety of ways. Initially, the opening tune settles the group, with no requirement to do anything although often there is already participation. This shows in small responses that demonstrate the beginnings of trust. Here a lady takes off her gloves, another puts down her handbag, an agitated person physically relaxes and closes his eyes. Another person smiles, engages in eye contact with a musician, a member of staff smiles at a resident, gently putting her hand on his arms. Each person in the circle is greeted by name in song, accompanied with personalised musical phrases or flourishes. A sense of being in a circle develops and musical relationships grow from here, sometimes instruments played together in duos or trios, sometimes pieces improvised for individuals, sometimes the musicians being directed formally by others in the group and at other times pieces developing spontaneously.

Musicians pay attention to space, textures, dynamics in their music, taking care not to overwhelm with textures that are too thick, or passages that move too much when not appropriate. They pace the session carefully, allowing time for responses particularly at the end of pieces when silence often allows the space to process what has been experienced and responses may occur, perhaps in comments or smiles or sometimes giggles of recognition. The session moves through different moods in response to gestures, facial expressions, movement, spoken requests: 'I want to fly like the swallow', 'Let's play!', I'm the boss'. The session is about enabling people to find something of themselves. For this to happen, the musicians and staff need to 'be themselves'. Integrity, respect, calmness, ability to relinquish control whilst maintaining a safe framework, all contribute to the extent to which connections are made. Hierarchies change in the sessions, where for example, staff can be led by people with dementia or musicians directed by staff. The workshop offers equal status and empowerment to all participants, an unusual position for those who live and work in a care home.

The session ends with the 'closing piece', a repeat of the opening improvisation, which emerges from a piece already being played. This often requires subtle key changes, changes of mood, reorientation in many ways to bring the session to a predictable close. The ending is as important as the opening and supports the transition that is about to happen - saying goodbye, moving from chairs, changing to another environment again, all of which can cause confusion and upset to a person with dementia.

Learning and Development

The pattern of this session is repeated over eight weeks. Each workshop hour is followed by an hour of debriefing both for musicians and for staff. Changes in behaviour and mood are noticed by staff and discussed with the dementia care trainer in the debriefing. Individual staff members are encouraged to share in the discussion, their own vulnerabilities are sensitively drawn out and gradually they may risk talking about their relationships with each other within the workshop or within their teams outside the sessions. Often, tensions are revealed, overlooked promotions discussed, poor teamwork addressed. Also compliments are paid, laughter shared, warmth and trust developed. The impact of the work on themselves is as important as for those they care for. Valuing feeling responses, reaching staff at an emotional level, raising their confidence and self worth has a direct impact on the residents. The trainer needs to work with the same level of integrity and sensitivity as the musicians, recognising that he too needs to improvise, working from the personal experience of each member of staff rather than arriving with a body of knowledge about dementia that needs to be transmitted. In encouraging questioning and discussion in this way, the trainer is laying new foundations for learning and the quality of life improves for the care staff too
The musicians need a period of debriefing too. It is not easy for them to withdraw from the session and look at it objectively as they too need a time of transition to surface back to life outside the intensity of this experience. A facilitator who has also observed the session, helps the transition and leads the discussion: talking about the detail of the session, the effectiveness of their planning, exploring the ways they have worked together and the affect on each resident. The detail of this discussion will influence the subsequent session and often raises issues which will need further thought and conversations over the next week. Support for the team is vital, just as it is for staff as they cope with the emotional rigours of the work and face the

occasions when connections are not made, as well as celebrating the progress of individuals.

Outcomes

Quantifying changes and outcomes is not easy. This level of engagement aims to encourage less isolation, a sense of being part of something, of being recognised and respected. Staff often report significant changes in behaviour. A lady who would spend all day every day in bed now gets up and comes out of her room each day to join others. A man who would bark out single words and walk out of the company of others, even frightening staff, now speaks in sentences and allows staff to touch him so he is able to receive hand massage and be led into the garden. Changes may reveal themselves slowly, sometimes noticed after the project has left. They are small and sometimes seen only in the absence of certain patterns, maybe a person has less need to search or wander around constantly, for example. There may simply be moments of connection in a workshop, which for that individual is a momentous event. The project is about endeavour, intention, and process. Music for Life is a tool for learning, a place to experience immediacy, to be respected and to give respect. The outcomes of the project are reciprocal; the beneficiaries are not only the person with dementia but the staff and the musicians too. Their personal and professional lives are affected by their relationships with each other, by the challenges they face through those relationships and by the skills they learn together. The interplay between the three promotes change, affects the communities they live and work in and enhances the lives of them all.

6.3 L   Christine Stöger

Head of Classroom Teachers' Training, Hochschule für Musik, Cologne, Germany

This Case Study is drawn from the experience of Christine Stöger whilst she was responsible for music teacher training for general music education at the University of Music and Performing Arts in Vienna. She is interested in developing innovative models of music teaching, including creative activities and building bridges between classroom teachers and their professional development. In 2003 she became Professor of Music Education in the Hochschule für Musik in Cologne. Christine Stöger is a member of the Research Group in Lifelong Learning in Music & the Arts.

Klangnetze Project in Vienna

Description of project

Klangnetze (1992 – 2000) was initiated by the Ministry of Art and Science in Vienna, especially to foster creativity and new music in the field of education. An expert in music education was selected to develop a concept and to carry it out. He first established a group of composers and musicians in the field of New Music for the project. Then teachers from primary and secondary schools were invited to participate with one of their classes.

The project phase started with a three-day workshop where teachers and artists came together to improvise and develop models of improvisation based on avant-garde sounds-noise and structures. Pairs of teachers and artists tried out their models in schools of the region and then reflected on the process.

After the workshop future partnerships were decided and the crucial phase started in selected schools. In a couple of workshops with the school classes, the classroom-teacher and artist team supported the pupils to create their own piece of music. Since most of the children did not play an instrument, they experimented with voice, body percussion and materials like paper, glass, etc. to create the music. The music pieces were finally performed in one of the large Viennese concert halls. All the participants and their families were invited. A person moderated the concert, which was especially necessary to prepare the audience for the unusual experimental and interdisciplinary creative products.

The most demanding point was how to build up a partnership between these two very different groups of people – teachers and artists. The project initiators worked against big prejudices with a long tradition. Some of the teams failed or in the worst case, just gave up. But most cases reported enriching experiences and an unforeseen musical development of their classes. Most progress was found in the area of co-operation because as the project was carried out over a number of years, a culture of partnership could be developed.

Comments

There was an interest from the Ministry to bring artists, new music and new sounds into schools. There was a project manager from the educational side who chose a composer interested in education. A group of composers and music teachers from secondary schools was established and a class selected from each school for the project.
It was hard to bring the teachers and artists together as there was a lot of prejudice from both sides that went quite deep. There were two weekends of workshops in order to create small pieces for each school. The teachers and artists often worked on very elementary things without instruments. In the schools they tried out the workshop processes with different children over a five week period. At times this proved difficult to facilitate. It was also difficult to get some of the schools fully on board with the project.

In the end there was a concert in one of the largest Viennese concert halls. The introduction was important because the pieces were unusual and involved other disciplines including video. Each year the project became easier to deliver. Very slowly a long trail of communication and understanding developed which removed some of the former prejudices. The Klangnetze project stopped after five years due to a lack of money, despite the fact that it had established itself in a number of schools. The initiator of the project was the Ministry of Culture and it paid for the co-ordinator.

Learning points

Project money is not going to last for ever. How can one act proactively in order to ensure an initiative can become a sustainable programme?

- Having the right people in the organisations is critical. However, projects cannot be purely personality led.

- In the end, the initiator has to make themselves redundant.

- A criterion for ensuring the development of a project should be whether there is an increase and broadening of interest.

- 'Lead partners': the initial direction and motivation comes from a lead institution, but all partners must feel ownership.

Transcript of interview with Christine Stöger by Rineke Smilde on the Development of Sustainable Partnerships – meeting in Groningen on 22 April, 2006

6.3 M   Judith Webster

Director, Nuance Music Ltd
Course Leader, PGDip Creative Leadership, Royal College of Music

Journey to music therapy

Everything changed for me at the beginning of my final year studying music at Birmingham University. Like many musicians, I had mapped out my intended career. Following university, I was to go to music college as a postgraduate followed by a short career as a professional musician in an orchestra (maybe 10 years), followed by something more down to earth after I had fulfilled my lifelong dream and got it out of my system. Then I had an accident, crushed my left hand, and began to get to grips with the most important lesson of my life. You can't plan your own destiny, and if you try to, fate might get in your way, and you may well be blind to the most creative opportunities which lie right in front of you.

So, from the outset my personal journey towards being a music therapist was littered with judgements around quality and the hierarchies associated with different musical skills in the music world. The pinnacle was to be a player; if you couldn't do that then you would teach. I went abroad to have a think.

Music therapy was always a natural bringing together of two important aspects of my life in a truly creative context; my music, and my tendency to be drawn to challenging social contexts that forced me to think and grow – at that time evidenced through voluntary work. However, I had already considered and rejected music therapy as a career path, prior to university, as to me it felt second best. Now that fate had closed the door on a potential playing career (as a violinist), I had to take another look at who I was and what I might do. There was never any question about it being in music, but I have always been driven by personal conviction and was incapable of simply drifting into an alternative career if it did not feel right.

There followed a two-year journey towards music therapy, and subsequently, through the work itself, a discovery of my true musical and personal strengths and how they could be expressed in the context of music therapy practice.

The work itself

I studied at the Nordoff Robbins Music Therapy Centre and am therefore trained in that particular approach. This involves the therapist being based at the piano and building a therapeutic relationship with a client in music which is improvised together. The client is offered a range of instruments including percussion instruments, piano, and voice. The therapist is trained in clinical improvisation which is the language of the therapeutic relationship. The premise is that the way a person improvises communicates who they are as a human being and that through a therapeutic relationship with the therapist in music, interventions can be made and change is possible. Although change is facilitated and expressed in the language of music, it is an external expression of that which is fundamental to the person and not disconnected from them. Therefore, new possibilities which take place in the musical interaction should also be evident in the client's life and relationships beyond the music therapy session. The musical relationship, like any therapeutic relationship, gives the client an opportunity to work through and to explore different ways of being. The music therapist is therefore trained in improvisation skills, as well as in psychological processes, child development and so on. This enables the therapist to hear and understand what the client communicates about themselves and to work with that.

The key element in the music therapy process is to quickly establish a therapeutic relationship, as opposed to simply improvising or making music with the client. Whilst making music is worthwhile for its own sake, it is not the intent in this context. To establish this relationship, the therapist must 'play the client's music'. This involves improvising precisely what is communicated by the client in order to gradually heighten their awareness of themselves, and then of the therapeutic relationship. To do this, the therapist must focus completely on them – how they move, feel, look, vocalise, breathe etc. and play that music, the music of the client through clinically directed improvisation. The therapist might take the tempo of their walk, gestures, movements; take the pitches and phrasing of their voice; take the rhythm of their tapping, stamping, shouting; play with the same energy, play with the same tension, play with the same unease, suspicion, calm and so on. In so doing, the therapist communicates important messages which are the bedrock for the subsequent work. In this way, the therapist communicates acceptance of the client, that they are being listened to, empathised with, given space to be whoever they want to be, being understood. The client has an opportunity to reflect on themselves in this musical mirror, as played by and with the therapist.

As the relationship develops, the therapist can begin to offer new possibilities to the client in music, and to explore different aspects of how they present themselves. For example, a client who persistently plays very rapidly and loudly might be encouraged to explore the more lyrical side of themselves; a client who obsessively gets stuck in a certain tempo or pattern might be offered contrast through experimenting with different metre or phrase lengths, or unpredictable patterns and free improvisation. A client who presents themselves as introverted and withdrawn might be encouraged to find their voice and sing, or play with large physical gestures.

Quality

To recap then, it is the integrity of the therapeutic relationship, established in music, which is the platform upon which personal development takes place and change is possible. A number of key ingredients are essential in order to achieve this.

It is vital that,

> the therapist focuses 100% on the client and connects with them and their needs in music

> the therapist has sufficient facility on their instrument to be able to improvise in a clinical context to support the client

> the therapist records and analyses the session/music as a way of informing future development and future music

> the therapist is able to differentiate between their own personal issues, and those of the client, in order to work most effectively

> the surroundings are private with no interruptions

the session is confidential and provides a safe physical space for the client

the time of the session is respected in that it is a regular commitment at a consistent time each week

the music therapist is regarded as part of the team supporting the client

Already, it is clear that quality issues concern not only the interaction in the music therapy session itself, but the context within which it exists. Care needs to be taken to secure the right environment for the work. To do this, it is important to establish positive and collaborative relationships with the other professionals involved with the client, so that the work can be respected as playing its part in their development.

Context and meaning

As stated earlier, the music therapy session provides a relationship within which an individual can be understood, listened to, respected, supported and challenged, according to their needs. As the music therapy process unfolds, the therapist stands beside the client on their journey of personal development – offering them a different experience of themselves and their relationships with others. This is achieved through concrete musical interaction and developing new musical skills, but always in the context of personal development. The sessions do not focus on the acquisition of skills per se, but these are nevertheless a barometer of the client's development. It is the contextualising of these 'skills' beyond the music therapy session which demonstrates lasting change in the client and the real meaning. Without this transfer of skills and ways of being to external contexts, it could be argued that the music therapy process has been ineffectual.

In order to be able to assess this externalisation of the work and the progress of the client, it is important that the therapist interacts and collaborates with other 'communities' of professionals and carers who are involved with the client. It is through these interactions that they may have a fuller understanding of the client's context and the impact of their work, and that others may understand the contribution made by the music therapy.

In my own experience as a therapist, I found it crucial to work collaboratively and saw it as part of my professional responsibility to enable co-workers and carers to share and witness their client's development in the sessions, so that we could identify how this translated into their every day life, or not. I made home visits to parents of children with special needs, sharing extracts of recordings or videos with them to help them understand the process, and indeed to understand their own child more fully. As a therapist, these visits were a source of support to me, as they enabled me to contextualise my experience of the work and celebrate changes and developments in a client which I might not otherwise have witnessed. The context beyond the therapy room gave further meaning to the work in the sessions.

Personal reflections on quality

Having initially disregarded music therapy as a career, I found that the very skills I believed to be my own strengths were the most useful as a music therapist. I found it was something I could do well and with the conviction I needed. As a musician, I have always considered myself to be a strong communicator, placing the emphasis on my musicality rather than my technical wizardry. It seemed to me that this aspect of musicianship was deemed less valuable than overtly technical skills. In music therapy, it was the very musicianship I possessed, together with a real empathy for and sensitivity to people, that was valued most. When training, I could see how it was possible to be an excellent improviser with a high level of technical facility, without making a personal connection at all with the client in music. It was possible for clever improvisation to be a barrier to the therapeutic relationship rather than a facilitator of it.

Although no longer practising as a music therapist, the training and experience I gained have strongly influenced all of my subsequent work. It has affected the way I have approached the training of professional musicians, the way I set up community projects, the nature of my own musical involvement in a project and the way I have shaped a programme on behalf of an organisation or group of musicians. I could not have chosen a more appropriate grounding for the work I went on to do within the community and education departments of orchestras. It enables me to continue to expect change and innovation within highly traditional organisations for whom change is slow and not always welcome. It is that continual striving for integrity which enables me to grow and develop, finding new opportunities within old contexts, and believing in what might seem impossible for just a little bit longer...

6.3 N   Marga Wobma-Helmich

Director of Education, Participation and Programming National Ballet and Nederlandse Opera
Former Head of Education Het Concertgebouw, Amsterdam

Changing roles

Imagine a large meadow outside Amsterdam. On the horizon you see typical Amsterdam canal houses – a meadow in the middle of nowhere with cows, horses and a small stream. On this meadow a concert hall is being built. We are talking about the year 1882 when a few wealthy inhabitants of Amsterdam took the initiative to build a concert hall that developed to become one of the most famous and respected concert halls in the world, nowadays standing in the middle of Amsterdam. Situated in the middle of the city but also in the cultural heart of the city, with three galleries among which the State Museum and the Van Gogh Museum. The Concertgebouw, with its Recital and Main Hall stages, nearly 900 concerts per year visited by around 810,000 visitors. It is the main house of the Royal Concertgebouw Orchestra with its chief conductor Mariss Jansons. A great number of national and international chamber music ensembles, orchestras and soloists can be heard in our House.

Each year the Concertgebouw welcomes approximately 30,000 children following primary or secondary school. The education programme is set up to reach all those children who would never visit the Concertgebouw with their parents. There are parents who do bring their children to our special children concerts, approximately 30 concerts per year, but these parents still represent only a small part of our society. Through our programme for schools we reach children from all different backgrounds. It is not our main goal but we are proud of the number of children coming to our House. This says nothing about the quality, which is our main focus, but it says something about the scale of our work and the place that is given to it in our organization. We do care; we are passionate and invest in many different ways. Although the education programme has been running now for about nine years, it still feels as if we're just starting and that we still have a long way to go.

From 2009 education for adults has been brought under the responsibility of the Education Department, which was not the case up till now, and this aspect is going to be expanded and deepened. At the same time, we are developing an outreach programme in order to be able to reach out to those people in our city that have not been seen yet as our target groups but for whom we want to offer our building and musical resources. We are not primarily doing this in order to build audiences; we believe that we can only be part of our community if we can be of some value for more people than only the happy few. In this respect it should be noted that the Concertgebouw has an internationally high reputation but – however – its market is mainly local and to some extent national.

During the period since our school programme has been running, the perception about our role has changed a lot. We started with projects where we programmed concerts with carefully selected repertoire and with theatrical elements to make the music more accessible. For each project a series of lessons was developed to be taught at school by the school teacher. One of the issues we were facing was a lack of time and a lack of musical skills by the school teachers in order to prepare their pupils for the concerts. In teacher training courses there is less and less time for arts subjects and teachers feel more and more insecure in teaching music. The music method books which teachers can use are expensive and require some basic music skills and understanding. But perhaps more importantly is the pressure on teachers to spend as much time as possible on subjects like mathematics and language, which does not stimulate them to teach music on a regular basis.

At the same time our government has introduced some measures in order to stimulate schools to be more culturally active. It is seen as the responsibility of the schools as well as for the arts institutions. Instead of offering one-off projects, the arts institutions are expected to build up long-term relationships with schools and to help them develop an ongoing learning curve. Important ingredients are the three learning fields which are focused on the participation of the pupils in an active, receptive and reflective way. This role requires a major change in the way in which our programmes are constructed. But still, the main goal lies with the musical outcomes. Another change of role is using the arts more for social goals than artistic: for example, using the arts to strengthen cohesion in society, to improve learning outcomes for pupils and so on.

How can we as concert halls satisfy all these different roles? There are a lot of questions we ask ourselves. What elements are important in the music curriculum and how can we contribute to that as a concert hall? How can we make sure that we include all pupils from all different backgrounds? What can we offer as side effects of music education to our society and how can we bring this about? Who are our partners? How can we train and who should be trained to do the actual job?

To give you an idea of how we tried to realise our new role I would like to outline two of our projects. The first one is based on developing musical skills, the second one on social outcomes.

Papa pia is a singing programme for 7-years old and their teachers. A story is told through a series of songs which are being taught in the class and performed at the Concertgebouw. A jazz ensemble is involved; the songs are specially written for the project and are a mixture of jazz and world music. The project starts with a kick off for the teachers to teach them the songs, but more important to offer the teachers new skills to improve the quality of their vocal teaching. That is our main focus for this project: offering the teachers the ability to work on their own musical skills and motivate them to be more active with music in their class room. The teacher starts the project in the class and for a further two sessions our vocal teacher works with the pupils and teacher. This vocal teacher is the singer/actor who is leading the performance at the Concertgebouw. During the performance the pupils perform their songs together with the jazz ensemble, some songs are performed by all classes, but each class sings one song alone as well. The children love being part of the performance and visibly enjoy singing.

The second project is called *Percossa*. *Percossa* is a percussion ensemble and the project is named after this ensemble. It has been developed for pupils following pre-vocational secondary education where 60 percent of all pupils follow their secondary school education. There is an ongoing debate about the system because it brings pupils together from so many different backgrounds and needs. It's called the trash can of our school system, and again, 60 percent of all secondary school pupils follow this system! Especially in the big cities these schools are facing major problems having to deal with, amongst others, safety and learning outcomes. Most of these pupils don't relate in any way to the music we offer.

We did have a project for these pupils before we started with the *Percossa* project. This was a success for schools outside Amsterdam but not for those in Amsterdam. During one of the concerts in our Main Hall the pupils of two schools started to tease each other and it ended in a fight with knifes at the Central Station. The schools involved decided not to go outside the school with their pupils anymore and not to attend any cultural activities in the future.

This was the starting point for the *Percossa* project. Together with these schools we had long sessions and developed different workshops leading to a concert at the Concertgebouw given by the pupils, presented by the pupils. The scenery, the costumes, the cakes during the coffee break, the publicity – all were realized by the pupils themselves. Only one school at a time is involved in order to avoid problems between schools. And there is strong involvement of the teachers and the musicians of the ensemble who know how to communicate and work with the pupils. Their professionalism, the way in which they keep challenging the pupils, keep them concentrating and winning their trust was of great value for both the teachers and pupils involved. During the concert, with parents and friends present, the pupils performed to a very high level. For some of them, they could finally feel proud of themselves, standing on the stage and receiving the appreciation that they deserved. After one of the concerts I congratulated the director of the school with his pupils. He pointed out that for him the greatest value was for his teachers. The project gave a quality impulse on working with the pupils on a project basis, which he had been trying to introduce for several years but had not succeeded. He saw his teachers change and he realized the school could benefit from this in many different ways.

At the beginning of this text I asked you to imagine a meadow. Two years ago an animator from London was involved in one of our projects. She asked the children to imagine a meadow as well. Of course, she didn't end up with the meadow where the Concertgebouw was built. Together with the children she ended up picturing a meadow with the sounds of the animals, of the wind and everything else you can hear or imagine you can hear. A meadow as a metaphor for a musical piece to which the children could relate their creativity, and be challenged to express themselves and give sound to their emotions. Perhaps this is one of the most important aspects of our work, what we can mean to our society: inviting people to express, to be involved, to communicate, to enjoy making and listening to music.

6.4   **Personal perspective**

Guiding principles

As a postscript it has been suggested that I spell out the educational perspective that has acted as a thread throughout my professional life. My journey has been rich and varied as I have moved between schools, colleges of education, universities, conservatoires and a school for talented young musicians. Sitting comfortably within this seemingly fragmented life is a sense of continuity based on a continuously evolving educational philosophy.

At the centre of this philosophy lie certain principles, all of which underpin the main substance of this book. For example:

- Aiming to achieve parity of entitlement for all young people and students engaged in the arts and education.

- Providing a quality and integrity of educational and artistic experience that connects to its context and resonates with the felt needs of that particular community.

- Respecting and listening to the voice of each person as they deepen and extend the quality of their learning.

- Developing processes of reflection that are grounded in experience but which enhance the quality of educational and artistic learning.

- Deepening an understanding of what constitutes quality in different educational and cultural contexts.

- Fostering creative engagement through harnessing individual and collective vision, motivation, imagination and curiosity.

- Developing a breadth of perspective that enables each person to make connections and understand, if not always agree with, other points of view.

- Establishing partnerships and collaborative ways of working that are based on shared values and mutual respect.

- Ensuring that student teachers and emerging arts practitioners have a realistic view of how to integrate and function effectively within a rapidly changing workplace.

Shifting the culture of an educational or cultural organisation so that it becomes more responsive to change and begins to extend its horizons and make new connections.

Viewing a school, college or professional arts organisation as a hub, a crucible for educational and artistic engagement within its wider community.

Creating support structures for teachers and arts practitioners to engage in different forms of lifelong learning that extend their skills, deepen their reflective learning and strengthen their personal and professional development.

Teacher education

All these principles can be seen in embryo from my early development work in teacher education. My MPhil thesis, *A Concept of a College of Education* (Renshaw, 1969), presented a critique of teacher education. It examined the purpose, nature and idea of a college of education, focussing particularly on a reappraisal of the curriculum. My supervisor was Richard Peters, who was the influential Professor of Philosophy of Education at the University of London Institute of Education. His seminal book, *Ethics and Education*, published in 1966 became the backbone of much of my thinking. The '60s were heady days at the Institute of Education, especially in the areas of philosophy and sociology, both of which brought their critical edge to bear on educational practice. It was not long before there was a growing movement for reforming teacher education in England and Wales and this led to a public enquiry that culminated in the James Report (1972) on *Teacher Education and Training.*

Feeding into the James' Enquiry was a protest voice from a network of teachers, college and university lecturers, students in training, administrators and councillors from Local Education Authorities, who came together with the aim of seeking ways of raising the quality of teaching in schools. Groups met in different parts of the country under the auspices of the 'Society for the Promotion of Educational Reform through Teacher Training' – SPERTTT as it was known. In 1971 we published a book, *Dear Lord James* (Burgess, 1971), which was an appeal to the James' Enquiry to establish new priorities in teacher education.

My own contribution to the national debate examined the outmoded assumptions and curricular structures that militated against creating a quality teaching force with the skills and breadth of vision to engage with the next generation of children. The emphasis was on finding ways and means of enriching young people's learning and expanding their horizons. The quest for quality in teacher education was seen as a key priority. For example:

> Any college curriculum must be geared to producing teachers who can understand the demands of education and society in a rapidly changing world. It is little wonder that there is growing uncertainty about the validity of the present curriculum, for we ought to be training teachers to prepare children for a highly complex technologically based economy, in which they would be capable of coping with and generating change. The children of today are entering a dynamic 'regenerative' society, in which the pace of technological advance is accelerating, bringing in its wake a range of new social and economic demands, new organisational structures, new concepts, attitudes, systems, roles and patterns of behaviour. The needs of such a society must be reflected in any teacher-education programme. Colleges cannot afford to be bound by obstructionist traditions; the curriculum should continually be reappraised in the light of ever-changing conditions (Renshaw, 1971a, p.82).

A similar argument can be found in a number of publications addressing the challenge of changing the teacher education system at a critical time of flux and development (for example, Renshaw, 1968; 1971b; 1973).

Although written 40 years ago, the main thrust of this critique has a certain resonance with current debates about transforming the culture of conservatoires! The pace of change can be painfully slow, especially if people remain entrenched within the security of their silos.

In 1974 I became Editor of *Education for Teaching*, the Journal of the Association of Teachers in Colleges and Departments of Education. My first editorial raised questions that would not be out of place in the present fragile climate of trying to maintain and strengthen the quality and scope of educational provision in cash-strapped schools, colleges and universities.

> One point that has been stressed repeatedly in this journal is the need to raise standards within the teaching profession. Such a plea might be regarded as obvious, but it would seem that concern for the quality of the professional preparation of teachers is more important now than ever before in the recent history of teacher education. At present, those engaged in training the country's teachers are fighting to reconcile conflicting political, administrative, professional, academic and student interests, during a difficult period of economic constraint and national cutback in teacher-supply numbers. Although the present crisis has the advantage of concentrating the mind, it is only too easy for the interminable debate to become dominated by the apparent machinations of those Whitehall mandarins who are obsessed with rationalisation, contraction and economy.
>
> Fortunately, there are some people seriously concerned with reorganisation, who recognise that the quality of the teaching force depends on considerations that rise above the implementation of a few structural changes designed for administrative convenience. Such tutors and teachers have the vision to look beyond current political and organisational battles in their attempt to focus attention on the means and ends of teacher education. For example, some colleges and polytechnics have acknowledged that fundamental curricular change needs to be accompanied by a corresponding shift in the pattern of power within an institution itself. Thus, in some instances, diversification and curriculum reform

have resulted in the replacement of the traditional departmental structure by interdisciplinary schools or faculties. Furthermore, not only are some colleges becoming less isolated from the mainstream of tertiary education, but they are also forging strong working links with schools, who, quite rightly are beginning to play a more active role in the preparation of teachers. There are indications that such growing local involvement will be extended further to make colleges major resource centres within a whole community (Renshaw, 1974, p.3).

Most of these views on education and training were formulated during my period of lecturing in teacher education – between 1964 and 1975. Since then the principles and perspectives have been reformulated, strengthened and applied to different educational and cultural contexts, but the underlying mission remains the same: to provide future generations of children, students and staff with an education and training of quality, integrity and relevance – one that engages and connects both to them as individuals and to the world with all its challenges, possibilities and opportunities. It soon became clear that if these ends were to be achieved, whether in the domain of teacher education or in that of conservatoires, it is necessary for each institution, supported by appropriate professional bodies and partnerships, to re-appraise the principles underlying its curriculum, to reconsider its culture or mindset, and to re-align its priorities so that they reflect where the world is at.

The education of talented young musicians and students

The principles of connecting to context and broadening the horizons of students and young people have been two of the key threads through my engagement with education. When Principal of the Yehudi Menuhin School, from 1975 to 1984, I was keen to widen the social horizons of the talented young musicians by creating opportunities for them to perform in contexts outside the normal concert hall (see Section 2.3). I was well aware of the criticism that a specialist music school runs the danger of cutting the children off from the realities of the outside world and I wanted to ensure that they did not become excessively self-absorbed and disconnected from wider society. Therefore every effort was made to create opportunities for making music in different social contexts (see Renshaw, 1980). As has been discussed at different points in this book, the launch of the Music Performance and Communication Skills Project at the Guildhall School of Music & Drama in 1984 grew out of these early initiatives at the Menuhin School.

In parallel with my desire to ensure that young musicians and students do not become trapped in a self-regarding bubble was a strong commitment to opening up the closed culture in which many musicians learnt. Although in the last decade the workplace has changed considerably with musicians having to be flexible and adaptable within portfolio careers, the culture of conservatoires and orchestras, for example, can still generate crippling feelings of fear, failure and dysfunction.

For many young musicians and their respective schools and colleges, the gold standard of success is winning competitions. Of course, there is nothing intrinsically evil about competition. What matters is how individuals cope with it and how events like music competitions are perceived and used – or abused, when tarnished by the crude veneer of celebrity culture. The most pernicious competitions are those designed to promote the 'star' system with its implicit hierarchy of soloist, ensemble musician, orchestral player, opera chorus singer and teacher. Such competitions are premised on a narrow view of achievement and excellence, which tends to maximise failure rather than success.

The desire to succeed is only natural, but for many young musicians their motivation is intimately connected to the aspirations of possessive teachers and ambitious parents, whose egos are bound up with the success of their students or children. In their attempt to gain approval, too many students are motivated by feelings of fear, guilt and a sense of duty, rather than by a love of music. These feelings are often deep-seated and go back a long way in their personal history. Sometimes they are reinforced by a growing awareness of the emotional and financial investment made by parents. There are times, I suspect, when some young musicians might not mind 'failing', but in no way would they want to fail their parents and teachers. Therefore, when placed in a competitive setting, the pressure to succeed is enormous. The fear of failure can then be devastating, leaving some students totally dysfunctional.

Recognising the seriousness of this problem, there are an increasing number of teachers developing forms of learning and teaching aimed at building up self-confidence, self-esteem and a positive self-image. Nevertheless, within the existing competitive world many students become severely judgemental and consumed by self-doubt. At its worst, this leads to a lack of trust resulting in destructive attitudes and collective neurosis within an institution. A typical student response is to display an apparent lack of commitment, hiding behind a veneer of apathy and cynicism in order to protect themselves from the pain of perceived failure and from the power of their deeper feelings.

Any human inner world is fragile, and yet having the strength to share this vulnerability is an essential part of the artistic process. The danger is that the stress of competition and the pressure of trying to become a soloist can result in students playing a survival game which lacks artistic integrity and fails to embody any form of artistic engagement. This is not only psychologically damaging, but it is musically barren and bereft. Students and professional musicians must be encouraged to find their own creative energy which will enable them to take risks, to act in the moment, be spontaneous and put their own authentic stamp on their performance. Conservatoires and music organisations must ensure that students and staff are given the space, time and opportunity to become more rooted in themselves and their artistic life. In the final analysis, both their inner motivation and quality of engagement are central to what they have to say as artists.

Another way of putting this is that self-worth is too readily defined by what people 'do' rather than what they 'are'. The challenge to institutions is to create a climate in which staff and students can develop a positive relationship between a well-nourished sense of 'being' and successful 'doing'.

To achieve this, a more realistic view of student aspirations needs to be adopted. It is absurd that in terms of perceived value, high priority is still ascribed to 'winning a competition' for pianists, singers and strings, or 'getting a job in an orchestra' for wind players. The music world has moved on as can be seen from many examples in this book. Many young musicians will not work in areas of conventional performance and therefore it is critical that they do not see themselves as failures. All musicians need to value a diversity of performance possibilities, developing imaginative training opportunities to match the changing needs of the profession.

Most of these observations about the culture of failure stemmed from my experience at the Menuhin School and from working in conservatoires and with players in orchestras who were aiming to extend their professional profile. They formed the basis of a talk I gave on BBC 3 Music Matters in December 2000 under the title *Music Performance and the Culture of Failure*.

What is telling is that the BBC presentation concluded with the following statement that could very easily have been drawn from the main text of this book.

> We must never forget that music, along with all the arts, can help to transform our lives. It can open new doors, extend our ways of seeing the world and challenge us to redefine who we are through active engagement in artistic experience. By enabling the cultural bubble to burst, musicians would more readily connect to the changing world. We need to create conditions which will not allow failure to cripple a musician's life. Fundamentally, this is a moral as much as an artistic imperative for all music institutions (Renshaw, 2000).

Epilogue

The full force of this statement could be seen as a cri de coeur for all those musicians, artists and teachers working with young people and students. There is no excuse for allowing musicians' lives to be damaged by an unreflective and unresponsive institutional culture. Unfortunately, in some cases the 'system' remains stubbornly resistant to redefining its central purpose and to re-aligning its priorities. The legacy of past practices can only too easily act as an unnecessary constraint on change and development. This could be seen as irresponsible in relation to preparing the next generation of artists for a profession that is becoming increasingly more imaginative and daring in its practice.

The voices throughout this book demonstrate only too clearly what can be achieved when arts practitioners have a broad view of their role and are motivated to engage with the myriad of possibilities within the whole community. Their dual passion for people and for art lies at the core of their commitment. This passion must always be allowed to burn brightly as a source of their engagement. Personally, I have found their motivation, values and sense of purpose catching – our many conversations have certainly helped to keep my own flame burning. For this I feel deep gratitude.

Bibliography

Barenboim, D., & Said, E.W. (2002). *Parallels and Paradoxes: Explanations in music and society.* New York: Pantheon.

Church, M. (2009). A decade of hope. In *Programme for Prom 50.* London: BBC Proms.

Cleveland, W. (2002). *Mapping the Field: Arts-based community development.* Minneapolis: Community Arts Network, Reading Room.
www.communityarts.net/readingroom/archivefiles/overview_essays_all2/index

Cox, A., & Gelsthorpe, L. (2008). *Beats & Bars.* Music in Prisons: an evaluation. University of Cambridge: Institute of Criminology.

Creative Partnerships London North. (2007). *Exploring the Impact of Creative Learning on Artists and Practitioners.* London: Creative Partnerships London North.
londonnorth@creative-partnerships.com

Culture and Learning Consortium. (2009). *Get It: The power of cultural learning.* London: Culture and Learning Consortium.
www.cultureandlearning.org.uk

CUREE. (2005a). *Mentoring and Coaching Capacity Building Project: National Framework for Mentoring and Coaching.* Coventry: Centre for the Use of Research and Evidence in Education.
www.curee-paccts.com

CUREE. (2005b). *Mentoring and Coaching for Learning.* Summary report of the mentoring and coaching capacity building project 2004-2005. Coventry: Centre for the Use of Research and Evidence in Education.
www.curee-paccts.com

CUREE. (2007). *Effective Mentoring and Coaching: Leading professional development to make a difference.* Coventry: Centre for the Use of Research and Evidence in Education.
www.curee-paccts.com

D'Amore, A. (2009). *Musical Futures: An approach to teaching and learning.* London: The Paul Hamlyn Foundation.
www.musicalfutures.org.uk

Downie, R. S., & Telfer, E. (1969). *Respect for Persons.* London: George Allen & Unwin Ltd.

European University Association. (2008). *European Universities' Charter on Lifelong Learning.* Brussels: EUA.
www.eua.be

Flood, P. (2009). LSO Discovery. In *Zone Magazine, Issue 17.*
www.musiceducationzone.net/z17_lso_discovery?_c=1

Footman, T. (2009). *The Noughties: A decade that changed the world 2000-2009.* Richmond: Crimson Publishing.

Gardner, H. (2008). *Five Minds for the Future.* Boston Massachusetts: Harvard Business Press.

Giddens, A. (1984). *The Constitution of Society: Outline of the theory of structuralism.* Cambridge: Polity Press.

Goffee, R., & Jones, G. (2009). *Clever: Leading your smartest, most creative people.* Boston Massachusetts: Harvard Business Press.

Gregory, S. (2004). *Quality and Effectiveness in Creative Music Workshop Practice: An evaluation of language, meaning and collaborative process.* MPhil Thesis. London: Royal College of Art.

Guildhall Ensemble. (1989). *Guildhall Ensemble: Performance & Communication Skills Project.* London: Guildhall School of Music & Drama.

Guildhall School of Music & Drama. (2009). *MMus in Leadership and Creative Music Workshop Leading.* London: Guildhall School of Music & Drama.
www.gsmd.ac.uk

Hobsbawm, E. (1997). *Age of Extremes: The short twentieth century 1914-1991.* London: Abacus.

Holden, J. (2008). *Culture and Learning: Towards a new agenda.* Consultation Paper. London: DEMOS.
www.demos.co.uk

House of Commons Education and Skills Committee. (2007). *Creative Partnerships and the Curriculum.* Eleventh Report of Session 2006-07. London: The Stationery Office Ltd., HC 1034.

Joint Music Master for New Audiences and Innovative Practice. (2008).
www.jointmusicmaster.org

Kelly, J. (2010). Citizen Ethics. In *Saturday Guardian* 20.02.10.
www.guardian.co.uk/citizenethics

Killick, J. (1997). You are Words in *You are Words*. Also in *Journal of Dementia Care*. London: Hawker Publications Ltd.

Killick, J. (2008). Reasons. In *Dementia Diary – Journal of Dementia Care*. London: Hawker Publications Ltd.

Lave, J., & Wenger, E. (1991). *Situated Learning: Legitimate peripheral participation*. Cambridge: Cambridge University Press.

McMaster, B. (2008). *Supporting Excellence in the Arts: From measurement to judgement*. London: DCMS.
www.culture.gov.uk/reference_library/publications/archive_2008/mcmaster_su

Music in Prisons. (2009). *Autumn Newsletter*. London: The Irene Taylor Trust.
www.musicinprisons.org.uk

National Advisory Committee on Creative and Cultural Education. (1999). *All Our Futures: Creativity, culture and education*. London: DfEE/DCMS.
www.culture.gov.uk/pdf/naccce.pdf

Odam, G., & Bannan, N. (2005). *The Reflective Conservatoire: Studies in music education*. London: Guildhall School of Music & Drama and Ashgate Publishing Ltd.

Peters, R.S. (1964). *Education as Initiation*. London: University of London Institute of Education and George G. Harrap & Co.

Peters, R.S. (1966). *Ethics and Education*. London: George Allen & Unwin Ltd.

Polanyi, M. (1966). *The Tacit Dimension*. New York: Doubleday & Co.

Reimer, B. (1970). *A Philosophy of Music Education*. Englewood Cliffs, New Jersey: Prentice Hall, Inc.

Renshaw, P. (1968). A re-appraisal of the college of education curriculum. *Education for Teaching,* **75**, 28-34.

Renshaw, P. (1969). *A Concept of a College of Education*. MPhil Thesis. University of London Institute of Education.

Renshaw, P. (1971a). A curriculum for teacher education. In T. Burgess (Ed.), *Dear Lord James: A critique of teacher education.* Harmondsworth, Middlesex: Penguin Books Ltd.

Renshaw, P. (1971b). The objectives and structure of the college curriculum. In J.W. Tibble (Ed.), *The Future of Teacher Education.* London: Routledge & Kegan Paul.

Renshaw, P. (1973). A flexible curriculum for teacher education. In D.E. Lomax (Ed.), *The Education of Teachers in Britain.* London: John Wiley & Sons.

Renshaw, P. (1974). Editorial. *Education for Teaching,* **95**, 3-4.

Renshaw, P. (1980). The place of special schooling in the education of gifted children. In R.M. Povey (Ed.), *Educating the Gifted Child.* London: Harper & Row, Publishers.

Renshaw, P. (1984). *Proposal for Music Performance and Communication Skills Project.* Unpublished document.

Renshaw, P. (1992). Orchestras and the training revolution. *British Journal of Music Education,* **9**, 61-70.

Renshaw, P. (1993). *The Management of Creativity in Schools, Colleges and Arts Organisations.* London: Gresham College.

Renshaw, P. (2000). *Music Performance and the Culture of Failure.* London: BBC 3 Music Matters: Counterpoint.

Renshaw, P. (2001). *A Continuing Journey: An enabling framework for the future of the Guildhall School of Music & Drama.* London: Guildhall School of Music & Drama.

Renshaw, P. (2005a). Connecting Conversations: The changing voice of the artist. In M. Miles (Ed.), *New Practices: New Pedagogies.* London: Routledge, Taylor & Francis Group.

Renshaw, P. (2005b). *Simply Connect: 'Next practice' in group music-making and musical leadership.* London: The Paul Hamlyn Foundation. www.musicalfutures.org.uk

Renshaw, P. (2007). Lifelong learning for musicians: critical issues arising from a case study of Connect. In P. Mak, N. Kors & P. Renshaw, *Formal, Non-formal and Informal Learning in Music.* Lectorate Lifelong Learning in

Music, Prince Claus Conservatoire, Groningen and Royal Conservatoire, The Hague.
www.lifelonglearninginmusic.org

Renshaw, P. (2008). *REFLECT Creative Partnerships National Co-mentoring Programme: Evaluation report.* Gateshead: The Sage Gateshead.
www.reflectco-mentoring.com

Renshaw, P., & Smith, W. (2008). *REFLECT Co-mentoring Framework.* Gateshead: The Sage Gateshead.
www.reflectco-mentoring.com

Renshaw, P. (2009). *Lifelong Learning for Musicians: The place of mentoring.* Lectorate Lifelong Learning in Music & the Arts, Prince Claus Conservatoire, Groningen and Royal Conservatoire, The Hague.
www.lifelonglearninginmusic.org

Research Group in Lifelong Learning in Music & the Arts. (2009). Prince Claus Conservatoire, Groningen and Royal Conservatoire, The Hague.
www.lifelonglearninginmusic.org

Roberts, P. (2006). *Nurturing Creativity in Young People: A report to Government to inform future policy.* London: DCMS/DfES.
www.culture.gov.uk/reference_library/publications/3524.aspx

Robinson, K. (2009). *The Element: How finding your passion changes everything.* London: Allen Lane, Penguin Books.

Robinson, S., & Greenstreet, T. (2006). *Mission Unaccomplished: The place of education and learning in our national and regional performing arts and cultural organisations.* Provocation Paper. London: Mission, Models, Money.
www.missionmodelsmoney.org.uk

Schön, D. (1987). *Educating the Reflective Practitioner.* San Francisco: Jossey-Bass.

Smilde, R. (2009a). *Musicians as Lifelong Learners: Discovery through biography.* Delft: Eburon Academic Publishers.

Smilde, R. (2009b). *Musicians as Lifelong Learners: 32 biographies.* Delft: Eburon Academic Publishers.

Solbu, E. (2007). What is excellence in Higher Music Education? Presentation at the Seminar *Trends in the Music Profession in Europe: Lifelong Learning and Employability.* (DVD Lectorate & Polifonia: Dialogue in Music.) Lectorate Lifelong Learning in Music. Prince Claus Conservatoire,

Groningen, Royal Conservatoire, The Hague and Erasmus Thematic Network for Music, Polifonia.
www.lifelonglearninginmusic

Sound Links. (2009). *Community Music in Australia.* Brisbane: Queensland Conservatorium Research Centre, Griffith University.
www.griffith.edu.au/_data/assets/pdf_file/0004/169780/sound_links_brochure.pdf

Stöger, C. (2006). *The Klangnetze Project in Vienna.* Case Study taken from interview with Rineke Smilde in Groningen, 22 April 2006. Unpublished document.

Sweeting, J. (2009). *Music in Dementia Care.* In programme of Launch Event, Music for Life Wigmore Hall and *for dementia,* 14 May 2009. London: Wigmore Hall.

Tavistock Institute. (2002). *Review of Current Pedagogic Research and Practice in the Fields of Post-Compulsory Education and Lifelong Learning.* Report submitted to the Economic and Social Science Research Council.
www.tlrp.org/pub/acadpub/Tavistockreport

Tett, G. (2009). *Fool's Gold: How unrestrained greed corrupted a dream, shattered global markets and unleashed a catastrophe.* London: Little, Brown.

The Sage Gateshead. (2007). *Handbook: REFLECT Creative Partnerships National Co-mentoring Programme.* Gateshead: The Sage Gateshead.
www.thesagegateshead.org

Wenger, E. (1998). *Communities of Practice: Learning, meaning and identity.* Cambridge: Cambridge University Press.

Youth Music. (2002). *Creating a Land with Music. The work, education and training of professional musicians in the 21st century.* London: Youth Music.
www.youthmusic.org.uk

Biography

From 1945-54 Peter Renshaw was at Brentwood School where his musical life was enriched by singing for the Royal School of Church Music and playing violin in the National Youth Orchestra of Great Britain. In 1954 he gained a Choral Exhibition to Gonville and Caius College, Cambridge where he read music and history, and enjoyed an active life singing and playing in university orchestras and chamber ensembles. For National Service, 1957-59, he was commissioned into the Royal Corps of Signals and posted to Singapore, after which he spent a year in the Metal Box Company, first as a management trainee and then as a sales representative.

1960 was a pivotal year when he went to Oxford University to train to be a teacher. He started teaching history in a London comprehensive school in 1961 and three years later became a lecturer in history in a college of education. From 1964-69 he studied part-time at the University of London Institute of Education, specialising in Philosophy of Education. His MPhil thesis, *A Concept of a College of Education,* presented a critique of teacher education. Between 1967 and 1975 he developed the first courses in philosophy of education at Wall Hall College of Education, the University of Leeds Institute of Education and the University of York.

With his deep commitment to music, he became Principal of the Yehudi Menuhin School in 1975 and moved to the Guildhall School of Music & Drama in 1984, where he pioneered the innovative programme in performance and communication skills. From 1986 to 1993 he was Gresham Professor of Music, and he retired from the Guildhall School in 2001 as Head of Research and Development.

Membership of external boards and committees has included: Editor, *Education for Teaching* (1974-75); Editorial Board, *Gifted Education International* (1982-84); Arts Council of England (ACE) Music Advisory Panel (1985-86); Chair, Education Committee, ACE (1989-92); Warden, Music in Education Committee, Incorporated Society of Musicians (1997-98); Arts Research Advisory Group, ACE (1996-2000); European League of Institutes of the Arts Board (1998-2000).

He has a special interest in training and development, organisational change, lifelong learning and mentoring. In the '80s and '90s he was adviser to a number of orchestras aiming to extend their role: for example, the London Philharmonic; City of London Sinfonia; London Symphony Orchestra; Royal Liverpool Philharmonic Orchestra; City of Birmingham Symphony Orchestra; Royal Philharmonic Orchestra; BBC Phiharmonic; Royal Scottish National Orchestra; Royal Opera House and English National Opera.

He has devised and led mentoring development programmes for Prince Claus Conservatoire Groningen, the Royal Conservatoire The Hague, Guildhall School of Music & Drama, the National Institute of Creative Arts & Industries, University of Auckland, the University of the Arts, London, The Sage Gateshead, Youth Music and Yo! Opera, Utrecht. Consultancies have included Banff Centre for the Arts, Ontario Arts Council, Sydney Conservatorium, Queensland Conservatorium, the Irish Government (developing a new Irish Academy for the Performing Arts), Royal Scottish Academy of Music & Drama, the British Council in Tanzania, International Yehudi Menuhin Foundation, Brussels, Jeunesses Musicales International and the London Borough of Newham.

He has been a regular visiting speaker at conferences in Europe, Australia, Canada and Japan, especially through the auspices of the Association of European Conservatoires (AEC), the European League of Institutes for the Arts (ELIA) and the International Music Council (IMC). Areas of interest have included musically talented children, performance and communication skills, connecting conversations, the changing role of the artist, globalisation, identity, cultural diversity and sustaining a learning culture in Higher Arts Education institutions.

From 2001-02 he was Chair of the Steering Group for Youth Music's *Creating a Land of Music* and from 2001-03 he was Moderator of the EU Socrates project, *Sound Links*, on cultural diversity in music education. In 2004-05 he researched the work of Guildhall Connect, as part of *Musical Futures* for The Paul Hamlyn Foundation. Since 2004 he has been a member of the Research Group in Lifelong Learning in Music & the Arts at Prince Claus Conservatoire Groningen and the Royal Conservatoire The Hague. From 2006-08 he was the evaluator of REFLECT, the Creative Partnerships National Co-mentoring Programme, which was managed by The Sage Gateshead.

Formerly he was a Trustee of the London International Festival of Theatre, the Centre for Creative Communities, Share Music, Accord International and currently he is Chair of Nuance Music Limited.